Leadership of Organizations
The Executive's Complete Handbook

Leadership of Organizations
The Executive's Complete Handbook

Part III.   Integration

by   JOHN M. BRION

 JAI PRESS INC.

Greenwich, Connecticut   *London, England*

Library of Congress Cataloging-in-Publication Data

Brion, John M.
    Leadership of Organizations : the executive's complete handbook /
  by John M. Brion.
       p. cm.
    Includes bibliographical references and index.
    Contents: pt. 1. The social -- pt. 2. The technical -- pt.
  3. Integration.
      ISBN 1-55938-934-3   (set : alk. paper). -- ISBN 1-55938-937-0
  (part 3 : alk. paper)
      1. Leadership.   2. Executive ability.   3. Organizlational behavior.
  I. Title.
HD57.7.B745   1996
658.4'092—dc20

                              95-16384
                                 CIP

Copyright © 1996 JAI PRESS INC.
55 Old Post Road No. 2
Greenwich, Connecticut 06836

JAI PRESS LTD.
The Courtyard
28 High Street
Hampton Hill
Middlesex TW12 1PD
England

ISBN: 1-55938-935-4 (Part I)
ISBN: 1-55938-936-2 (Part II)
ISBN: 1-55938-937-0 (Part III)
ISBN: 1-55938-934-3 (Set)

Library of Congress Catalog Card Number: 95-16384

Manufactured in the United States of America

About the Author

John M. Brion, a graduate of Yale University (B. S. in Industrial Administration) with a recent MBA from Pace University, is well qualified to write on organizational leadership, having had some 30 years in organizational leadership positions himself, positions that gave him a comprehensive knowledge of the management technology essentials for organizational excellence plus a wealth of people experience: District Sales Manager to V.P. of operations in one of the nation's largest metals distributors ($100 million sales), General Sales Manager of a metals rolling mill, Manger of Sales and General Administration in the Engineered Products Group of Crane Company, V.P. of a prominent New York consulting firm, and in-house management consultant at Johns-Manville Corporation (now Manville Corp.). The American Management Association published his *Decisions, Organizational Planning and the Marketing Concept* and John Wiley his *Corporate Marketing Planning*, both translated into Spanish. He has also been published by the American Marketing Association on Wholesaling and by the Marketing Communication Research Center on how 40 leading firms develop and introduce new products (in-depth analyses of each).

After Manville he spent the next 12 years researching the causes of the poor performances he had found in so many of the companies he had worked with. His book *Organizational Leadership of Human Resources* published by JAI Press in 1989 presented the good and bad of the human side of the subject; this one covers the total of organizational leadership, advancing the art-science of it to the new paradigm sketched in the third paragraph of the Foreword.

CONTENTS

PART II.   THE TECHNICAL

Foreword

There's a new corporate world out there very different from but a few years ago and changing for the better at a rapidly expanding pace—Leadership, followership, strategies, structures, operating techniques, everything. Leaders and those hoping to be leaders who don't keep up will be dropped by the wayside.

The reader will find here the "how," all aspects of the subject with the latest developments needed by an executive to personally excel and lead an organization to competitive superiority. It is essentially the logical follow-on of the author's 1989 book on human resources leadership recommended by Harvard's organization behavior pioneer, Chris Argyris, this handbook containing the most advanced findings of research, technology and operating experience.

Leading an organization of course entails decisions and actions that account for all the variables of both the internal and external environment; thus, included is all the important knowledge required down through middle management on how to undertake successfully leadership development, upgrade as needed an organization's culture and climate, minimize bureaucracy, plan strategy, structure, operating systems, corporate policies, process teams and team development (at three levels), to reengineer with the latest information technology, computer networks and groupware, and to flatten the organization optimally for best performance. Supplementing this are many illustrative examples, including the changes and progress in such majors as GE, Motorola, Xerox, Texas Instruments, AT&T, IBM and GM.

And because some 50 percent of organizational leadership is leading and motivating its people, one therefore must first understand humans and their behavior, so all of the beginning, all of Part I, is dedicated to helping on at least the basic requisites.

It is primarily an executive's handbook but no less a college text, directed at not only executives, managers and staff but also students, any of all who are interested in finding out how to maximize organizational performance in corporations or non-profit institutions, with the assumptions that he or she has had some organizational experience or management courses.

The titles of the three Parts manifest the simple truth about what the executive has to do: gain an in-depth understanding of the **Social** factors of the organization, especially what makes the individual tick—personality, values, behavior, motivations, etc.; about the **Technical** (management technology, principles, systems, skills, control, planning), with how to mold and operate the organization keeping employee needs and aspirations in mind as well as organizational goals; and finally the **Integration** of the social and technical for best performance and industry leadership.

There is of course the problem of just how much can be gained solely by reading, and to judge, it might be helpful to review briefly a comparison of the strengths and weaknesses of learning by reading with those of the other well-known educational alternatives believed worthwhile. Then, whichever is chosen, or before choosing, one can decide how best to proceed, and, how to fill the gaps left by any of them, virtually all having gaps, some very large.

There are essentially four choices extant, not including the school-of-hard-knocks, the sink-or-swim on your own still the policy of many traditional organizations, the results obvious enough to need no more comment. The four: (1) graduate business schools, (2) vendor leadership programs, (3) corporate in-house programs, and (4) the reading.

(1) A comprehensive critique of today's graduate business schools is covered at the end of Chapter 17 to which one should refer, particularly before deciding which school to select if you want to go to one. The large majority are not worth the investment for leadership development, but the good ones are now fairly effective, especially for building awareness of the demands of organizational leadership and the teaching and integration of the functional skills. Three major problems: the limited number of leadership skills that are teachable, the difficulty of changing

unacceptable behaviors by classroom instruction, and the problem of transferring what is learned back to the workplace. See the elaboration in Chapter 17.

(2) A recent book *Learning to Lead*, by J.A. Conger,[a] gives an excellent description of the various types of professional vendor programs on the market and ticks off what he called an "ideal" against which one can evaluate each (and also apply to the schools and in-house programs). The ideal program will:

a. begin with a conceptual overview of organizational leadership, including the required skills and behaviors;
b. provide feedback on where participants stand with regard to each skill and behavior;
c. work on building the skills that are teachable;
d. for the very difficult skills to teach and the unteachable ones, focus on awareness building with the idea of participant self-development of what is needed over the long run back on the job as opportunities present.

Conger explained that there are broadly four categories of leadership training that vendors apply (he seems to deliberately avoid the word "development," perhaps because it takes considerably longer than the 5-10 days of vendor programs to achieve): training through personal growth, through conceptual understanding, through feedback, and through skills building.

The "personal growth" ones are based on the assumption that most managers ignore an inner calling to realize their potential to become leaders, and programs in this category aim to awaken the drive by outdoor adventure activities (e.g., mountain climbing, group camping) intended to arouse reflection on one's values, behaviors, motivations, interpersonal skills, and desire or not to lead others. They've helped some on self-awareness but clearly fail on all four of a to d.

"Conceptual understanding" programs are essentially off-site or on-site classroom courses covering all the basics like Theory Y, teamwork, participation, contingency models, etc., doing it via lectures, cases, discussion and review of what successful leaders have done. Skills building in these courses is also in lecture form with role playing for feedback but no real-world skills application. They are generally 4 to 5 day seminars or "workshops" that at least encourage thinking about leadership and what's involved.

Programs that are predominantly on "feedback" are also based on an assumption: that most of us already possess leadership skills in varying degrees, so the idea is to learn more about one's own, strengthen those that are weak, and develop what's missing. In one comprehensive program extensive feedback instruments are filled out before attending by the participants, by their job peers, subordinates, and bosses, then five days of skill exercises are given in class with class feedback, and on the sixth day each individual goes through a session of feedback back in the company from staff and class peers in discussions on what was learned and what more to work on, using all the pre-session feedback instruments to aid evaluation and the planning of a back-home program. A while later the peers, subordinates and boss may be asked to fill out new progress instruments, a program counselor contacts the participant, the two review them and replan the back-home program.

The designers of "skills building" programs generally recognize that it's difficult if not impossible to teach psychological and "vision" skills in the 5-day time they normally have for their programs, that in fact leadership skills that are teachable are largely limited to management technology skills (systems, planning, problem-solving, effectiveness techniques, etc.), plus a number of supporting social and interpersonal skills that are commonly taught by a combination of lectures, discussion, videotape of realistic examples, practice, class feedback, and planning utilization of the skills on the job. One program has structured 19 skill areas in 5 clusters, each cluster a function of the attending participants, for example, clusters on developing team performance, managing innovation and change, total quality management, and interpersonal skills. And since many skills even among these are too complex to teach, there's more stress on awareness building than training with the hope that the participants will be inspired to work on them over time back on the job.

As one can see, all types, except the "personal growth" ones, apply some of each of the four categories, one category being dominant, but there are some vendor programs that are quite comprehensive. An example: one has basically five parts: (a) each participant is assigned a "process advisor" who becomes a coach, friend, advocate, and support; about a month before the program the advisor sends the participant a pre-course packet to be filled in on the individual's life purposes, self-evaluation, and organizational situation and experiences; shortly after (still before the course) the advisor contacts the person, offers help on the packet and starts a friendship. (b) One of two full-time weeks of classroom sessions are attended, the advisor spot-checking to help as deemed needed, and 3-person teams of participants under the advisor are formed at the end for feedback, reinforcement, and planning. (c) Back to work for three months, during which the participant keeps a journal on leadership experiences, and is called occasionally by the advisor on progress and for discussion. (d) The journal is sent to the advisor just before the second session of 3-5 days and is used by the advisors with two other participants advises for evaluation, feedback and reinforcement. (e) Back on the job "change partners" are set up among participants who are encouraged to provide each other critiquing, support and truth for as long as they feel the urge.

(3) Increasingly large firms are undertaking corporate in-house management and leadership development programs for a variety of reasons: close control of program content and quality, designing to fit the needs of the firm, the program length governed by company objectives (not principally to be made cost-attractive to prospects as on vendor ones); though the cost is too high for smaller firms, it's less expensive than other options when applied to full management teams in the thousands; and career-length development cohesion is possible so that the individual can build competence through the years to cover increases in job "scale" and "complexity" as the person rises in the hierarchy, the way GE does it (described in Chapter 17); GE's assumption as well as goal: "good material entering at the bottom will emerge exceptional material at the top.".. and they make it happen.

The good firms manifest the recognition that education must be a lifetime pursuit for all of us, and both national and global competition has made on-going human resources development and use of the talents of all employees mandatory for corporate survival let alone corporate leadership. It's a lucky person who works for such a progressive one.

(4) Finally, the reading. Tragically, the vast majority of managers feel (a) they're too busy to read books (one survey found that no one up through middle management in its large sample even knew the title of a current business book, only a handful of progressive senior executives did); (b) their managerial success in getting as far as they have implied to them they already knew enough. But of course, as said, it's a very different and much more complex ballgame than but a few years ago, and reading up-to-date books like this one can not only show what new should be learned but what successful competitors are doing and why they're succeeding.

Granted, the total of the three parts in this one adds up to an enormous amount of reading, but you're in fact not ready for leadership if you don't realize how huge and complex it is. If you are ready, consider that completing one chapter every two weeks will cover it in a year's time, after which it can be a very useful handbook on the office shelf or desk to refer to.

This is not to deny that reading is frequently seriously distorted by the reader's subjective vanity and misconceptions, that it cannot teach skills or *self-awareness* and that it lacks reality testing; but a good comprehensive book (or set of them) can go a long way toward the *skills* awareness-building mentioned and give important guidance as well on how to gain the needed self-knowledge along with all the other subjects herein.

A treatise of such magnitude certainly should be introduced by describing the framework of the basic approach, the key factors being the *technical* and *social* described, two words that concisely package what only a few business schools have successfully integrated, which probably explain along with the omissions why they've commonly developed only able number-crunchers rather than good leaders of people.

A major issue covered within the approach will be a fundamental flaw in many organizations produced by authoritarian or "directive" styles and ignorance, one that would be appropriately called *The Individual-Organization Gap,* labelling the appreciable difference between the attitude and feelings of employees about their work and those of the organization represented by superiors with such styles, and an inevitable consequence is that performance suffers, sometimes terminally.

Expertise in the technical is quite common now, and thanks to the behavioral sciences we know a great deal about the social and have many excellent books on how to manage it for better results, some in fact promising that competent management of the social is the key to maximum performance.

Experienced educators, however, readily agree that there's much more to it, and their teaching techniques are generally designed to embrace fully the technical and social together in a sociotechnical system as in the standard problem-solving procedure taught in many business schools. The procedure has in fact been made a pervasive feature of the text as it advances on both the social and technical through its stages, clarifying the steps and aiding a sense of continuity. Also, to help one relate the discourse and cases to one's own situation, it will be assumed that its performance could be a lot better (so the initial problem manifestation=unsatisfactory performance), that it has decided to undertake a project to define the problems (e.g., for one, what is the gap problem underlying its manifestations?) and what can be done about them; then it assigned the project to one of its best and most thorough executives.

Such a person would probably think immediately of the standard problem-solving procedure as an efficient way to go about it, so presuming all this has happened, it will be used:

Standard Problem-Solving Procedure

Step 1. *An informal investigation.*[b]
    a.   An analysis of the manifestation(s)
    b.   Preliminary information search
    c.   Problem identification
    d.   Problem definition

Step 2. *Conceptual preparation:*
    a.   A statement of the assumptions

> b. A model of the problem's system (structures, process, human resources) and its functioning
>
> c. Hypotheses of the probable solution

Step 3. *Formal investigation*: the information search

Step 4. *Analysis*: study of all the most probably causes uncovered in the investigation; appraisal of their individual and collective contribution as causes of the problem; verification, or correction, of the systems model as consistent with the formal investigation findings.

Step 5. *Design*: development of the most probably alternative solutions other than the hypotheses that were suggested by the analysis.

Step 6. *Choice*: test of the alternatives and the hypotheses in the final system model and selection of the one that yields the best results.

The ultimate goal of the project, one can see, will be the Step 6 *Choice* for the solutions and decisions showing the management team how to implement each, including how to account for the multiplicity of organizational complexities and to deal with the realities of power, authority, and organizational politics.

One comment about the 6-step procedure might be helpful. Analysis is naturally a continuous process during an investigation, so that the write-up of the three Parts will include the analytic reasoning relevant to the details of each as the investigation progresses. The *Analysis* of Step 4, however, is essentially the final summary stage of it that leads to Steps 5 and 6, all of which will be undertaken in the last chapter.

NOTES

a. Conger, J.A., *Learning to Lead* (San Francisco: Jossey-Bass, 1992).

b. la through 1d are the steps for problem search if that is first necessary, after which the whole procedure is applied.

John M. Brion
Author

Part III

INTEGRATION

Introduction

On completing his research and analyses in Part II of *The Organization*, the hypothetical problem-solving executive felt it was time again to summarize the most crucial points of the Part as an aid to moving ahead. His selection:

1. *Control:* managers have to accept it as their fundamental means of achieving the organization's purposes, and that in order to fully succeed the potentially undesirable negative consequences must be avoided, which can be done only by imbuing an in-depth understanding of the relevant abstracts (power, authority, compliance, punishment) and a competent application of the control techniques and devices with an enlightened management philosophy (Theory Y and System 4) to evolve mutual agreement on ends and means; the result: leadership that gains commitment concurrent with the needed control.

2. *Communication:* organizations with the most effective communication have demonstrated that it is basic to producing optimum performance, the effectiveness based on a comprehensive understanding of group dynamics, the 9 forces on group performance with leadership at the top (Figure 8.1, page 268), and the impact of structure, how to design in order to facilitate communication upward, downward and laterally, the overall goal: a "freed-up" or "organic" organization (pages 447-448), participation and the "Team Philosophy" (pages 584-599) being fundamental. A fact all managers must always keep in mind: you cannot not communicate.

3. *Decision making:* the imperative elements for superior organizational results are not only the ability to develop good decisions but to motivate subordinates to implement them as intended; the requisites: understanding all the dynamics of the function: certainty, risk, uncertainty, ignorance, futurity, quantitative/qualitative content, importance, uniqueness, and how computers, computer networking, groupware, and the Internet can help; knowing all the necessary inputs and the process and the psychology of individual and organizational behavior (which of course includes the group dynamics in #2 above).

4. *Corporate planning:* Organizational continuity and success through the years requires periodic formal planning, usually quarterly and/or annually, in all 12 key result areas (p. 630), structured to cover all 10 areas of the Plan for Planning, the dual goal of the competitive strategy planning being competitive advantage and shareholder value and return.

5. *Structure:* Designing it entails essentially two parts: (a) The design basics applicable to virtually all organizations (the principles, jobs, units, span, decentralizations, staff, and functional, market and process/team structuring); (b) advanced design: accounting for contingency factors, the industry, the environment, and the utilization of one or more of the 9 types of lateral processes... in all cases ensuring the four-way fit of person-job-organization-industry.

6. *Human resources management:* Given that at all levels the social part of leadership (behavior, values, ethics, psychology, personality, motivation, culture, climate, norms) is "half" of what it takes to make the organization successful, it behooves the top leadership to ensure its effectiveness by institutionalizing the responsibilities and their implementation, thus the HRD as described in Chapter 17, the purpose of the department being to help all levels of the line to perform that "half." Each leader-manager should be aware of those responsibilities and how to implement them, and can be by a careful study of the chapter.

The major intent of Part II, recall, was to cover the key relevant technical knowledge and the general social considerations required for the first stage of the indirect technical-social integration, the initial unilateral planning Of the organization's or unit's goals, structures, and processes that have only indirect impact on individuals.

With that completed, it's now possible to move on to the next step needed to be successful on the indirect, how to undertake the OD second stage of accounting for the specific social consideration of those who will be affected in order to gain their commitment, the part that requires participation.

And as pointed out in Chapter 2, OD itself has to have two steps to achieve any significant improvement in performances: when managers as superiors are inclined toward Theory X the way the preponderant are, their thinking and behavior has to be changed first before subordinates will change their own.

So the problem-solving executive began by looking into how *Individual Change* can be induced (Chapter 18), which when achieved would make possible both *Organization Change* by the second stage (Chapter 19) and the direct integration of the organization's goals and the individual subordinate's needs, the direct explained in Chapter 20.

Finally, to produce a solution for the defined problem, the technical and social complexities described of operating an organization have to be melded—a complete integration of all those technical and social factors—and that's plainly the function of *Leadership*, Chapters 20 and 21 summarizing and/or completing all in the book on the subject.

By the end of the four chapters, all of the problem-solving Step #3 and much of Step #4 (page xxiii) will have been carried out, leaving still to be done the completion of #4, the design of alternatives in #5, the testing of the alternatives and the hypothesis in the model in #6, and the final choice. What the executive did on these remaining tasks will be described in Chapter 22.

Chapter 18

Individual Change

The fact that society and its organizations appreciate the importance of planning and managing change is well manifested by the Part II chapters, all aimed primarily at change for better **performance** through structures, processes, and incentives external to the individual. But the removal of dysfunctional **behavior** that may be impairing the performances has been only a hoped-for result of the motivation incorporated in the planning. The idea of removing it directly by *Individual Change* of behavior has until recently been considered impossible.

Indeed, the psychological consequence of even suggesting someone's behavior was wrong and should be changed seemed to be sufficient reason for giving it up. The word *change*, technical or behavioral, is itself emotionally loaded for most organizational people when it touches on one or more of three very sensitive concerns:

> Security (job, self-confidence)
> Economics (the threat to present or future income)
> Personal worth (including self-image and dignity)

Mix the complexity of personality with these and the outcomes of a change request can range from acceptance to the unpredictable traumatic. For example, asking a self-confident subordinate to change a technical method usually gains immediate unemotional compliance when it's perceived to be feasible; yet the same request to an insecure one might arouse doubts about all three; and a diplomatic recommendation for a *behavior* change to even a confident top executive by the CEO can almost put the person in shock.

When the emotional upset of opposition does occur in a work organization, it is, we know, the result of either the dysfunctional social or the technical-social conflict defined on page 31, and recall that an overview and the basics of the skill of *leading/managing conflict* for dealing with them was presented in Chapter 11 (pages 504-513).

However, it was also pointed out that pragmatic managers recognize that, in dealing with subordinates, there are three parts to the subject

1. Minimizing the potential for conflict,
2. Dealing with the overt dysfunctional,
3. Handling the dysfunctional that has advanced to non-compliance;

and the skill (italicized above) is by definition dedicated to only the second, the #1 minimizing being built into the job of effective leadership and climate development and the #3 an issue of control.

Nevertheless, it's easy to see now that success on both #1 and #2 would be no less than success on behavior change in its most elementary form, that is, by information education (the #1 type on page 191), which has to be the first step of any change effort, nothing more being necessary if it works.

But for most people, the potential for conflict (#1 above) is more than initially meets the eye in that it's present in virtually every interpersonal event; so it has to be a major concern of every leader both before and during those events (which to the skillful becomes intuitive habit). Indeed, the text has given many recommendations and techniques that do have some to considerable indirect minimizing effect along with their positive values; for examples, the interpersonal concepts within or with regard to:

- Understanding the individual's personality and needs (Chapters 3 to 7)
- Organizational culture and climate development (8)
- Relationship development (8 and 11)
- Participation principles and techniques, especially "team philosophy" (13)

- The Interaction Method (13)
- Structures and processes (16)
- Human resources management (17)
- Training and development (started in Chapter 17 and to be continued in 20).

And it will be seen that the OD to come is also not only a minimizer but may at times be used to resolve overt conflict, though the techniques were designed mainly for the linked dual purpose of problem-solving and behavior change as the deliberations show change is needed, during which problem-solving constructive conflict of ideas (debate) is stimulated toward consensual solution.

Also, recall that the basic knowledge for minimizing conflict was presented in Chapter 11, and as said on page 507, a knowledge also of the psychology of conflict can be an important aid to both the #1 minimizing and the #3 non-compliance handling as well as being a basic to the first step of behavior change (changing the superior). Here are the salient points.

The psychology of conflict

Especially important, every leader/manager must be continuously aware of the fact stated in Chapter 11 that conflict is not only inevitable in organizational relationships but is an essential potentially positive phenomenon as well as a negative one.

Also, there are the complications that can arise between the two, e.g., that a constructive one can suddenly become dysfunctional because of an injected misunderstanding or a slide-over occurs by bringing in threats to psychological needs or aspirations, subordinate behavior generally telling you clearly enough in either case.

An example of the slide-over would be a superior's attempt to teach a subordinate manager a better way to do a technical task, the subordinate candidly disagrees, demonstrating the advantages of his or her own way—constructive technical conflict. The superior yields, and the subordinate's technique fails. In the next discussion the subordinate tries in anxiety to justify the use of the technique, and dysfunctional technical-social conflict involving fears of inadequacy and penalty begins to dominate, a frequent scene in periodic appraisal sessions where all technical, social, constructive and dysfunctional commonly become entangled.

One of the most helpful explanations of the psychology was started with the comment that "Conflict can be more readily understood if it is considered as a dynamic process...a sequence of episodes."There are five of them, the pace and extent of advance depending on the situations and personalities.[1]

- *Latent conflict*—a conflict that is built into the situation but has not as yet been perceived, felt or manifested.
- *Perceived conflict*—one at the conscious level but not yet implemented; it has been accepted as fact without any bad feelings, and may be only a misunderstanding.
- *Felt conflict*—a perceived one that has been "personalized" with emotions and is the prelude to manifest conflict.
- *Manifest conflict*—the implementation of conflictful behavior.
- *Conflict aftermath*—if it is not genuinely resolved to the satisfaction of all participants it might be suppressed back to the latent, perceived or felt state, ready to explode by even unrelated aggravations. An aftermath naturally affects the course of succeeding episodes.

And the researcher charted the sequence of the episodes and the major influences on each with the diagram in Figure 18.1 below.

An "environmental effect," the upper right hand box, might be an unpredictable factor that resolves the latent conflict at that state, such as a limited resource situation in which more is found so there's enough to go around, or it might amplify the conflict; for example, part of what is available is accidentally destroyed, raising the level to perceived, felt or manifest.

A "strategic consideration" could be the decision to risk a fight and lose a relationship as better than lose the issue and win harmony.

A "manifest conflict" understandably depicts a range of behaviors in reaction to an action taken or a decision or command that has been made. While a successful resolution might produce

The dynamics of a conflict

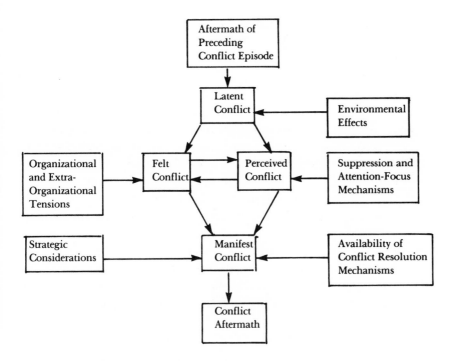

Figure 18.1

(a) in the list below and a less than wholly successful one produce (b), (c) to (g) describes increasing degrees of manifest dysfunction. Interestingly, withdrawal or apathy (e) can also be at the latent state, and apathy's potential for future manifest conflict is commonly overlooked.

- a. Enthusiastic acceptance
- b. Reluctant acquiescence (resistance perceived)
- c. Persistence (on one's viewpoint)
- d. Compromise
- e. Apathy
- f. Open verbal resistance

    g. Non-compliance in the forms of withdrawal, open rebellion or aggression

Recall that Figure 11.2 on page 478 portrayed the full range graphically. Referring to it, one can see that anything below 50 percent acceptance is "manifest" and includes (c) to (g) above; (f) is 50-25 percent, and (g) is below 25 percent, both (f) and (g) being non-compliance.

Finally, the bottom box in Figure 18.1, "Aftermath," is particularly important to the entire conflictful situation, because the residue from a conflict tends to generate latent conflict in the next potentially conflictful event (usually similar); moreover, one will guarantee the occurrence of this carryover when applying any of the four conventional approaches to a manifest conflict: force an opinion or decision, evade the issue, smooth over the conflict, or compromise (the (d) in the list above referred to the other party's concession). And a little experience will show that there are situations in which any one will in fact be the best solution, given the trade-offs; but, the most effective way to handle the large majority of conflicts (as will be shown for groups in Chapter 19) is the confrontation technique, which is no more than open, objective, honest discussion of the problem, but still so difficult for many that OD specialists have to provide training on how to do it.

However, the choice among these is only the decision for handling an actual manifest conflict, whereas managers in a potentially conflictful situation should consider the total interpersonal approach to prevent it from going that far in the first place if possible. Assuming an intention to make a request the subordinate may not be "indifferent" about (Barnard's zones, page 496)—so it's a potential "latent conflict" situation—relate the recommendations for compliance on pages 476-481 to this discourse somewhat along the following lines:

●   evaluate the probable difficulty of acceptance re Figure 11.2 on page 478 in light of the variables in the chart, and give thought to the mode of communication recommended by the chart;

- try to judge what personal needs and goals of the individual might be involved (at least make an educated guess);
- ask yourself, are my own aims wholly performance-relevant and objective? (of course try to make them so if not).
- consider participative "confrontation" (after learning how to do it) to arrive at a mutual social exchange and do it if not faced with a crisis of time or circumstance.

If the result still leads to the "perceived conflict" or "felt" stage:

- consider the possibility of peripheral "dissatisfiers" that, if changed, might make the request acceptable—policies, procedures, physical environment; if changes are feasible, bring them up in the discussion;
- consider whether or not a cooling off period should be given to allow time to acquiesce, with an awareness that it might instead give time to build to rebellion.

Then if the "manifest" arrives either as the resistance of (f) or aggression of (g):

- Quickly apprise which of the conventional approaches would be best (force, evade, smooth-over or compromise) or will more confrontation discussion help?
- Also consider: (a) changing the form of the request, (b) changing the content, (c) adding a reward or increasing it, (d) adding a penalty or increasing it, or (3) abandoning the request.
- Throughout, keep in mind that only a decision acceptable to the person will avoid aftermath for the next event.
- If then open defiance (the g) occurs in spite of these efforts: separation—remembering that, where performance has been otherwise satisfactory, *removal from the premises manifests, in the last analysis, a failure of leadership.*

Needless to say, only Theory Y inclined managers would consider such an approach, and at that, seldom is there time to consciously go through all of it. But like all management education, it pays in the long run to have all the principles and facts in the back of one's head for the neurons to refer to in given situations—the reason why experienced Theory Y executives intuitively go through many of the steps in a fraction of second and with superior results.

Having the principles and facts about behavior change back there too will do the same for all interpersonal skills.

Behavior change[a]

Any awake person knows that, throughout life, we constantly change on our own our values, assumptions and beliefs, the bases of behavior, as we see it to our benefit, doing it by conscious processes as well as through unconscious adaptation to the tide of events. But we object strongly, almost automatically, when someone else tries to make us change any of them. Since the beginning of civilization people have found that such efforts of others have almost invariably not been for their own benefit but for the benefit of the others. Consequently, it's virtually a cultural learning to oppose any direct effort to do so.

Interestingly, attempts at change by any traditional formal "direct instruction" methods of education, training or current management development face no such opposition. Of course it's because the teaching is presented impersonally to the group, it's predominantly technical, the behavioral parts are subdued or hidden, one can take or leave the change attempt, and there's no clear penalty for non-compliance.

In those instances, values, attitudes and behavior in fact undergo little change, no identification with specific jobs or their goals is developed, and no commitment is induced; the change, if any, is solely the acquisition of new knowledge that is used only when found advantageous.

So it became generally accepted that attempts to change behavior were a waste of time unless the long drawn-out psychoanalysis and therapy that evolved from psychodynamic behavior theory were applied, the well-known technique developed for the mentally disturbed.

The technique's inappropriateness for the normal in fact was quite evident to some psychologists, who recognized around the 1930s that what may be right for the mentally unhealthy and neurotic is not necessarily right or even practical for normal people. Much of dysfunctional behavior in normal people, they observed, is not due to deep-seated personality problems but to value misconceptions, incorrect assumptions, and/or current social conflicts, and they should be amenable to change, acceptable change, through less protracted methods.

The logic of it was too strong to ignore, and the reasoning led to the initial OD and encounter group experiments that evolved into what is now called *social change theory*, in reality a combination of the phenomenology and social learning theories described in Part I.

One of the best descriptions was given by contrasting it with the psychodynamic approach.[2] To paraphrase the essence of it with the summary table below, psychodynamic theory holds that undesirable behavior is primarily due to internal subconscious forces (1)—internal emotional conflicts, defenses and unknown motives—built up since birth that must be uncovered and changed first, for only by doing so will the undesirable behavior then change. To do it requires the professional skill of a therapist in a one-to-one doctor-patient relationship (2), probing the individual's past (3) toward understanding these forces and changing the basic personality factors causing the behavioral problems; thus the therapist engages in maximal change (4). The client is expected to see via reasoning (5) the errors of his or her ways in terms of specific recalled incidents (6).

Psychodynamic Theory Emphasis	Social Change Theory Emphasis
1. Problems primarily internal	1. Problems primarily social
2. Client-therapist	2. Group experience
3. Historical reconstruction	3. Present behavior
4. Maximal change	4. Minimal change
5. Reason	5. Reason and emotion
6. Content	6. Content and process
7. Therapist change responsibility	7. Client change responsibility
8. Low maintenance concern	8. High maintenance concern
9. Time: 2-5 years	9. Time: 1-2 wks. for individuals, 2-5 years for organization
10. Cost: high	10. Cost: comparatively low per capita

Numbers (7) and (8) (on the left) are related: the behavior change clearly depends on the authority and supportiveness of the therapist, and, because of it, a high measure of therapist-dependence is created, and it cannot help but be at the expense of post-therapy self-reliance and new-behavior maintenance. On cessation of therapy the client not only misses the support but faces an old-behavior vacuum with an inadequate linkage of new-behavior to real world experience... possibly a reason why therapists commonly see the need for the sessions to go on and on.

The social change theorists, on the other hand, while agreeing with the importance to personality of deep internal forces, hold that much behavior, especially in organizations, is due to social interaction (1 on the right) in group (with one or more others) experiences (2); it's seldom due to the isolated behavior of individuals; and it concerns mainly present problems, such that the undesirable behavior is an adaptation to the present (3), so change efforts should be limited accordingly (4).

Also, new knowledge has made apparent that emotions are as important as reason (5) and that the person must understand what caused the behavior in question, the content and processes behind it (6), because (i) any change must be made by the person himself or herself (7), no one else can do it, and (ii) after it is made, one has to know the processes to be able to be flexible to subsequent changing circumstances.

We now know additionally that much of peoples' behavior in organizations is in reaction to both social and technical (management technology) aspects of the sociotechnical system they're in, and changes made for the better will undergo extinction if each of the following three actions are not undertaken (8):

a. the social part of the system must be made congruent; if coworkers are not brought around to the same opinion their behavior will constantly pressure a changed individual to revert;

b. the technical part of the system must be made congruent; structures and processes that frustrate desirable behavior have to be corrected;

c. the new behavior of the changed and coworkers has to be continuously reinforced because of normal human inclination to revert as explained in Chapter 4.

The superiority of social change theory on (9) and (10) certainly needs no comment.

One can see that the two camps were interested in entirely different subjects and had in mind two different levels of conflict; in fact, the approach of neither is effective in the other's arena. The psychodynamicists' paramount interest was (and is) abnormal or seriously neurotic people and their *internal psychological conflict* caused by what they believed to be aberrations of personality. Understandably, they concluded that the way to change the aberrant behavior is to change the personality.

Social change theorists however are concerned about dysfunctional behavior of otherwise normal people and are convinced that most of it is due to *social conflict,* either on its own or in association with the technical or technical-social conflict, caused by current situations.

It can be seen that the latters' interest therefore is in the first two of the three values change solutions listed on page 191, the third being up to society:

1. Fast-to-change—by new information
2. Medium—social change by behavioral techniques
3. Slow—change by cultural conditioning over a long period.

As said earlier, Kurt Lewin and his associates were the ones who pioneered the second, and the first is built into it to the degree that it is needed. Change by social change is obviously a learning process, and it can be very slow or not occur at all if not consciously and systematically induced. This team discovered that the small group could be used to greatly speed it up if the group starts unstructured and the members are allowed to develop the structure, the process itself opening the door to and effecting value and behavior changes.

Further, they found out that the reason for the changes that did take place were due to what was labeled the "unfreeze-change-refreeze" process; in outline form as described by Edgar Schein:[3]

1. The elements essential to **unfreeze** are:
   - disturbance of the person's stable equilibrium to make him or her ready for change; he called it "destabilizing";
   - removal of support for old attitudes;
   - saturation of the environment with new attitudes to be acquired;
   - minimization of threat of or resistance to change and maximization of support for any change in the right direction.

2. During **change**, which must be applied closely after unfreezing, a description of the desired change is presented and the two basic processes of learning new views are examined:
   - *Identification*—identifying with and emulating some other person who holds the desired new attitudes (e.g. a superior who does it). It can result in the adoption of a desirable set of organizational attitudes, but is not flexible to diverse problem-solving nor is it durable; it usually evaporates when the emulated person departs;
   - *Internalization*—learning new attitudes by being placed in a situation where the new attitudes are demanded of the individual to solve the problem at hand. If he or she solves the problem during identification the two processes can occur concurrently; in any case, internalization is more common when the *direction* of change is left to the individual.

3. The **refreeze** is the integration of the new attitudes into the individual's personality. It occurs when they fit naturally because (a) they are or seem self-discovered, (b) they solve the enigma(s) to the person's advantage, and (c) they are supported by the social environment (superiors, subordinates, peers).

(Schein elaborated in greater detail what it takes to "unfreeze" in a recent article; the main thoughts are given in the next chapter for application to OD task forces.

Social change techniques thus are learning methods that target specific social behaviors, taking into account the total social situation, utilizing the context, and engaging at least the general concepts of this process.

However, a leader who wants to change in a subordinate manager some bad methods or habits should try to discern first whether or not this entire process is necessary. For example, young managers who've not been long at managing, are eager and open to learning, usually haven't developed strong convictions about their methods, and are frequently amenable to the abbreviated one used by good courses for leaders on how to do it, courses sometimes optimistically entitled "how to motivate subordinates" though they only deal with this single issue (correcting a bad method or habit). But certainly it's a most important one; the course steps in general:

1. The leader first has to learn how to avoid criticizing the undesirable behavior when confronting the person about it, learn how to describe it, and in doing so be specific—what was done where and when. Trainers have exercises for teaching this.
2. Proof of the negative impact on the person's subordinates has to be given the person. A survey of the subordinates' opinions is best, but if not available or feasible, the next two steps often make it self-evident.
3. Both the undesirable and desirable behavior for the task is presented in training material with the results of each, a film showing them being particularly helpful.
4. The subordinate practices the desirable, role-playing it with either the leader or peers,[b] taking the time in subsequent days to repeat the role-playing until the leader feels it's been imbued, the leader reinforcing progress then and on-the-job with suitable reward, the course covering the numerous reward options.

One can see that it leaves out some very important parts of the Lewin process, indeed gives no attention at all to values, such that it is more a performance change procedure than behavior change. Note, for an example that it is in general what McClelland and Burnham applied to Prentice and Blake, on page 274.

When, on the other hand, the subordinate manager has been managing people for some time, has an essentially authoritarian style and a batch of the misconception of page 118, and the manager feels sure the misconceptions have helped his or her success, a combination in virtually all experienced conventional managers—for them the full unfreeze-change-refreeze is necessary, the often-mentioned Stranger T-grouping commonly considered *the* technique.

It is indeed crucial but only part of what is required. With that alone, the participants are usually insufficiently informed about values, behavior, communication, and interpersonal psychology in general, they rarely have been exposed to interpersonal ethics, and only the values and behaviors that come to the attention of the group members during the sessions are directly addressed.

Nonetheless, along with the self-enlightenment and social understanding gained from the T-group, the process brings about a major beginning in learning self-evaluation (introspection) and empathy, thinking that tends to be carried forward by each individual both on and off the job.

For the full complement of requisites (to change in traditional managers the values [and consequent behavior] that are amenable to behavior change techniques). There are, as said, two steps, consistent with the fact that there are two parts to such conflicts, one being the most frequent cause of the other: (1) change the superior's values and behavior that are causing subordinates' dysfunctional behavior, then (2) change (or remove) the technical factors contributing to or supporting the dysfunctional behavior, factors that are usually due, at least to some degree, to the first. This second step, one may recall from page 264 is clearly also the two-stage indirect integration, and only when these two steps have been successfully undertaken will the subordinates themselves be open to any efforts toward lasting change in *their* behavior.

In sum, an ideal comprehensive first-step behavior change program for traditional-minded supervisors or managers that can supply the social requisites of leadership:

1. Sufficient education on values, organization behavior, and communication

2. Stranger T-grouping
3. Ethics education and training: philosophies, sensitivity, applications, and the skill of ethics analysis (page 178)
4. Interpersonal skills psychology and training

Plainly and befitting the chapter, the first step is with respect to *individual change,* the order of #1 to #4 preferable but not essential; the next chapter covers the indirect of the second for *organization change,* and the direct is (completed) in Chapter 20.

T-Group

The word "stranger" now has to be inserted in front of it for the particular technique described above because of the several forms that have evolved from the original one developed by Lewin and his research team. The initial T-groups were laboratory workshops set up at Connecticut State Teachers College in the summer of 1946 as a research project to see if the participants could learn about their own behavior by experimenting with the interpersonal relations of the group in a certain way (thus the "laboratory training" label that led to the T-group abbreviation). The results were so promising the National Training Laboratories was organized the next year and established at Bethel, Maine, where the procedure was refined, the several forms subsequently added, and many of the other OD techniques developed.[c]

The stranger T-group is the original pure concept and still the most important. A description of it is best presented in four parts: (1) general characteristics, (2) the trainer, (3) the goals that were added to the original sole behavior-change goal, additions that grew out of T-group experience, and (4) the process.

(1) A social group—the stranger T-group in this instance—provides unique learning advantages over the one-to-one method: learning via the processes of a real-life situation that involves emotions as well as reason, where the information is self-gathered from listening, observation, coping and defending, where the feedback is convincing (especially when all others react the same way to one's behavior), and where alternative behaviors can be tested on the other individuals or the whole group.

Because a major obstacle to open exchange of opinion and information in normal social and organizational settings is fear of adverse consequences—loss of friends, a superior's respect, a job—the group was composed of participants who had never before met, had no need to meet again, and could not afterwards have any influence on the job future of other members of the group. The other characteristics:

- 8-12 people meeting in a secluded off-site location for 5½ days, the sessions 8 hours/day with the last day the half day.
- As mentioned, there is no group structure at the start: no leader, titles, roles, rules, agendas, tasks.
- The group "finds its way" by learning to understand each other and the group as a unit via the process in (4) ahead.
- In contrast with a therapy group (which it is not), it presupposes normal emotional health, and some of the experiences may be traumatic for those who are not, so they should be identified in advance and kept out.
- A "trainer" (or OD consultant) is present, the person's role described next.

(2) A very substantial measure of the success of a stranger T-group depends on the trainer's competence and sensitivity, so great care has to be taken to be sure the person is well trained, temperamentally qualified and with a record of successful experience.

He or she starts each meeting with a few wake-up exercises (it's 8 or 9 AM) and, in the first few days, a short talk on the psychology of interpersonal relations. After the talk the trainer acts as a group facilitator during each session, making helpful comments, keeping down confusion, helping individuals in trouble (such as getting more negative feedback than they can handle), preventing amateur psychoanalysis (criticisms are allowed only on observed behavior), telling members when they're getting bad feedback if they don't recognize it, and pointing up insensitivities.

(3) The initial T-group goal of behavior change[d] via upgrading participant values and assumptions has been considerably expanded as a result of experience with it, so that it now includes the subgoals for the participants of:

a. Greater self-awareness and greater sensitivity about their own conduct, prejudices, myopias and non-verbal behavior;
b. Greater awareness of others and sensitivity to their feelings, needs, opinions, rights, communications;
c. Greater understanding of group processes by experiencing them;
d. Learning how to accept and give constructive feedback without threatening the self or the other(s);
e. Learning some of the main reasons why one is ineffective with certain kinds of people.

(4) The general characteristics presented in (1) of course also described the conscious visible process, but the really significant process necessary to achieve the stated goals in (3) is the subconscious psychological sequence of events.

Two OD pioneers, Bennis and Shepard, uncovered it in the study referred to twice before because of its broad organizational significance (page 468 and 531), a study that demonstrated not only the value and efficacy of the stranger T-group technique but that the experience can be very appealing and stimulating to anyone with a little intellectual curiosity.[4]

Freud had postulated long ago from his observations of interpersonal relations that its two basic forces are "dependence" and "interdependence," and that people have to resolve their dependence problems, fears and frustrations before they can move on to the resolution of their interdependence ones.

Bennis and Shepard found, however, that the members of their study initially applied to those forces the negative behaviors they developed in their authoritarian hierarchical organizations, developed to accommodate the organizations' climate of mutual distrust, threat, fear, and coercion:

Dependence (authority relations): any of competing for power, rebelliousness, submissiveness or withdrawal.

Interdependence (personal, or intimacy relations): exploitiveness, competitiveness, destructiveness, or again, withdrawal.

The consequence is group immaturity in the beginning and an inability to advance toward the desired state of maturity described on page 532.[e]

What you and I see in the first 2-3 days of a T-group experience is how the group, oneself included, tries to cope and make sense of its existence under such a condition, which is aggravated further by its reaction to the trainer.

Having learned back on the job how to succeed with its structure of traditional authoritarian techniques (power, status, rules, intimidation, punishment), when told by the trainer that there'd be no structure at all—no leader (with authority and status), functional goals, rules, or guidelines—the members refuse to accept it and in fact look to the trainer to supply it, especially to supply the leadership (the way technical trainers usually do and have to), holding to the traditional assumption that irresponsibility and chaos will reign in any leaderless group (per the authoritarian ethic on page 169).

But they find that he or she refuses and just acts passively along the lines of the description in (2) above, attempting to function only as a mirror to the members, reflecting their conduct by verbalizing now and then the assumptions they reveal and their significance.

Frustrated, the members eject (figuratively) the trainer from the group, attempt unsuccessfully to elect a leader, and succeed only when they turn to an (one or more) "independent" for help, thus making the person (one of them) a kind of informal leader, all of which starts the evolution of some group authority and solidarity. Independents are those who are more objective, not highly dependent on authority, but not rebellious against it, and as a result tend to be catalysts toward logical thought and action.

About now though, the members are beginning to sense what they've actually been doing and the absurdity of it: competing for power and attempting it with ineffective means. Without the conferred authority and status of one's organization, the traditional techniques, they find, are useless; without them leadership, authority, and respect have to be earned; even a posturing of strength or an intimidating voice gain them nothing.

Their whole world of values and assumptions about leadership and how to achieve their own personal goals through competition and at the expense of others evaporates, as does the traditional structure they'd imposed of mistrust and threat, leaving a gaping values/assumption vacuum. Also, a realization correspondingly begins to develop that they are mutually responsible for what has happened and for the fate of the group.

As said, this is the early sequence of events we see and experience; Bennis and Shepard discovered the psychology behind it and explained it as the *Dependence Phase* (I) of authority with three subphases:

Subphase 1: *dependence-flight*—warding off the anxiety of the unfamiliar situation, typical self-oriented social behavior.

Subphase 2: *counterdependence-fight*—two tight warring subgroups tend to form, "dependents" who want to structure the group with Leadership and "counterdependents" who are unwilling to give up control to anyone; hostility, embarrassing incidents, disillusionment with the trainer for refusing to lead, bids for Leadership, attempts to structure; the brink of disaster.

Subphase 3: *resolution-catharsis*—a turning to the independents; the trainer "evicted" (possibly by independents' suggestion or behavior); a developing awareness of the behaviors and acceptance of mutual responsibility-for the group's fate.

By this time the members are realizing the folly of their conduct, the emptiness of their traditional concept of how to become a leader, and that they can't gain their own personal goals of acceptance and advancement in any regard without the collaboration of the others—which leads to the recognition that the others can't serve as resources unless they themselves are open and genuine. The result is a subtle movement to the *Interdependence Phase* (II) of intimacy, in which three more subphases were identified:

Subphase 4: *enchantment-flight*—at the outset contrived harmony, laughter, patching up differences, planning outside activities; but a new ambivalence emerges: which is better, solidarity and cohesion or self-identity that may be lost by giving in to them?

Subphase 5: *disenchantment-flight*—anxiety over the dilemma results in the formation of two subgroups again but not necessarily the same as the ones in subphase 2: the overpersonals who believe in self-esteem through commitment to the group and counterpersonals who believe the reverse and that intimacy breeds contempt; the latter dominate.

Subphase 6: *consensual validation*—the warring groups come close to disaster again and turn to the independents (who's self-esteem is not threatened by intimacy) who suggest a collaborative appraisal of what's been going on, and the experience of it at this point seems to free-up the whole group; fears of rejection dissipate, discussion becomes open, and consensus is reached (though probably not verbalized) on their interdependence and how to capitalize on it.

Indeed it becomes apparent that *trust* is the central issue; what we observe is the group finally building a structure of trust with acts of trust: expressing and listening to feelings, showing empathy and supportiveness, accepting differences, and acting as resources to one another with questions, observations, suggestions, and efforts to help rather then dominate.

The earlier perception of a no-resource no-win situation is replaced by one of abundant resource all-win. Empathy and intimacy replace distance and defensiveness, interpersonal conflicts are greeted as challenges to problem-solving rather than occasions for compromise or win-lose polarizing.

In sum, we see in Phase I the group emerge out of the heterogenous collection of individuals, and in Phase 11 the *individual* emerge out of the group, in a process through which the climate changes from fear and closedness to trust and openness, and the participants move

> from faulty values and assumptions,
> > to serious disequilibrium,
> > > to self-reevaluation,
> > > > to new values, assumption and attitudes,
> > > > > to new behavior.

Not all individuals and groups navigate and weather the passage successfully. Groups may falter because of a poor trainer, but often it's because of the disruption by one or more individuals with less-than-normal deep emotional problems. As said, the technique is based on the assumption of normalcy, and screening them out is a responsibility of the organization conducting the T-group. Any who slip through are in fact quickly noticeable (usually a hostile attitude and disturbed emotional attacks on the trainer or others) and should be taken aside and persuaded to leave with fees returned.

Significantly, managers who have successfully traversed the sequence are the best proselytizers of the technique. Some executives admit to going several times. However, consultants, managements and participants themselves have repeatedly complained that often when stranger T-group managers return to the job, either they have quickly reverted from the improved behavior back to the old ways, or their efforts to stick with it confused others as inconsistent, unpredictable and out of step with the rest of the organization.

One Harvard professor of business administration described in an article some actual examples he'd encountered in his off-campus consulting. A typical one: a successful tough-as-nails division manager goes through a stranger T-group week; "from being proud of his toughness, he became ashamed of his psychic brutality;" back on the job he changed, but no one then knew for sure which man he was going to be at a given time, things fell apart, then he did.[5]

The professor-writer stated that a person's interpersonal skills, "those matters which are central to his private personality," are not appropriate subjects for attack with research and teaching, for manipulation, that one's "style" finds the job-slot it's best suited for.

This is as much as to say that short-range visible quantitative management success is what's important regardless of the social or long-range impact of methods, that the manager, the subordinates and the organization would be better off if he'd remained the brutal s.o.b. Aside from the immorality of it and the invisible long-run systemic quantitative and personal cost, learned behavioral values and attitudes are apparently confused with and taken for "constitutional" traits (page 46).

The point totally missed by the professor, the manager and the personnel department that sent him was the maintenance requirement of behavior change, that new behavior must be compatible with and supported by the social environment (superiors, peers, subordinates) back on the job, otherwise either everything falls apart as in this incident, they suppress their learning, or they allow it to fade away. A major reason: "If coworkers (superior, peers, subordinates) are not brought around to the same opinions and attitudes, their behavior will constantly pressure a changed individual to revert" (item "a" on page 958).

The man should not have been sent unless his associates both up the ladder and down—his boss and his subordinates—could also attend within a closely spaced period in order to change the climate on the job to one approximating the trust, openness and supportiveness developed in the person's T-group.

Naturally it adds up to T-grouping the whole management team in a short time span, which, to the traditional way of thinking, is out of the question on cost alone. The present practice therefore of those firms who do decide to try T-grouping is to start at the top of the company, division or major unit as it should be, but at the most carry it only 1-2 levels down, and at that, applying it to only part of each team, with the hope that it will trickle across and further down from there.

Few organizations are willing to go further, have yet truly accepted the idea that their managers are their most important resource and worth the expenditure and a week off—less than a quarter of the agency cost of hiring for the middle echelon. So to appease them, organizational behaviorists have, to get them started on at least something, skipped the stranger T-group and started them with variations on it: the "cousin," "peer," or "family" T-groups that they've been able to sell as cost-cutting batch-process options.

The "cousin" is composed of people from the same organization who have no working relationships, may not even know each other but have fairly similar status. The "peer" type would be all members of the same level, and some or all might know each other. The "family" is the superior-subordinate actual working team of two to three levels, ranging from 5-10 members.

The savings, one can guess, are in group lodging and miscellaneous expense control,[f] and if the organization is large enough to have in-house trainers, savings are possible there too. Even so, the intangible costs of taking such short-cuts often far exceed the savings; examples (assuming no prior stranger T-groups have been attended, in which case there is the typical low trust of conventional organizations):

- Fear that one's behavior will get back to others on the job is always present.
- For fear of opening up in all these types, no one gets past the stage of role playing in their standard effort to maintain an image or create an impression.
- The competition for leadership and the personal attacks in the cousin and peer groups can clam up the group so tight it doesn't resolve itself beyond subphase 2; indeed, none of the types really get started on the three-phase unfreeze-change-refreeze principle.

- The power, status and emotional problems of the superior-subordinate relationships in the family type are so dominating that trust and openness is impossible; commands by bosses to be honest have such a cruel effect, at least one subordinate member can usually be counted on to lose face, quit or be transferred.[8] And of course it's a great opportunity for subordinates to brown-nose.

These should raise some serious doubts about not only the cost/effectiveness of any of these three types before undergoing stranger T-grouping, but also the ethics of placing people in such situations.

Nevertheless, the rationale of the family T-group in particular has been so compelling that it's become the most popular, and if the superior and most of the members have had prior stranger T-grouping, important values changes do occur when they're guided by a highly regarded professional. For example, six months after Chris Argyris put a team of 11 top executives through the family process, most of whom and the CEO had had prior stranger T-grouping, he asked them (in a survey) about the wisdom of dealing with interpersonal problems, feelings and emotional disagreements in their group. Before the sessions, approximately 90 percent said they should be suppressed; after the 6 months, some 80-90 percent said they should be aired and resolved.[6]

Importantly, further interviews in the tenth month revealed a new development: though "the executives had not lost their capacity to behave in a more open and trustful manner, they had to suppress some of their learning because the corporate president and other divisional presidents, who were not participants in the laboratory, did not understand them."

Thus, not only must the individuals in a family T-group be made intellectually and emotionally ready first (by the stranger T-group process), other managers and groups they associate with have to be ready for what happens also.

Warren Bennis suggested the following readiness checklist:[7]

1. The core of the target system (the on-the-job) values must not be too discrepant with the lab training values.

2. The legitimacy for the change must be gained through obtaining the support of the key people (especially re misunderstandings by upper executives who learn belatedly about what's going on).
3. The employment security of the change agent (when an in-house person) must be guaranteed.
4. The voluntary commitment of the members to participate may be a crucial factor.
5. The legitimacy of interpersonal influence (decision participation) must be potentially acceptable.
6. The effects on the adjacent and interdependent subsystems must be carefully considered.
7. The state of cultural readiness must be assessed.

Some complications: it should now be evident that executives with authoritarian bent are not likely to go along with #2 and #5, precluding #1, and experience with them has shown they often will not go along with #4. If the new "team philosophy" and process/team approach to organizational effectiveness is or has been adopted—requiring significant values change of such individuals—these executives must be persuaded to undergo at least the T-grouping first step to values upgrading—refusal being good reason for removal.

NOTES

a. On this subject the assumption is always made that the persons involved are normal.

b. An advantage of group training of subordinate managers by a training specialist, videotaping and group critiquing adding persuasion.

c. The Research Center for Group Dynamics at MIT that included Kenneth Benne, Leland Bradford and Ronald Lippitt.

d. Now the NTL Institute located in Arlington, VA (22209) with 31 development seminars in its catalogue that every top HRD executive should be familiar with.

e. To repeat here for reading convenience: to mature, a group has to—overcome its obstacles to valid communication, resolve its internal conflicts, be able to mobilize its resources, and be able to take intelligent action; and only when this has occurred will it be able to develop methods of achieving and testing consensus without useless and ultimately troublesome disturbances of self-esteem. This was the hypothesis of the T-group study.

f. Travel costs should now be a minor concern because sessions are available near every major city either from universities or NTL Institute's nationwide programs.

g. The old anecdote about Sam Goldwin, who is said to have told his executive team in a meeting, "I want you to tell me what's wrong with our management even if it costs you your job!" Examples of these effects are given under "Packaged programs" on pages 1012-1017.

REFERENCES

1. Pondy, L.R., "Organizational conflict: concepts and models," *Administrative Science Quarterly*, September 1967, pp.296-320.

2. Margulies, N. and J. Wallace, *Organizational Change* (Glenview, IL: Scott Foresman, 1973), pp.6-20.

3. From E.H. Schein's description of the Lewin process in "Management development as a process of influence," *Industrial Management Review*, May 1961.

4. Bennis, W.G. and H.A. Shepard, "A theory of group development," *Human Relations*, Vol.6, November 14, 1965.

5. Levitt, T., "The managerial merry go-round," *Harvard Business Review*, July-August, 1974.

6. Argyris, C., "T-group for organizational effectiveness," *Harvard Business Review*, March-April, 1964.

7. Bennis, W.G., op.cit. (1969), pp.77-75.

Chapter 19

Organization Change

FUNDAMENTALS

To repeat for reading convenience the breakdown of the technical-social integration process on page 264 it's comprised of:

Direct integration—in all interpersonal negotiations.
Indirect integration—in two stages:

- **The first stage:** planning the structures and processes of the organization incorporating the *general* social considerations—the unilateral part.
- **The second stage:** finding out the *specific* social considerations of those concerned and affected by means of OD and incorporating them in the planning and decisions to both their satisfaction and the organization's—the participative part.

The functional activities of the *direct* have been covered (job planning in Chapter 8, goal-setting in 10, career and development planning in 17), the underlying thinking, as said, postponed to Chapter 20 because it's basic to all interpersonal leadership skills, and Part II presented the first stage of the *indirect*; now we move on to the second stage—keeping in mind that if superiors are Theory X inclined, they must remove their aversive and obstructive values and behavior before the OD techniques to be described will work, doing it by the individual change techniques of Chapter 18, that can serve them also as subordinates to *their* superiors.

Perhaps a brief review, with the aid of Figure 19.1, of the technical along with its interaction with the social covered to this point can help pull it all together and make more apparent what the goal of the whole integration effort is. Note that box #2 represents the technical functions of Chapters 11 to 15, which naturally follows the #1 of Chapter 15; box #4 is the HR management of 17, and box #3 the factors within or impinging

Organization Planning/Operating Flow Chart

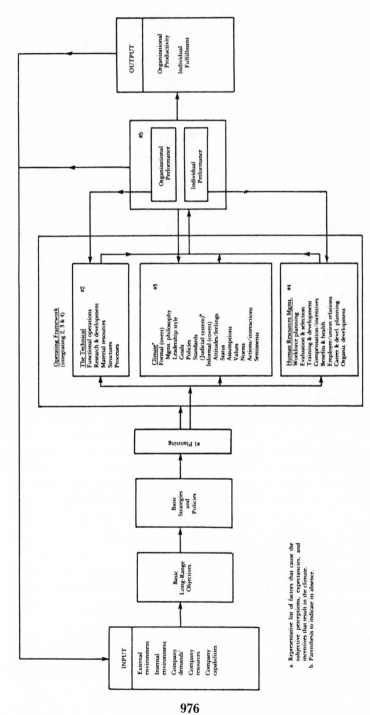

INPUT

External environment
Internal environment
Company demands'
Company resources
Company capabilities

Basic Long-Range Objectives

Basic Strategies and Policies

#1 Planning

Operating Framework
(integrating 2, 3 & 4)

#2 The Technical
Functional operations
Research & development
Material resources
Structure
Processes

#3 Climate[a]
Formal (overt)
Mgmt. philosophy
Leadership style
Goals
Policies
Standards
(Judicial system)[b]
Informal (covert)
Attitudes/feelings
Status
Assumptions
Values
Norms
Actions/interactions
Sentiments

#4 Human Resources Mgmt.
Workforce planning
Evaluation & selection
Training & development
Compensation/incentives
Benefits & health
Employee/union relations
Career & devel. planning
Organiz. development

#5
Organizational Performance
Individual Performance

OUTPUT
Organizational Productivity
Individual Fulfillment

a. Representative list of factors that cause the subjective perceptions, expectancies, and incentives that result in the climate.
b. Parenthesis to indicate its absence.

Figure 19.1

on individuals from Part I. The technical-social integration goal: bring subordinates around to acceptance of the technical in boxes #1 and #2 by the methods in #4, that include modifying the #1 and #2 to mutual satisfaction, such that their perceptions of #3 will result in optimum results in #5.

The result will be optimum if all elements of the four-way fit of *industry organization-job-people* (pages 813) are attended to. The planning of box #1 and on its left must first ensure the industry-organization fit and box #2 the organization-job fit; then with conducive policies and actions for the other items of box 4, OD is the discipline of supplementary techniques that can bring about the people fit; indeed, they're the only ones so far that have been able to (except for charisma, the commitment inspired dying when the inspirer leaves).

The reasons why OD can and participation alone cannot are pertinent: as commented at the start of Chapter 10, participation only sets the stage and presents an opportunity to negotiate an agreement without changing the values and behavior that may be at the bottom of the problems, without fostering an agreement (it may only amplify a disagreement), and without altering the associated technical changes necessary. OD can do all three.

Lest the last, the technical change, be underrated, an observation of two of the consultants involved in the Harwood-Weldon case cited in Chapter 13 (page 565) is worth quoting:[1]

> The social system must not be merely compatible with, but integral with, the system of work roles and the systems for operations control. In the Weldon case, the technical changes of considerable scope were initiated early in the program...destroying the physical basis for continuing old relationships and providing an atmosphere in which further changes were to be expected. The changes in the technology of scheduling, of information generation and flow, of work-load balancing, allocation of staff services, and the like, nearly all had features that aided social changes of the desired kinds and in turn were made possible by coordinated efforts to change individual behavior and to change the relations among the Weldon people. Where the linkage was lacking or weak, the change program faltered.

One can see that the consultants actually engaged first in a lot of unilateral planning of technical change the way traditional managements do but built in the necessary *general* social considerations. Those affected were then brought into the process before putting the changes in place to find out the *specific* ones they wanted, came to an agreement on them, and jointly planned the modifications.

However, a reading of the case will also show that neither stranger T-grouping nor direct integration were undertaken. The former omission commented on in Chapter 18 is common for current OD; the latter is a universal one critiqued ahead. Here they used for the former an abbreviated family T-group format, 2-3 day sessions with the limited goals of reducing hostile tensions and misunderstandings and improving interpersonal competence.

But the progress that was achieved is testament to what a well-organized and implemented effort at indirect integration alone can do in a situation so bad there's a lot of room for improvement. It's not possible from the project text to discern the short-range loss of omitting either of the two techniques, and publication was too soon after implementation to see the long-range effects, but a reading of it would still be invaluable to anyone interested in advanced human resources management.

Incidentally, a glance again at Figure 17.13 (page 905), Schein's tabulation of problem-solving at different growth stages, would be a helpful reminder of how in the real world top managements have tended to resort to OD and other options to solve their organizational problems associated with expansion, maturity, stagnation, decline, reorganization, etc.

Before going into the OD techniques (the "interventions") however, one needs a more comprehensive understanding of what OD entails, its character, its dynamics, and the preliminary considerations that should be taken into account.

Character of OD

No official definition of OD has yet been agreed to, but the basic elements have and can be assembled in this way, formalizing the q on page 30:

> *Organization development* is systemic planned change to improve the culture, climate and performance through the collaborative management of the organization's management technology and human resources, using

behavioral science techniques that stress participative processes, problem solving and self-renewal.

And it's applicable to organization any size, embracing all of individual change, group change and as stated, technical change, the three often occurring essentially at the same time as will be shown, and two inevitable consequences: climate improvement (the subjectively perceived and experienced qualities of the environment—p. 27) and culture improvement (some deep-seated assumptions).

OD is capable of so much because of several basic characteristics: (1) it functions integral to the organization's work such that the organization and its individuals virtually change simultaneously; (2) it is governed by humanistic values that extol the individuals involved, motivating their commitment; and (3) it capitalizes on the powers of interpersonal forces and social exchange to bring about ends and means that are mutually agreed to by the organization and its members.

The overall concept of both the direct and indirect integration illustrate the first. Each is undertaken:

1.   on the job,
  2.   learning by doing,
    3.   of actual managers,
      4.   working on real problems,
        5.   with jointly researched facts,
          6.   in the participative process,
            7.   relying on feedback
              8.   and employing behavioral science knowledge.

Moreover the discipline as a whole is (should be), as stated in the definition, built into the management system and achieved through structures and education such that the application of OD thinking and appropriate techniques become spontaneous, fitting the needs they can serve (a section on the building in is near the end of the chapter).

The consequence is that individuals, groups, structures and processes are all changed together. A comparison of traditional management development and OD illustrates it in terms of OD's educational approach. One can see in the table below that management development is only concerned with a limited part of human development and is disinterested in groups, in the interpersonal relations of the situation, and in the feedback needs of the relationships (no correlation between the two columns; they are but lists according to the left-hand column subjects).

	Management development	Organization development
Goal:	Individual effectiveness	Individual and group effectiveness
Focus:	The individual	The individual, the team, and the total organization
Methods:	One-way direct instruction Batch-process classes One-to-one feedback Examples Experience	The Lewin principle (p.959) Social Change Theory Action research and survey feedback (ahead) Confrontation techniques (ahead) On-the-job interaction within and between groups
Subjects:	The management technology and skills Managerial judgment Personality style Organization policy	Social education Interpersonal sensitivity Behavioral alternatives Group and intergroup processes Problem-solving Policies Goal-setting Indirect integrationa Leadership style
Learning time	Duration of class or study	Continuous and long-ranges
Transfer to the org.	Difficult	Built-in

Plainly, management development is restricted to unilateral "direct instruction" plus some role playing practice, which can do a good job on the technical and personal skill needs of managing to which it is largely limited, but it is unable to improve personal conduct, *group* performance, or the management technology-to-person fit.

The very principle behind it is in fact the reason why it can do no more: it accepts the organization and its management as they are, good or bad, and tries only to change *individual* performance and change it to fit the requirements of the organization without regard to the wide variety of forces influencing it—leadership, structures, processes, relationships, human needs and aspirations, and all the technical-social conflict going on.

On the second OD characteristic (page 979), humanistic values, unquestionably an application of them to the workplace is the fondest dream for operating of every subordinate, and spelling them out details at the same time the specific objectives required to achieve the stated broad purposes of OD:

OD Values and Objectives

The organization

- The psychological needs and aspirations of members are considered as important as their material needs, so they are a major management concern, one that translates into a high respect for their welfare and rights and attention to opportunities for individual growth.
- The ultimate character of the organization and its parts toward which the management is aiming is the description of "System 4" provided by Rensis Likert (page 576).

Leadership

- Theory Y (page 16) and humanism (page 176).
- Rank imposes obligation with regard to the welfare and growth of subordinates as well as of the organization.
- A readiness to share power with one's team and a habit of transcending power struggles, allowing individual subordinates to take the lead in instances of demonstrated superior knowledge or competence.
- Decision-making should be as close to the source of information as feasible rather than by position or status.
- Feelings and sentiments are recognized and accepted as significant components of attitudes, opinions, performance, satisfaction and commitment, and the consequence of honoring them is more effective problem-solving, planning, decisions, and action.
- Both the leader of teams and members realize that the formal leader cannot perform all leadership and maintenance functions alone, thus the concept of participation and collaborative management of the management technology and culture are legitimized out of necessity as indispensable to optimum functioning.

Interpersonal and intragroup relations

- Conflict is a normal occurrence between people, much of it constructive, that should be dealt with openly and as objectively as possible; win-lose conflict, however, is one type that seldom contributes in the long-run to effective organizational relations, and of course destructive conflict never does.
- Most interpersonal and intragroup problems are resolvable by the parties working together to produce agreement on effective solutions.
- A climate of trust, openness, supportiveness and the sharing of relevant information is crucial to interpersonal and group processes, so their development must be initial as well as constant concerns.

- Behavior change of an individual must be accompanied by similar change of coworkers and change of associated structures and processes for the individual change to be maintained.

Intergroup relations
- The sources of conflict between interacting and interdependent groups—inappropriate competition, functional differentiation, goals, value differences, personalities, etc.—mandate collaborative resolution of the conflicts for mutual modification of their interaction behavior toward greater cooperation and effectiveness.
- There are two reasons why a linking-pin participative decision-making system is essential to the effectiveness of any organization: (a) the decisions, policies, practices and events of the organization as a whole influence its subgroups and vice versa, and (b) the positions of managers as both subordinates on the teams of their superiors and as superiors of their own makes the operation of the linking-pin function crucial for the transfer of valid information for decision-making at all levels.

And the third OD characteristic on page 979, effecting a mutuality of ends and means through interpersonal relations and social exchange, introduces the dynamics of OD one needs to know to carry out the techniques.

OD dynamics

The experiences of the Lewin research team at Connecticut State Teachers College in 1946 evolved what was labelled the *action research principle* that essentially formalized the (I) to (8) elements listed on page 979 as the heart of OD dynamics and what should be the core of a basic process for all OD intervention techniques.

To be historically more precise, Kurt Lewin died in the Fall of 1947, at which time his organization was transferred to the University of Michigan's Institute for Social Research (ISR) headed by Rensis Likert, and shortly after Floyd Mann converted the elements of the principle to the accepted basic process, which became known as the *survey feedback* technique, refining it and applying it first in the landmark Detroit Edison case (1948).

At the utility Mann found that intensive team analysis by managers and their subordinates of a survey of the subordinates' attitudes about the group's and company's leadership, structures, and processes (the survey undertaken by an outside consultant) could bring about significant improvement of the group's attitude, climate and performance; further, if the analysis conclusions of the organization's groups at each level were fed up from level to level then back down according to the linking-pin function (page 573); there was an interrelated increase in the improvements of the individual groups and the organization as a whole.

Using the flowchart below, a scenario of the technique would read like this. The reason for doing it: ordinarily a top executive of a unit or the company who has at least done a little reading about OD, faced with unsatisfactory performance, concludes that is may be due to the way the subordinates have been functioning as a team or in managing their own subordinates; technical malfunctions may be suspect but be considered a result of it.

Flowchart of The Surveys Feedback Technique

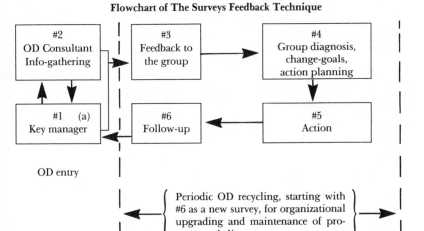

The executive calls in an OD consultant (1), and the consultant suggests a survey of what the subordinates think the problems might be and their solutions (2). The results of the survey—always with respondent confidentiality whether by written forms or personal interview—are reported back to the executive, and the consultant recommends reviewing them with the subordinates to go over the responses, diagnose problem causes, get their ideas on what the best solutions might be, and jointly plan corrective action.

The meeting is held (3); the group studies the data, comes to agreement on what the problems are, sets goals for change, and plans a program to achieve them (4);[b] during all this the consultant acts as a passive aide and facilitator and the executive presides.

The plans are carried out (5), the group members themselves being responsible for their parts, the executive for his or her part, such as policies, structures, processes or changes of personal behavior. A while later a follow-up reading is taken of the results (6) and fed back to the manager and group. If OD is permanently established as an organizational function, the technique is made a standard problem-solving and periodic climate improvement/ maintenance method.

Clearly, the word "research" in action research is used loosely, not scientifically, to refer to the combination of the survey and subsequent analysis, and the "action" is the planning, implementation and reiterative improving and updating of plans and decisions through feedback.

One can see that all of the steps in the standard problem-solving procedure on page xxii are carried out: the survey is the "informal" investigation"; the problem assumptions and models are at least in the team's heads during the box #4 diagnosis (though the diagnosis should spell them out) when the formal investigation, analysis, design and choice take place sequentially.

However, the differences for (A) the assumptions and (B) the consequent processes (between conventional problem-solving and survey feedback) are the reasons why one cannot solve behavioral problems and the other can.

A. The conventional technique makes the three assumptions: (1) there is a specific answer to the problem at hand; (2) an outside (of the group) specialist can identify the problem and design the answer; and (3) applying the answer will solve the problem as with a technical malfunction.

In other words, the consultant does the diagnosis and design after Step #2 in the flow chart above, recommends an alternative, and walks away. Though the three parties—the consultant, the executive and the subordinate group—are all involved, nothing happens until the executive exercises unilateral power and orders the group to implement the recommendations. It is an arrangement that authoritarians feel comfortable with, but if the problem is behavioral as suspected, a unilateral order to correct it would obviously be a waste of time.

Action research, on the other hand, makes three very different assumptions: (1) when dealing with behavior there are too many variables for there to be specific, clear-cut answers to its problems; there are no pat solutions.

(2) The truthful *problem* and *cause facts*—the "valid information"—is not obtainable by an outside expert with even the most competent interviewing of the subordinates partly because of the one-to-one nature of the procedure and partly for lack of trust. The valid information can only be generated in the interpersonal interaction of the group probing the symptoms, problems and solutions together (assuming the superior has established the minimum trust necessary).

And (3), behavioral problems are not solved once-and-for-all by correct answers the way technical ones can be; they are solved by changing attitudes that are in themselves obviously neither final nor clear-cut, are subject to change again or regression, and the changes need maintenance.

B. Discernible, each set of assumptions cannot help but lead to totally different problem-solving processes, and three differences in the two approaches are particularly significant, the differences of (a) power distribution, (b) research and decision responsibility and (c) the problem solving length of time.

(a) In contrast to the absence of power-sharing extant in standard problem-solving, once a superior has conceded to go ahead with an action research-based process, some unilateral power has willingly been given up to allow the group to share in collaborative diagnosis, goal-setting and planning (box #4). A cybernetic, adaptive technique has been created that makes possible all of valid information, acceptance of solutions, and commitment to results.

(b) After a survey feedback start-up (box #2) the potential for cybernetic collaboration created is made a reality by having the diagnostic research and decision-making done by the group and superior together instead of respectively the consultant and superior alone, and because of the joint effort the group acquires a sense of ownership and responsibility for success—commitment.

To explain (c), the standard procedure, we know, not only has time delays between its six steps and the transfer between people, but the action step (box #5) may not even be reached if the boss does not like or act on the recommendation.

In the survey feedback techniques all delays are eliminated by having all steps done by the same people in essentially one step; moreover, implementation is automatic if the boss follows the rules, which is hard not to do after the process is allowed to start.

In summary, the survey feedback technique is a consequence of a total view of the causes of group performance problems—that they're most often due to all the interrelated social and technical forces together, not just individual behavioral, skill, or task inadequacies. Thus, in engaging systematically all the elements and influences that impinge on the problem, improvement has a high probability when the technique is managed well.

Additionally, when it's applied to the whole organization through the linking-pin function one has a major solution to the "organizational feedback learning" need described in Chapter 4 (pages, 99-101).

Of course the technique is nothing new to progressive firms. it's estimated that well over 100,000 employees up through senior management are experiencing it annually to solve a wide variety of operating problems. In G.E. alone over 20,000 now go through it each year.

A major caveat: don't ask for the survey if you're not willing to complete the process—share the information, plan correction together, and act on the plan. A survey always raises expectations, and failure to follow through on results generally sends morale to a new low.

Preliminary considerations

Before managers decide to use OD they should give serious thought to four OD issues to avoid problems on them:

1. The use of an outside professional
2. The manager's own cultural state of readiness,
3. The prospects for success:

    (a)   The dominant problem: the situation's susceptibility to OD treatment,

    (b)   The point of entry,

    (c)   The present state of the climate—its conduciveness or not to success.

  4. The organization's growth stage.

1. The use of OD in a company or organization for the first time has almost invariably been due to the selling and effort of an outside consultant, because, still, few managers are convinced of its potential, those who are often see a threat or too high a risk, and conventional personnel departments are not up to proposing it or educating on it. So if you've decided to go ahead on it, it's only natural to wonder whether or not that person or any professional should be hired to help apply it. There are three reasons in particular why the answer is yes, at least in the beginning.

First, recall the psychological subtleties and potential pitfalls of OD described in Chapter 18 (and more in "Problems" ahead); particularly, is the risk of damaged relationships worth the cost of trying to do-it-yourself?

Second, since all OD involves participation and collaboration, you as superior may be faced with the problem of believability by subordinates in suddenly suggesting these activities. An objective independent catalyst is needed.

And third, the participation and collaboration of the group virtually mandate that the real concerns of the group be on the agenda for any intervention. The gathering of facts of this sort in confidentiality by a reputable consultant is one of the best solutions, often the only one.

However, you may have heard about, been warned about, or experienced the dependency that less-principled consultants try to develop. Page 1028 on the client-consultant relationship will describe how to prevent it and what else to guard against.

It is important to keep in mind too what their experience is. Clients should not look to them for substantive personnel management or personnel policy advice; they're seldom experienced management executives or seasoned decision-makers.

Furthermore, if a manager starts asking for substantive decision advice and is emotionally pleased with what is heard, it's easy for the person to slide into the very dependence feared. In fact the more astute consultants know better than to give it: if the advice proves later to have been wrong, scratch one client.

2. Cultural readiness refers to one's ability to accommodate the values of OD that have been described.[c] For most managers OD requires at the least some philosophic and attitudinal change, change that will result correspondingly in:

(a)   A shift of some authority and influence toward subordinates for the collaboration on analyses, decisions, planning and action.

(b)   The opening up of communication to provide the desirable freedom in all directions: up, down, laterally, diagonally.

(c)   A looser control over the subordinates with more delegation and more motivation of self-control.

(d)   The release of much information to them that may have been previously withheld.

Generally, the event that paves the way is the "pain" or frustration that induced the invitation to the consultant, who must at that time persuade an acceptance of the above points. Then, the first sign of probable readiness is the concession to carry out the feedback and joint discussion of the initial survey. When a manager begins to take this small interest in subordinates' views and feelings and moves in the group meeting toward genuine listening, (a) above has begun to occur, and (b), (c), and (d) tend to follow shortly after.

Judging this cultural readiness and educating about it is of course a responsibility of the consultant. During the preliminary meetings when the manager is getting the feel of the consultant's competence and experience, the consultant must be sizing up the client at the same time through questioning and should, before closing the deal, present the evaluation, discuss the four points above, and make a go-no-go decision on his or her own part based on the prospects of success. If, for example, the manager turns out to be strongly authoritarian, and further, one who wants to use the OD manipulatively, the success probability will obviously be very low, and the consultant had better withdraw.

3a. The reason for the withdrawal is not just for the consultant's reputation; the first OD project must be a success for the company's sake.

If it fails, it's apt to be a long time before OD is tried again due to the emotional costs of failure, and the benefits that must be foregone during the wait while competitors move ahead can be telling.

The consultant therefore has to try hard to plant the seed in the organization where it will start a chain-letter multiplication of other projects, an event that will occur only if it is both clearly visible and successful. Ten situations were listed by one behavioral consultant as particularly susceptible to OD and therefore good start-up candidates: where there is a need to (and management recognizes it or is helped to by the consultant):[2]

- Change structures, and roles, often the aim of a new top executive.
- Change a major managerial policy and its subsystems such as decision-making, personnel policies, or compensation policies.
- Open up the communication system, the central problem of most organizations.
- Do better planning—broader involvement and showing managers down the line how.
- Improve the motivation of parts or all of the organizations.
- Adapt to a changed or new environment, e.g, changed market, economic or sociological condition.
- Change obstructive values, norms or attitudes, such as those about authority, conformity, control (others on page 118).
- Improve intergroup collaboration, especially groups that are competing harmfully.
- Cope with problems of merger, e.g., the human problems on integrating different cultures, goals, expectations, resources.

3b. Behaviorists refer to good points of entry as "leverage points" and rank them as to accessibility and linkage to other parts of the organization.

Entry at the top of a company or division naturally affords the best leverage for decision control, organization influence and multiplication down the ladder; and, restating here the importance of top executives' personal commitment and involvement (and the consultants' effort to inspire it) is not overdoing it. Time and again failure has occurred because they have wanted it for their teams but, in their emotional insecurity, feared their ability to handle the openness, typically leading to last-minute excuses to miss key OD sessions. Subordinate executives see the evasion as meaning a low priority and follow suit, the effort falls to pieces, OD is blamed, and the discipline is blackballed in the whole organization.

Successes have started at the department level also. A manager "in pain" and/or with a new awareness of OD's potential gets permission to explore and implement it; then success encourages the superior to take an interest, recommend it to others in the division, and perhaps get personally involved. This is the way it happened at TRW Systems, the most outstanding continuous success, the initial impetus coming from the industrial relations department using an outside consultant.

Sometimes too a bright OD-educated HRD staff person, smart enough to look for the combination of a good leverage point and progressive line executive, exposes the executive to the behavioral solutions, and OD is started.

3c. Concerning the conduciveness of the climate, plainly it's a function of the superior's philosophy, values, attitudes and readiness, and close behind are those of the group members, all of which determine relationships, norms, feelings, etc. But some clarification is needed.

What counts is that the minimal amount of trust, openness and supportiveness be present to fit the OD technique used, and the key to the minimal is how deep behavior is to be probed.

It will be seen ahead that some OD interventions can do a lot at a fairly shallow level, as for example the survey feedback above and the "diagnostic" and organization-wide "confrontation meeting" techniques to be explained; it is for this reason that they are good introductory projects. But in some others, like intragroup family team development, there is a need to bring to the surface attitudes, opinions and assumptions in order to reconcile differences...which, as explained in Chapter 18, requires indispensable preliminary behavioral preparation.

Perhaps it should be repeated too that the maximum depth of any intervention technique in probing attitudes and opinions must be observable (that is, by eye or ear) behavior without digging into motivation. It takes some practice under the instruction of a professional.

4. One will recall that in the "Succession" section of Chapter 17, E. Schein, it was stated, had advised that when deciding the candidates for succession in an organization with or anticipating serious problems due to the nature of the culture (assumptions, values and beliefs that fundamentally govern decisions and behavior), the candidate selectors should give consideration to the growth stage of the organization (the three ones in Figure 17.13), because the stage tends to mandate the mechanism most effective for culture change.

Of course the goal and function of OD is to change those factors, factors that generally manifest themselves as climate consequences, one of which is stultifying bureaucracy. Interventions of OD can be effective in both stages II and III, but OD is but one of eleven mechanisms, the circumstances, environment and problems often bringing about the need for specific ones to achieve successful change, and success on a number of the ten depends on the personality, character, experience, initiative, and competence of the CEO in charge. The selection of a new one free of the constraints holding back the current CEO has commonly been crucial to the changes for the better the board wants implemented.

The thumbnail sketches there of 8 of the mechanisms explain their nature, and the detail on OD follows.

OD INTERVENTIONS

To summarize why managers need to be familiar with these, it's been shown that, assuming reasonably good unit technical competence (not performance), any attempt to improve the unit's performance must be done through the change of behavior, structures or processes, or the change of two or all three of these where there's an interaction or interrelationship of the two or three. Further, when behavior is involved, the behavior of normal people can be changed fairly quickly via social change theory (pages 957-958). OD interventions are the theory in action, the structured behavioral science techniques in the definition of OD on page 978, able concurrently to effect the change of all related and associated influences through developed participative procedures.

And, although OD professionals are needed to introduce, teach and guide the start-up of interventions, the superiors must always do the leading from the beginning, eventually undertake them entirely on their own.

The principal interventions are the ones listed below, grouped in their four categories of improvement (change for the better), multiple-use shown by the repetitions:[d]

Interventions	Directed at
Stranger T-group Direct integration Role prescription	Individual development
Survey feedback Family team diagnostic meeting Role prescription Family, cousin, peer T-group Process consultation Family group team-building meetings	Intragroup development
Survey feedback Process consultation Intergroup team-building Organization mirror	Intergroup development
Survey feedback Top management diagnostic committee Confrontation meeting Tailored multiple-intervention)	Total-organization development

Having described earlier those in the "individual" category, the discourse here will move on to the others, giving first some general principles of design for guidance, needed because all the descriptions are basic formats that it require some degree of fitting to the situation. One OD text phrased the major ones as follows:[3]

- Structure the activity so that the relevant people are there, those who are affected by the problem or opportunity being worked on.
- Structure it so that it deals primarily with a real problem or opportunity of the participants, generated and defined by them.
- Structure it so the goal of the problem or opportunity and the goal of the intervention are clear and such that the processes of reaching them are clear.
- Structure it so that there is a high probability of success on each. The task can still be hard, complicated, taxing but it should be attainable; and if there is failure the reasons should be searched for and made clear to avoid failure repetition.
- Structure it so that it contains both experience-based learning and conceptual/theoretical-based learning that puts the experience into a broader framework.
- Structure it so the participants learn both how to solve a particular problem and "learn how to learn" at the same time; chief methods: "time for reflection" and/or "critiqing" the process. A devotion of as much as half the time to one or both may be advisable.
- Structure the climate so that the individuals are "freed up" rather than anxious or defensive, expect to learn together and are willing to experiment for better alternatives.
- Structure the activity so that the individuals are engaged as whole persons, not segmented persons. This means that the role demands, thoughts, beliefs, feelings and striving should be called into play, not just one or two of these, to enhance the individual's ability to cope and grow.

Intragroup development

Three of the interventions in the list are principally for *diagnosis* alone: the diagnostic meeting, role prescription (p. 94), and process consultation; while the team building is for *development*, two steps that are applied also in the intergroup and total-organization development.

The family team diagnostic meeting. Like the "survey feedback" it's a good introduction to OD for superior. It is only a problem identification procedure, the probe is not deep, and if the superior is fairly open and participative with subordinates, it can be successfully undertaken without preliminary psychological or emotional preparation (e.g., Stranger T-grouping).

An OD consultant or trained in-house (HRD) facilitator familiarizes the manager in advance with the technique, explains that its purpose is only to identify and discuss the team's strengths and weaknesses, not solve problems uncovered (forbidden) and ascertains the superior's willingness to lead it and do it participatively. The issues examined:

> The clarity of the team purpose and goals
> The degree of mutual support and trust
> Collaboration vs. interpersonal competition
> Group dynamics
> Operating processes

The group dynamics refer to norms, cohesion, group roles, actions, interactions, and sentiments; the operating processes are those of communication, collaboration; goal-setting, problem-solving, decision-making, planning, conflict resolution, role performance, control methods, leadership.

It requires that the team spend about a day in a secluded location free from interruptions, and the facilitator does no more than his/her title indicates.

The Family Team Diagnostic Meeting

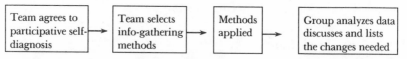

Although capable enlightened managers inexperienced with the procedure can do it by the book, the third party assistant is strongly recommended even for them for the first two or three applications, because a good one greatly reduces the uncertainty for all, and he or she has a wide variety of devices to ensure progress, methods to bring out problems not easily recognized, to generate valid data, resolve complications an inexperienced group might have difficulty with, keep the meeting from bogging down or getting dull, and generally maintain momentum; among them: fishbowling (page 1002), collages,[e] polling, drawings, charting, critiqing, interviewing, subgrouping, pairing.

After two or three such projects with the facilitator's guidance managers usually find themselves able to initiate and undertake the technique on their own. For an excellent "ice-breaker" each time, they might try the simple polling a questionnaire in Figure 19.2 designed by Douglas McGregor rating each factor from 1 to 7.[4f]

One can see that, like the survey feedback, the diagnostic meeting is another way for an organization's teams to develop effectiveness and vitality but do it more quickly and less expensively.[g] This one, however, requires that the teams have somewhat more openness, cohesion and desire to collaborate.

Correspondingly, it's an ideal technique for a *new* team after a few weeks of its operation or one that's just experienced a significant change—the leader, members, responsibilities, environment—to help it adjust and/or become effective within days instead of months—again, assuming a genuinely participative leader (which the facilitator first verifies). Examples of its capabilities in this regard:

- Getting them better acquainted and collaboratively working together.
- Learning about the leadership style and expectations of the leader.
- The members learning with the leader how to make their expectations and aspirations congruent.
- Clarifying team goals and priorities.
- Defining authorities and responsibilities, perhaps using "role prescription."
- Determining structures, processes, policies, procedures and communication.
- Getting the feel of norms.
- Getting a running start.

1. Degree of mutual trust:
   High suspicion ———————————————— High trust
         (1)   (7)

2. Degree of mutual support:
   Every man for himself ———————————— Genuine concern
                                           for each other
         (1)   (7)

3. Communications:
   Guarded, cautious ——————————————— Open, authentic
         (1)   (7)

   We don't listen to   We listen; we understand
   each other ————————————————————— and are understood
         (1)   (7)

4. Team objectives
   not understood by team ———————————— Clearly understood by team
              (1)   (7)

   Team is negative   Team is committed
   toward objectives —————————————————— to objective
         (1)   (7)

5. Handling conflicts within team:
   We deny, avoid. or   We accept conflicts and
   suppress conflicts ————————————————— "work them through"
         (1)   (7)

6. Utilization of member resources:
   Our abilities, knowledge,   Our abilities, knowledge,
   and experience aren't   and experience are fully
   utilized by the team ————————————————— utilized by the team
         (1)   (7)

7. Control methods:
   Control is imposed on us   We control ourselves
            (1)   (7)

8. Organizational Environment:
   restrictive; pressure   Free; supportive;
   toward conformity ———————————————— respect for individual
                                            differences
           (1)   (7)

Figure 19.2

The second diagnostic method listed, *process consultation*, is capable of greater depth, which may be necessary for any progress on well established teams, like most of those at the top, that are firmly imbued with deep-seated habits and norms difficult to uncover just with open discussion.

The depth is achieved by a behavioral professional analyzing the group processes (page 994) as illustrated on pages 197-198, where Chris Argyris tape-recorded three operating meetings of a progressive top management team that had worked on team development for several years and critiqued the tapes with the playback in an educational way: having them listen to their own behavior in the playback to judge for themselves, giving an objective professional explanation of the interpersonal consequences holding discussions of alternative behavior and their consequences, letting them draw their own conclusions.

Family Group team-building meetings. Many consultants call team-building the most important of all OD interventions and with good reason: the first requisite of making an organization healthy and effective is to make its sub-groups, especially its management teams, function well internally. The technique is particularly good for both problem-solving and maintenance in this regard. Some typical situations that might prompt superiors to use it:

- Frequent bogging down or lack of progress in discussions;
- Visible interpersonal friction;[h]
- Dissatisfaction with the team's cohesion, openness, commitment or productivity;
- Dissatisfaction with the functioning of any of the processes listed on page 994;
- Concern about one's own personality style and how it affects members.

The procedure is also the same as the survey feedback on page 983 with these important differences:

— The survey feedback is superior/consultant planned, while the most effective of these is participatively planned with

the team members: goals, information gathering method, agenda, and so on.
— The gathered information in the former is an attitude survey of fairly general nature; in these it's a specific opinion survey in depth on any or all of the diagnostic meeting (which is a good preliminary) subjects listed above believed to be hindering progress.
— The former is usually used before the climate of the team(s) has been ascertained, so the participative discourse (in box #4) is as expected fairly shallow; these must be in depth to achieve better than the diagnostic meeting, so being freed-up is essential.

Again as for diagnostic meetings, a third party professional during the first two or three applications can be invaluable and for the same reasons. McGregor himself warned that an attempt to do-it-yourself should be with great care and an awareness of the dangers[6] (more on team development in Chapter 20).

Intergroup development

Where the organization or system has two or more interdependent groups, departments or divisions that should cooperate toward a common goal, the needed teamwork, we know, is not always present.

The signs are excessive delays and errors, arguments, missing information, negative we-they attitudes, stereotype labeling, hostilities, etc., and Murphy's law in full force: anything that can go wrong will. They may even be competing instead of cooperating. The conventional solutions have been:

- *Stricter rules*—the Theory X manager's reaction to unsatisfactory performance.
- *Hands off*—let them fight it out; the winner lays down the rules (producing deeper hostilities).
- *Negotiation by the managers*—the arguers are not satisfied, the causes remain, time is wasted in repeated negotiating.

- *Criss-cross panels*—negotiation by representation resulting in compromise not touching the causes, technical or behavioral.
- *Exchange of members (followed by return)*—those strongly negative or positive do not change, only the neutrals do; those important to operations cannot be given up for the exchange; emotional attachment to home base tends to keep mental doors closed.
- *Consolidation of the groups under one manager*—group heads can learn to cooperate, but with functions still specialized and the same tasks to be done, the attitudes of the others seldom change.

The essential ingredients are missing in each: the participation of all subordinates affected (at least the majority or key ones), the joint analysis, a mutually acceptable agreed-to solution. Intergroup team-building is the most effective approach to supply them for the two groups, and the organization mirror, also usable for two, is particularly good for three or more (intergroup conflict management is covered in Chapter 20).

Intergroup team-building. The process is both diagnostic and developmental in one technique. The goal must be not only to (a) diagnose and resolve all dysfunctional issues and disagreements but (b) build a greater awareness of the interdependence and (c) identify and rectify any structural or process impediments to cooperation, such as an absence of sufficient intercommunication, the need for rewards that foster cooperation instead of competition, or the presence of unnecessary red tape.

Every group or department of a division of course must cooperate closely with, at least one other—sales and manufacturing, R & D and engineering, headquarters and field, line and staff, and also purchasing externally with suppliers and sales with customer groups. All are subject to misunderstanding, friction, parochialism and are therefore prospects for this treatment.

But a perceptive analysis first of the overall problem is important. An organization planner, for example, might easily prescribe a "lateral relations" structure as a solution, assuming it to be a "differentiation-integration" problem (pages 821-832) when in fact this solution may be what's needed because the dysfunction involves all in the groups. There is the possibility too that it may be a necessary preliminary for a lateral relations structure to succeed.

The TRW Systems procedure described by Fordyce and Weil and shown in Figure 19.3 is a good example of the technique:[7]

1. *Setting up the objectives* by the planning committee of the two group managers and the consultant or HRD staff person.
2. *Collecting the information,* done by the consultant or staff the same way as for the survey feedback process.[i]
3. *Conducting the meeting—*
    (a) Each group in a separate room develops 3 lists:
        *   A positive feedback list—what they like about the other group (it makes the climate in the next steps more receptive and congenial).
        *   A bug list—what they don't like.
        *   An empathy list—a prediction of what the others are listing as (a) and (b) for themselves. (This accentuates the gap in perception between the two groups that has to be filled).
    (b) The groups reconvene, and each presents its lists, after which, without discussion, they combine the two bug lists and rank the items as to importance.
    (c) Subgroups, half and half from the two teams, are formed and instructed to work on each item.
    (d) The subgroups reconvene and report their conclusions, and the total meeting formulates a list of action items that it commits itself to perform; the items are assigned and scheduled.
4. *Follow-up—*crucial to success. A shorter meeting 4 to 5 weeks later in which the same subgroups make progress reports, evaluate the maintenance of open communication originally obtained, replan and reschedule.

Procedure for the Intergroup Team-building Meeting

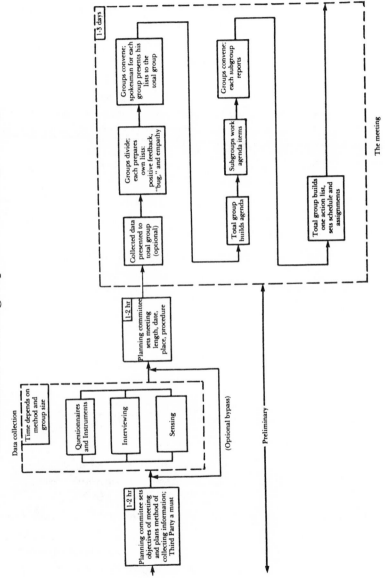

Figure 19.3

The authors added the following suggestions from their own experience: the managers must accept lead responsibility for the meeting. They must set the standard for candor. Don't go into a group meeting if you haven't solved serious internal personal problems; they contaminate the process. Restrict the scope to those things the group can do something about. Use 1/2 to 2 days, more if necessary to substantially achieve the objectives.

Organization mirror. The organization mirror applies principles similar to those of intra- and intergroup team-building in a way that places the emphasis on the feedback to representatives of one organization, called the host, from representatives of two or more others with which the host has, or should have, considerable interaction.

The "fishbowl" is the basic concept. An inner circle (the seating) of guests discusses the collected information showing problems, complaints and compliments about the host, while it as the host around the outside listens and takes notes; then they reverse the roles.

Fordyce and Weil listed these typical applications:[8]

- Staff groups that service the line organization where there's low use of the services or undue conflict.
- An organization being by-passed.
- When things seem too good.
- When the product isn't being bought.
- When a group received no information about its performance.
- When a group receives undeserved criticism.
- When ability to perform is impaired by other groups.
- When interface problems embrace a number of groups.

The guest should be composed of highly regarded members of their units, capable of insight and communicating and willing to help. The consultant or HRD staff person interviews them before the meeting to describe the technique's nature and get their opinions about the host, encouraging positive as well as negative comments.

The total number of participants including the host should not exceed 20, with about an equal balance of guests-to-hosts for a subgrouping balance, and the meeting should take a full day, two if needed.

The host manager leads the entire operation starting with an introduction of the meeting purpose and a presentation of the meeting's schedule. The rest proceeds as below:

Organization Mirror Procedure

Step
1. The host manager's opening.
2. Third-party presentation of interview data.
3. Outsiders fishbowl, in inner circle, discuss data, the host group listens and takes notes.
4. The host group fishbowls, discusses the data and the outsiders' comments.
5. Summary by total group.

Lunch

6. Mixed subgroups determine and rank the top 5 desirable changes.
7. Total group reconvenes, integrates the results in one list.
8. Mixed subgroups work on solutions, action plans, assignments, schedules.
9. Total group recommence, subgroups report, joint planning of actions.
10. After a short break, the host manager summarizes and commits the host organization to carrying out the planned action.

In step #5 only summarizing is done, no work on solutions, after which the meeting usually goes to lunch. The mixed subgroups in #6 also do not work on solutions, only select and rank. The rest is as described.

like team-building, and even more so, follow-up action is crucial to return on investment, and here, to future relations with the guests. Progress reports to them one month and six months later, possibly including short meetings, can importantly improve future cooperation and regard. Typical after-meeting reactions:[9]

Outsiders: "I think they finally heard what we have been trying to tell them."

"I was encouraged by the way they paid attention to our comments. I don't know if I could have listened to that kind of stuff."

"I have a better sense of all they have to put up with. I'll be a little more responsive in the future."

Host individuals: "I was surprised at the number of good things they had to say about us."

"We sure have a lot of work to do!"

Total organization development[j]

The four interventions listed on page 992 in this category were, recall, the survey feedback, the top management diagnostic meeting, the confrontation meeting, and the tailored multiple-intervention approach. And within the last, there are a few ready-made packaged programs, the best known being "Grid OD," that warrant separate consideration.

The survey feedback, illustrated with the Detroit Edison project on pages 982-983, though the first application of OD to industry, remains popular and will continue to be for its limited intent because it succeeds, but if, as was there, many groups in a large organization are to be engaged, the technique is time-consuming and expensive. There are instances when a top management only wants a "temperature-taking" or progress report at low cost and others when it must have fast results on at least the major problems. The "top management diagnostic committee" complies with the low cost temperature-taking, and the "confrontation meeting" gives the fast organizational results, each with important limitations.

Top management diagnostic committee. A committee of this sort can be for a one-shot project or be a relatively permanent OD advisory committee to the top of a company or division, one that utilizes a survey, interviews, or sensing once a year to evaluate OD progress, problems, and needs for OD projects.

The CEO or executive v.p. heads it and has as members the top administrative and HRD officers, an outside consultant for interviewing or a survey if either is the fact-gathering choice, and about a half-dozen rotating temporary members, progressive highly regarded executives from the key position ladder in different divisions or departments.

The procedure is the familiar one: the committee meets to decide the data collection method and administrative detail, the data is gathered, the committee evaluates and recommends.

It is as effective as the CEO wants it to be and feels OD is important, and the participation can be a material factor in sustaining OD interest and commitment throughout the organization involved. It has to be kept advisory however to prevent offensive authority intrusions that can lead to resentment.

Confrontation meeting.[k] Given that confrontation is the best way to handle most conflicts and interpersonal problems (page 823), getting a management group or an organization's whole management team to do it in a specific systematic way is called a confrontation meeting.

Richard Beckhard constructed the original procedure to solve a particular problem in one of his consulting projects a problem that commonly occurs: a period of major change or stress in which the top management must quickly assess the state of the organization's general health and get valid information on what should be done if anything.[10] Typical incidents of change or stress where it can be appropriate:

- A new CEO takes over
- A reorganization
- A merger
- Loss of a key customer shaking up the firm
- An important technological change in the industry.
- Start-up of a major new product.

Beckhard described a common occurrence in a change of command: in the beginning the top group tends to spend a lot of time together planning the changeover and future; with a good leader it builds its own team cohesion and commitment, but it is so busy, communications with middle-management are slighted; anxiety sets in lower down over what's being planned for them, morale and productivity suffer.

If the CEO were to instruct the top team to communicate better with them it might fill the void, but can a new CEO count on its effectiveness and rely on a new team to feed back the negative as well as the positive (when considering what any CEO normally gets) and do it all soon enough?

CONFRONTATION MEETING

Here is a detailed description of the seven components which make up the specific "design" for the day-long confrontation meeting.

Phase 1. Climate Setting (Forty-five minutes to one hour)

At the outset, the top manager needs to communicate to the total management group his goals for the meeting, and his concern for and interest in free discussion and issue facing. He also has to assure his people that there is no punishment for open confrontation.

It is also helpful to have some form of information session or lecture by the top manager or a consultant. Appropriate subjects might deal with the problems of communication, the need for understanding, the assumption and the goals of the total organization, the concept of shared responsibility for the future of the organization, and the opportunity for and responsibility of influencing the organization.

Phase 2. Information Collecting (One hour)

The total group is divided into small heterogeneous units of seven or eight people. If there is a top management team that has been holding sessions regularly, it meets as a separate unit. The rest of the participants are assigned to units with a "diagonal slice" of the organization used as a basis for composition—that is, no boss and subordinate are together, and each unit contains members from every functional area.

The assignment given to each of these units is along these lines:

> Think of yourself as an individual with needs and goals. Also think as a person concerned about the total organization. What are the obstacles, "demotivators," poor procedures or policies, unclear goals, or poor attitude that exist today? What different conditions, if any, would make the organization more effective and make life in the organization better?"

Each unit is instructed to select a reporter to present its results at a general information-collecting session to be held one hour later.

Phase 3. Information Sharing (One hour)

Each reporter writes his unit's complete findings on newsprint, which is tacked up around the room. The meeting leader suggests some categories under which all the sheets can be located. In other words, if there are 75 items, the likelihood is that these can be grouped into 6 or 7 major categories—say, by type of problem, such as "communications difficulties"; or by type of relationship, such as "problems with top management"; or by type of area involved, such as problems in the mechanical department"

Then the meeting breaks, either for lunch or, if it happens to be an evening session, until the next morning.

During the break all the data sheets are duplicated for general distribution.

Phase 4. Priority Setting and Group Action Planning (One hour and fifteen minutes)

The total group reconvenes for a 15-minute general session. With the meeting leader, they go through the raw data on the duplicated sheets and put category numbers by each piece of data.

People are now assigned to their functional, natural work units for a one-hour session. Manufacturing people at all levels go to one unit, everybody in sales to another, and so forth. These units are headed by a department manager or division head as that function. This means that some units may have as few as 3 people and some as many as 25. Each unit is charged to perform three specific tasks:

1. Discuss the problems and issues which affect its area. Decide on the priorities and early actions to which the group is prepared to commit itself. (They should be prepared to share this commitment with their colleagues at the general session.)

2. Identify the issues and/or problems to which the top management team should give its priority attention.

3. Decide how to communicate the results of the session to their subordinates.

Phase 5. Organization Action Planning (One to two hours)

The total management group reconvenes in a general session, where:

1. Each functional unit reports its commitment and plans to the total group.

2. Each unit reports and lists the items that its members believe the management team should deal with first.

3. The top manager reacts to this list and makes commitments (through setting targets or assigning task forces or timetables, and so on) for action where required.

4. Each unit shares briefly as plans for communicating the results of the confrontation meeting to all subordinates.

Phase 6. Immediate Follow-up by Top Team (One to three hours)

The top management team meets immediately after the confrontation meeting ends to plan first follow-up actions, which should then be reported back to the total management group within a few days.

Phase 7. Progress Review (Two hours)

Follow-up with total management group four to six weeks later.

Figure 19.4

A survey could also tell the principal concerns and prevailing attitudes, but it takes a lot of time, is essentially unilateral, does little to relieve the stresses or anxieties, and solves none of the problems. The confrontation meeting can achieve all of these and do it in one day for a unit or management group running in the hundreds—the survey of attitudes and concerns, a two-way participative feedback, valid information, relevant corrective plans of action, and the whole management involved and committed to the plan. One of the best descriptions of the procedure is appropriately Beckhard's own in Figure 19.4.

The conditions necessary for success however should not be taken lightly. The top team itself must be mature, cohesive, OD enlightened, committed to the success of the intervention, and a convincing example to others down the line of the openness and candor the technique requires.

And there are some important cautions: expectations have to be constrained to match the short time frame and degree of depth— it is more apt to surface manifestations than causes; it cannot get into major problems of policy and performance; and it will only bring out what the participants are willing to confront, which may take some bravery since OD will rarely have gone below the top group. Still, much of importance can and does surface.

Beckhard added these two warnings:

> If the top management team does not really use the information from its subordinates or if there are great promises and little follow up action, more harm can be caused to the organization's health than if the event were never held.

> If the confrontation meeting is used as a manipulative device just to give people the "feeling of participation" without the action, the meeting can boomerang. They will soon figure out management's intentions, and the reaction can be severe.

Senior management program. The confrontation meeting, one can see, is a good technique for achieving specific goals on subjects like those listed on page 1005, a fairly shallow approach to provide some education to a total management group and develop an action plan for the subject. However, an organization with a major problem like needing to be "turned around" can best-start with a more comprehensive confrontation approach on the key executives, taking say 4-5 days, to establish clearly in their minds the corporation's purpose, strategies and goals as a base on which they as the leaders can move the *whole* management team into the on-going long-range leadership development program needed to truly change the organization and its culture.

The program carried out by the Xerox Corporation provides an excellent example of how to do it successfully.[11] Waking up after their steep decline in the 70s due mainly to Japanese competition, they restructured their centralized organization into strategic business units (SBUs) for different market segments, and the CEO, D.T. Kearns, considering that the past practice of sending executives to business schools was inadequate, that they needed an in-house program tying the learning close to the firm's own needs, ordered the HRD to interview the top 12 executives for their reactions and ideas on the strategic direction he had planned, design from the results the program (adding their own professionalism), and in the process get the executives involved to motivate their commitment; several even wound up as faculty members.

A number of common themes emerged from the interviews: (a) the crucial need for senior management to understand the firm's total strategy and the financial demands of the strategy; (b) the need to develop a united purpose, set of goals, and consistent management style; (c) the need to develop specific action plans to implement them; and (d) the need to understand the critical success factors of each SBU. Five objectives emerged:

- To clearly articulate and ensure the understanding of the corporate objectives and strategies, stressing their global application.
- Top management (the 12) to show how the firm plans to implement them and what executives down the line have to do for success.
- To identify key opportunities, roadblocks and the critical success factors, and develop plans on what to do about them.
- To build teamwork across organizations and functions.

• To state, clarify and demonstrate the management style and practices desired by Xerox.

A 5-day program was designed—Figure 19.5—and applied initially to the 12, the first four days having workshops on information technology, return on assets, TQM, technical strategies, customer satisfaction, and human resources leadership. For the last, an anonymous opinion survey of subordinates on their superiors was prepared in advance to provide individual feedback, an eyeopener to each, supplying points on how to improve their leadership style. Three style goals stressed: participation, openness, and the feedback process in general.

The success of the program was unquestionable and so it was quickly applied to the rest of Xerox's top management, and it became the introductory program for on-going leadership development of all managers along the lines of the Northern Telecom schedule in Figure 17.15 (page 926). The action plans on all these major subjects increased the $2 billion revenue at the start to $18 billion by 1992.

A parallel learning system. Edgar Schein has pointed out that the learning process in all organization change programs can be greatly aided by setting up a transition group, that in fact the learning "will not spread across the entire organization unless a transition group is created that will be accountable for the organization learning process" and serve four critical functions: provide a supportive environment for learning, create and monitor task forces to tackle specific change programs, communicate what to change, why and how, and represent the organizational culture, giving the task forces a sense of psychological safety and freedom to make errors, all of which structures a parallel learning system.[12]

The group is in effect a "change management" group, commonly called a steering committee, that functions similarly to those previously described: those for developing self-directing blue collar teams and the ones that handle the variety of parallel organization goals on page 835, and it will be recommended again ahead as a major aid to building OD into the management system, in each instance using much the same method, and with due

Xerox Senior Management Program

MONDAY	TUESDAY	WEDNESDAY	THURSDAY	FRIDAY
• Program Introduction and Overview • Business Environment - 1992	• Information Resources Strategy • System Strategy	• Asset Management Workshop	• Leadership through Quality • Human Resource Issues	• Action Planning (Continued)
LUNCH	LUNCH	LUNCH	LUNCH	LUNCH
• Financial Condition and Implications • Corporate Strategic Direction	• Reprographics Strategy • Strategy Issues Workshop • Strategy Panel	• Technical Strategy • Customer Satisfaction Panel	• Management Practices • Action Planning	• Present & Discuss Issues • Closings Remarks • Program Summary
DINNER	DINNER	RECEPTION & DINNER WITH THE CUSTOMER	DINNER	
			• Action Planning - (Continued)	

Figure 19.5

authority and influence because of a composition of senior executives, often including the CEO, and the top HRD executive. Of course the first task of the committee itself is to learn what has to be changed, getting it from consultants, joint training, benchmarking, etc. It is thus also able to perform the function of the top management diagnostic committee described.

Tailored multiple-intervention approach. Beckhard's book on organization development presents a description of one of his consulting projects involving five of these OD interventions: family team diagnostic meetings (incorporating survey feedback), confrontation meetings, T-grouping, family group team building, Grid OD. The case is well worth repeating—Exhibit 6[13] in the appendix—because many managers can vicariously see problems of their own in the described organization, examine how the diagnosis and interventions might fit their needs, and note how the interventions were integrated to turn a large organization from the road to decay into a dynamic motivated firm from top to bottom...and see how it could be the first step toward solving the "moral mazes" case in Chapter 1.

The initiating top executive (Mr. A) could not have asked for a more demanding change because it required both technical and social change of extraordinary proportions—

1. from centralized family leadership to professional management,
2. from heavily production-oriented to heavily marketing-oriented,
3. to begin the change from a System 2 toward a System 4 organization.

In effect, a cataclysmic change in the organization's goals, values, assumptions, behavior patterns, climate, structure, and culture.

Particularly interesting, its industry had been in earlier years a stable generally mechanistic one with the usual low interest in autonomy and participation; but the growth of competition brought it up to the characteristics of the plastics industry with its more uncertain environment demanding marketing orientation, strategies, and attitudes.

However, one also notes in Exhibit 6 the absence of direct integration again, sees the mixed emotions caused by delayed Stranger T-grouping, and wonders how much aversiveness occurred in the Grid OD since only senior management had gone through the T-grouping (to what extent was Mr. B's remarks a few years later rationalizing?). But a radical change-over was apparently achieved to a far greater degree than would have been possible only a short while ago for lack of OD.

Packaged programs. Although several have been reported, little is known about any except for two: Gordon Lippitt's "ITORP" on which he wrote a book[14] and "Grid OD" that the designers, Robert Blake and Jane Mouton, have written often about. The latter moreover has been extensively critiqued in research journals so is the one that can be the most reliably described and, in fact, does illustrate the common nature of packaged offerings.

Grid OD is probably the most comprehensive of all the packages, attempting to cover for an entire organization every aspect of technical and social change, short and long-range, and doing it in six phases that take 3-5 years to complete. A great many firms have gone through phases 1 and 2, but very few beyond, and less than a dozen seem to have covered all six. It has three particularly distinguishing characteristics:

1. The Grid teaching tool.
2. It's stress on setting high performance goals—both technical and social—early in its processes and keeping the focus on them.
3. It's comprehensive coverage of the technical requisites of corporate performance as well as the social and emphasis on the *indirect* technical-social integration.

The Grid, in Figure 19.6,[15] is one of the first things an interested executive is introduced to, because it presents a visual picture in the simplest manner of the technical-social factors and interactions every manager of people must manage. How the manager does it is of course an important part of the person's personality style.

The Managerial Grid

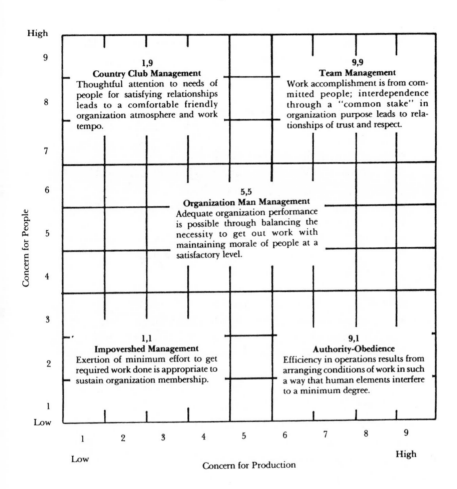

Figure 19.6

Here are some thumbnail sketches that illustrate the five basic "style" descriptions given in the figure; obviously 9,9 is the paragon model:

9,1: Authority, obedience
- Organizational goals best attained by applying Theory X to subordinates.

- An aversive climate with suppression of opposition, buildup of resentment, alienation.

1,9: Country club management

- Good relationships misconceived as the whole of organizational health.
- Conflict evaded, smoothed or compromised; "don't say anything if you can't say something nice."
- Climate of complacency and no trust.

1.1: Impoverished management

- Indifference to the organization, subordinates, performance, job satisfaction.
- Main concern the pay check and security.
- A wholly negative as well as aversive climate.

5,5: Organization man management

- Maintenance of status quo; little innovation; mediocrity.
- Accommodate, compromise, accept, adjust.
- Don't pressure, but don't appear too soft.
- Climate: conventional to unhealthy bureaucracy, most often the latter (pages 447-448).

9.9: Team management

- Joint pursuit of personal and organizational growth and excellence.
- Commitment equally to high technical and high social performance of the organization.
- Climate: freed-up, positive, self-actualizing.

When a Grid OD consultant is called in, it is usually an action of the top CEO or a relatively autonomous top executive of a large division or department in a situation where performance has been unsatisfactory for some time.

The interested top executive is asked by the consultants to go to a week-long orientation seminar at their home office, where the first thing done is to take the Grid questionnaire that determines the individual's present "style." Seldom does it come out 9.9, so it's easy for the executive to see that improvement is either possible or needed.

Then instruction, exercises and workshops teach the basics of organizational behavior, team building, problem-solving, evaluating an organization's culture, etc., enough to get a good understanding of what the six phases will do for one's own organization.

At the end, the top executive is encouraged to persuade two other associate executives to go through it, so that when they complete it and return to the firm the three can jointly evaluate whether to recommend going ahead on the full organization. If the three agree to institute it, more executives are sent, two of whom also attend an "Instructor Development Seminar," after which the two teach the other line managers back at work; thus the whole organization is eventually put through the seminar entirely by in-house personnel. The orientation seminar is the same as, and is labeled, phase 1 when the decision is made to give it to the whole outfit.

Phase 2 is the application of the family team-building throughout management, Phase 3 the intergroup team-building, and Phase 4 a top management project, the design of an ideal long-range "Strategic Corporate Plan" requiring from six months to a year to complete. Phase 5 is the implementation of the plan at all levels, which may take 3-5 years, and Phase 6 is a "systematic critique," a progress review.

The superiority of the package for achieving the 9.9 thumbnail sketch above compared to conventional management consulting methods at their best *could* be striking. Phases 1-3 are capable of introducing thoroughly the social side that all conventional organizations ignore and can upgrade the organizational modus operandi to a self-renewing, "error correcting" set of behavior patterns. Phase 4 and 5 can then improve the management systems technically while participatively incorporating all the social considerations that should be.

The statement is conditional however because Grid OD as now designed falls considerably short of its potential, due principally to three flaws Grid OD's own literature reveals, flaws that one suspects are the main reason for the failures that have occurred and the low number that have gone beyond Phase 2:

1. No bona fide values change effort incorporated (only the Phase 1 "direct instruction"), such that participating managers retain their traditional views and behavior, precluding development of the mutual trust essential for the Phase 2 team building where Grid OD has been grinding to a halt.

2. The premature heavy reliance on do-it-yourself in Phase 2.
3. The absence of education and training on the *direct* integration.

And one can see that the three are able to reinforce each other negatively.

Any attempt to design a consulting service program as comprehensive as this is admittedly a formidable project: how to include all the essentials and still keep the size and price down to a sellable, viable commercial product. The answer here has obviously been short-cuts.

But the need in #1 for Stranger T-grouping and in #2 for initial professional guidance should go without saying. The possible range of the consequences of their absence was well illustrated in a Harvard Business School case. The case writer, in writing up the Grid OD experience of a division of a large firm, interviewed its top executives after its Phase 2 and these comments about it which were representative of the group:[161]

> *Participant #1:* I must admit we weren't very candid. Perhaps its because it's not natural to make a lot of negative statements about a man you work with every day. Still, we did get quite negative. Yes, we cleared up a lot of little problems and identified a number of basic problems to work on.

> *Participant #2:* It was great; a real opportunity to improve our effectiveness as a team. Some thought it was real blood-letting and didn't like it. Personally, I wasn't bothered by it.

> *Participant #3:* I'll admit I damn near went 1,1. It didn't help me a bit; in fact I found it demoralizing. Part of the problem was that I didn't feel like revealing myself to these people. I just didn't want to open up.

Any person familiar with Stranger T-grouping and the typical environments of managements that haven't had it would not be surprised.

The neglect of direct integration (#3 above) is a flaw of all current OD programming, Grid OD is simply following suit. Without it managers are being expected to be committed to organizational goals when they have doubts that their superiors will deliver on or let them achieve their own personal ones. Obviously, the superior leading Participant #3's group above had a crying need for both values upgrading and education on the direct integration technique.

Another risk of program simplification (the three flaws being over-simplifications) that has to be guarded against is the manipulation of the simplifications adopted. The "managerial grid," for example, is an admirable easy-to-understand educational device through which managers can learn important things about themselves and others. At the same time, unless duly apprised of it, they're not apt to recognize that plenty of executives with Theory X philosophy are capable of contriving a 9.9 "style," that one can behave that way manipulatively without being able to elicit the trust necessary to develop a team to maturity.

Good packaging, however, *can* make a significant contribution, and it is a distinct asset of Grid OD. The comments on it have been extensive mainly to point out that a total-organization effort filling the technical social needs is possible. Grid OD itself sells a good framework and the long range perspective that, with proper preliminary preparation and professional guidance, would cover all the essential elements and do it well enough for any moderately sophisticated management group to handle.

A main drawback, one of any package, can be insufficient flexibility to tailor it adequately to the needs of the specific organization, the way it is done in the Beckhard Exhibit 6 illustration. Though tailoring is not necessary for all, it is very important for many.

Building OD into the management system

This is a requisite by OD definition for good reason: the OD process is not achieved and successful—therefore is not development—unless the process is such that it is sustained in the organization or unit. Isolated applications of OD interventions do not produce enduring results because the problems they're applied to always involve people and their behavior that, as said, is subject to rechange, regression or extinction for lack of support, changed circumstances, mismanagement by the superior, or for units, the opposition or indifference of the larger organization.

Organization development therefore cannot be said to have been achieved unless the changes for the better that are made are maintainable by design and maintained in practice, which can only be done by making the management system itself keep on top of it, constantly support the new behavior, and make OD thinking and processes the spontaneous response to the needs they can serve. The failure to do so is plainly a major reason why there's still so little OD practiced.

A description of how to build in the OD naturally must include the two elementary parts, the prerequisites and the structuring, the former being no more or less than an extrapolation to the whole organization of *the prerequisites* of success for individual and group techniques to this point. In sum:

- A Theory Y philosophy throughout the management team resulting in a high regard for the individual, trust, openness, mutual-support (OD being a discipline of principles and techniques for translating Theory Y into action).
- All managers have been educated about the human side of organizations (Part I), group dynamics, participation, OD and its techniques.
- All managers have had effective training in interpersonal skills and team development and leadership (Chapter 20).
- All are competent in the technical part of their responsibilities (essential to the success of the technical-social integration process as well as functional success).

Needless to say, they comprise an ideal; the realistic prerequisites are that management is determined to pursue them, has them as goals of management training and development, and is in the process of succeeding.

For the second part, *the structures*, just as traditional structures have to be modified so that they support and not obstruct behavior change, the same has to be done in this instance to ensure the ongoing practice of OD wherever needed, the parallel structure described in Chapter 16, and thus that also of the parallel learning system above, being the best approach that's been devised for it. The specifics are as follows; some of the ten, like the basic three parts of parallel structures, are essential, not all, but each can significantly increase the odds:

1. A published "management philosophy," a "basic human resources policy," (Chapter 21), a QWL goal for the entire organization, and a team philosophy (Chapter 13).
2. An HR Management Committee of the top team in each major unit to make, manage and monitor HR policies (as at GM—page 583).
3. A competent HRD providing the appraisal and HR services described in Chapters 9 and 17.
4. Professional OD talent and services in HRD available to all managers on request.
5. A norm or participative leadership and team decision-making and problem-solving where decisions and problems have an important impact on employees, those affected participating in the resolution or represented on the team.
6. A permanent Top Management Steering Committee to hear ideas from anyone anywhere in the organization for the improvement of any aspect of managing, communications, relations, or innovation, the committee authorizing and guiding task projects decided on as in the example on page 835-836.
7. "Open communications" structuring as may be advisable, including lateral processes (a to i on page 821).
8. An adequate MIS—one that supplies managers with the operating, performance, feedback data computers and programs they need.
9. Open personnel, appraisal, pay and selection systems.
10. Periodic (preferably bi-annual) opinion surveys of the entire organization and climate surveys of the units, to be followed by the survey feedback process.

The automatic consequence of these two sets—the prerequisites and structures—would plainly be the institutionalizing of an *integrative climate* (the page 282 definition), one in which technical-social integration would be significantly achieved by both intuitive and conscious processes.

It might be well to note again the design difference this structure can take to suit different degrees of technology, that what is described here is for *all* organizations regardless of degree, with the, intention of achieving the operational goals of, #2 through #7 on page 835 (and of course all the "objectives" on pages 981-982), whereas medium- and high-tech firms *add* the new product development activities described on pages 835-839 to achieve the goal #1 as well (thus all seven) with essentially the same structure, activities the low-tech do not include.

PROBLEMS AND THE FUTURE

It must be apparent from the behavioral science nature of OD that no chapter or single book can show managers how to do it all on their own. It can advance the application sophistication of those already experienced with OD, but for managers without the experience, reading can understandably only help them become aware of OD's potential, see how the processes can lead to solving both technical and social problems, and become acquainted with the prerequisites and environmental conditions essential to success.

A recent book on OD surprisingly does purport to show managers, regardless of their experience, how to do it all on their own, with a checklist of criteria and instructions on how to pick out techniques and implement them. One need only consider a managers' inability to be sufficiently objective to point up the fallacy of it. Then what about the executive's philosophy, leadership style, and cultural readiness, the conduciveness of the situation to success, identifying the specific problems, contiguous power pressures, and so on? The expertise of a professional is essential in the beginning and for some time thereafter.

Indeed, the leading predicament of OD has not been its principles or tools but the way the tools have been poorly used or misused— and in fact at times misused under the guidance of consultants! The do-it-yourself book is one example; undertaking team development with inadequate preliminary preparation as described is another.

In fairness to those consultants though, due weight should be given to the fact that OD is still a young discipline; there's much yet to be learned, and that leaves a lot of room for strong opinions drawn from good and bad personal experience with it. The conflicting attitudes about T-group alone must be sorely confusing to those who've read several authors.

Another difficult problem has been the fact that because of OD's infancy, its qualitative intangible nature, its long-range dimensions and its heavy dependence on erudite sciences, it doesn't sell easily. The pragmatic prospective customer is used to buying only quantifiable short-term results, and usually with at least a 0.7 probability of success. The absence of a success probability estimate alone (mainly because of its dependence on the manager/climate factor) is more than many can bear.

So the more the prospective client learns about the subject in advance from reading about it and attending seminars, the more will OD's value and scope be appreciated, the more realistic are the expectations apt to be, the less need will there be for a sales pitch, and the better will the consultant and client be able to collaborate as to goals, design and implementation. It's important too that the enormous potential of OD presented be balanced with an awareness of the limitations, subtleties, weaknesses and problems that have to be accounted for to optimize results. These categories become so enmeshed it would be appropriate to use for them that convenient umbrella word "complications."

Complications

Among the many, the complications of eight in particular should be given the most attention:

1. The difficulty of learning interpersonal skills.
2. The dependence of OD on the top management
3. The dependence of OD on trust and openness.
4. The present inaccessibility of most organizations.
5. The applicability of OD to mechanistic structures.
6. The client-consultant relationship.
7. The absence of direct integration.

8. Criticisms of the ethics of OD.

1. Chris Argyris has pointed out a number of reasons why the core element, *learning interpersonal skills*, is difficult, and an awareness of them can help one improve project design and management:[17] (a) present concepts of interpersonal competence (e.g., competition, winning, one-upmanship) are deeply ingrained in us, are strongly supported by society, and are believed to be and often have been the key to managers' personal organizational success (regardless of the consequences for others and the organization) in the dog-eat-dog culture as it is now; (b) the compensation system presently supports these concepts and rewards managers accordingly; (c) managers are embarrassed to realize they have to learn a completely new language (trust, openness, concern, emotions, experimenting) and one that cannot be learned in the usual "direct instruction" manner; they are also displeased to find they must genuinely feel the rightness of the new attitudes or they will come over as unauthentic (see page 1024 quote) and phony; (d) we are culturally programmed to behave in ways that inhibit OD, especially to minimize expressions of feeling, to down-play individuality in organizations, to accept distrust as part of life, to avoid helping others be open, to minimize experimenting and risk-taking.

2. *OD's dependence on the top manager* is a considerable complication to the OD consultant and, at the same time, a constant threat to the program.

It is of course in the nature of all hierarchies that a major purchase in dollar amount be made or approved by the top executive, minor ones by subordinate managers; but when an OD program of any amount, even free, is undertaken to change values and attitudes, as they all are, and in so doing appears to the boss to threaten the amount or nature of his or her authority, logically the person will be aroused. If a subordinate manager were to implement one independently, an awake superior would be quick to see what's going on and step in aggressively. Entry must be at the top or at least have obtained the full support of two levels up (cardinal rule: don't let your superior get in trouble with his boss because of your actions).

The dependence of project success then on the head of the organizational unit implementing it presents the OD consultant with a far more difficult selling job than any other type of consultant or sales person ever encounters. In addition to having to overcome the mentioned difficulties of selling indefinite, long-range results without even a figure of success-probability, the consultant has to be a super motivator, to motivate (therefore sell) the manager to commitment, experimentation, continuous involvement, personal leadership of the project, and a significant change of leadership behavior on the way to 9,9.

Only occasionally have managers called in the consultant on their own; the managers are generally solicited. And rarely are they culturally ready at that point; yet they must be convinced enough on the benefits and long-range promise of OD not to buckle under criticisms of associates, through economic ups and downs, and in moments of doubt. As any experienced OD consultant knows, a month's serious drop in sales, the loss of an important customer, a factory fire, any number of things can abort a program if the appearance of commitment is only an appearance.

Then as often said, there is the dominant importance of the model at the top, such that it's best to try first to bring the CEO's values sufficiently in line with OD's values for the person to want to implement it, after which they have to be helped over the difficult hurdle of putting their upgraded values into practice. The second step is in fact a major problem because those who in mid career have changed to congruent "espoused theories" of behavior, as Chris Argyris has called them,[18] are still sorely inhibited from putting them (their upgraded values) into action because of fears of the consequences.

3. A subtle complication is the **dependence of OD on trust and openness** for its success, making it very difficult for OD processes to get started let alone function at all in some situations. Four facts are responsible: (a) their universal absence and the reasons for it, (b) the "norm of reciprocity," (c) the nature of the organization, which in some cases militates against trust and openness, and (d) the on-the-job congruence requisite for OD to succeed on the job.

(a) Their absence of course goes hand-in-glove with the universal authoritarian climate of organizational life; trust is certainly out of the question in the pattern described in Chapter 1 (pages 6-8) as typical for many large organizations. Managers might consider the extent to which the value misconceptions and assumptions on page 118 can build to such an interlocked maze of distrust.

(b) We naturally all approach new situations and encounters with some mistrust and usually test the safe degree of trust one can adopt. Sociologists call it "the norm of reciprocity." We give a little to see what will be received in a social exchange and develop the character of one's communication and the relationship with the results in minds.

Unfortunately, mistrust functions like a disease. Let it get started, it spreads rapidly, and the norm of reciprocity assures that it takes a long time to cure unless trust is targeted by OD.

Certainly being "open" with a subordinate will itself generate some trust reciprocity that can lead to greater openness, which raises the questions of how open at any one time one should be, and how far has one a right to expect another to go. Argyris gave an explanation using it also to illustrate what "authentic" behavior and an authentic relationship mean:[19]

> Note that it is not recommended that an individual be completely open, or show complete trust. The key is for A. for example, to be open to the extent that it also permits B to be open. Openness, therefore, is not something in an individual. True openness and trust exists only in interpersonal relationships. One asks therefore how open the relationship is between A and B, not how open A or B is.
>
> This implies that A adjust his degree of openness to how he believes he will be heard most accurately and completely by B, and what will help B express himself most accurately and completely. If A believes that B is not open to as much relevant information as A has, then A can explore the issue with B as to how to widen the channels of communication.
>
> To say what you believe is to be honest; to say what you believe in such a way that the other can do the same is to be authentic.

Of major significance to corporate management: a recent study found that when reciprocal trust in a group is high, the quality of its managerial problem-solving is substantially higher than when mistrust prevails.[20] Of course additional consequences are not only a higher quality of organizational life but an important competitive advantage.

(c) Assuming the CEO has elected to try OD, it can have a difficult time getting started not only because of all the obstacles described in #1, 2, 3, 4 and 7 on page 1021 but also when the environment is one of politics or power struggles, which in some cases is endemic to the organization. In those mistrustful circumstances OD can be promised trouble unless it is managed with consummate skill, as Warren Bennis described it:[21].

> Organization development seems most appropriate under potential conditions of trust, truth, love and collaboration. But what about conditions of war, conflict, dissent and violence. "All's fair in love and war." It really is, but you really must know what you're playing... OD systematically avoids the problem of power and the politics of change...The deficiency is serious, for the OD consultant tends to use the OD truth-love model when it may be inappropriate and he has no alternative model.

There has to be at least some desire and effort toward truth, trust and collaboration for OD to build on, a condition not likely where the top leadership is weak (e.g. in handling interdepartmental conflict which is often hostile), the management is politics-infested, or the philosophy is authoritarian.

Also, some organizations, we know, are by their nature political, such as bureaucracies headed by short-term nominated or elected officials, and others have a diffuse authority structure, little management training, and often much professional myopia, such that they are difficult to control, e.g., universities, hospitals, and community activities. OD will fail in any of them if the truth-love formula is force-fed without due allowances for their special nature. Bennis' recommendations to help consultants in such situations are actually applicable anywhere though more so in those:

- Recognize that collaboration is a learned achievement (in other words, if it's absent it will have to be taught, the best methods being via OD).
- Conflict is not to be avoided by the change agent; seek to channel aggressive energies toward personal and social gain for all.

- Power is not a bad thing. Social action depends on it. Nothing changes in human affairs until new power is generated or until old power is redistributed.
- Where coercive power and conflict exist don't just condemn or ignore them; account for their dimensions in your program model toward the OD objectives.

(d) The requisite of co-worker values congruence for successful behavior change to be sustained was stated in (a) on page 958. When considering the application of OD to or by an individual manager, the cultural readiness of the subordinates, superior and interrelated departments must also be considered (criteria on pages 972-973. Can they be sufficiently attuned? The example on pages 969-970 illustrated what is apt to happen when not done.

4. Ignorance of OD's nature and potential is still by far the principle reason for its slow acceptance, but after it becomes widely known, plain *inaccessibility*, already a serious roadblock, will take the lead, inaccessibility caused by (a) top management value differences and (b) an absence of the pain-values combination.

(a) The values of many managers are so strongly dead set against Theory Y principles that they not only refuse to go to seminars on values and philosophy, they won't even concede to discuss the subjects.

An incident in one of Argyris' projects is typical. It was a top management team of ten; seven were Theory Y with Stranger T-group experience, three Theory X without it. It took the CEO three diplomatic attempts, doing his best not to be coercive, to persuade the three just to talk about their philosophy differences with the group, but they agreed only with the provision that there'd be no discussion of group processes or feelings and that they would not be required to undergo T-group.[22m]

(b) The pain-values combination requirement refers to a linkage that usually has to occur before a manager will consider OD entry: the pain caused by the situation plus possession of enough of the values of OD on page 981 to lead to it. The implementation of OD has, as mentioned, seldom been based on an objective in-house finding through a realization of the need for it; a painful operating or profit condition has almost always had to first exist; then if the awareness is at a level below the top, average managers have to be at rope's end before they're willing to risk rocking the boat (e.g., the boss's regard) by calling in a consultant, especially an OD one. But, a good OD consultant can often help pave the way at both levels.

5. Concerning the *applicability of OD to mechanistic structures*, the organic nature of OD principles may at first seem to rule it out. The Part II Introduction pointed out that a correlation exists in a general way between the industry's technological characteristics and the structure of the organizations in it; for any organization there's an optimum point on a continuum from the extremes of mechanistic to organic for the best performance in that industry.

Most firms are in the middle area as to what is needed in their industry but even in those that should be heavily mechanistic, it's the rare one in which the managers do not need what OD can do for them. One can summarize the effects of OD as producing *trust, openness, collaboration, participation, teamwork* and *problem-solving*. What outfit doesn't need all? Virtually every medium-to-large organization, mechanistic or not, has some of the conditions in which these factors can make a big difference in effectiveness and profit. All the italicized factors are especially important where:

- any management teamwork is required or any functional interdependence exists;
- interpersonal skills are important in any activity;
- cooperation and fast feedback will aid coping with external uncertainties of markets, competition, technology, economic change.

So being mechanistic is not a "complication;" it's listed here only to be sure it is not seen as such blocking the use of OD.

This is not to say that OD will not affect an organization's existing location on the mechanistic-organic continuum, for it will. To the extent that the above italicized qualities are increased in amount, it will become more organic, but the increases will have rectified a past imbalance, and the movement will not be beyond the desirable point if properly applied; as the organization will simply be "freed-up." (see descriptions on page 448).

At the same time, OD is quite capable of adding some missing mechanistic factors, such as needed job descriptions, policies or rules for better interpersonal communication and understanding.

6. The success of *the client-consultant relationship* depends on a mix of fairly obvious interpersonal requirements that may need verbalizing for some and also depends on a few moral obligations of each to the other.

Successful OD efforts are a process of mutual influence (of client and consultant), not an imposed program from any direction,"[23] and it naturally only develops when both parties have taken time to build a mutual trust and confidence that the other will do his or her part. Included would have to be the consultant's openness and honesty about one's own relevant held personal values and goals, giving the client an informed free choice, the consultant not imposing his or her own philosophy, and on the client's side a frankness about intended use of the OD and the consultant. One day spent together may be enough for some, several necessary for others, and since all subordinates will inevitably interpret the observed relationship as how they will be expected to function interpersonally, the goal of the two should be to make it a small scale model of the relationships expected in the organization.

Needless to say, the foundation of the client's confidence should be the consultant's competence regardless of the consultant's charisma that too often closes the deal. Any good consultant who hasn't already established a reputation and record that speaks for itself is quite willing to verify competence in writing to the extent that it can be:

- scholastic degrees; what fields? A Ph.D. is not necessary if there have been significant verifiable OD successes;
- number of years in OD consulting, supervision of what OD techniques for what organizations (phone check of results); at least experience as an assistant to the supervisor in several verifiable successes is a minimum;
- publications on the subject;

- some line or staff business experience in addition can be valuable but it is not necessary.

. . . and the willingness of the consultant to submit to two or three interview sessions. Try to determine, with a highly-regarded HRD executive present, the person's maturity, perceptivity, diplomacy and general knowledge of the subject involved.

Then there are the caveats for the client. A sensitivity to three spurious consulting practices is advisable: (a) selling an OD package that doesn't fit or isn't OD, (b) the building of dependency, and (c) not following through after starting a project.

(a) There are those who have packaged a bright idea around a personal forte, and like the ancient philosophers, they try to sell them as a cure for every ailment; if it fits, fine; but this chapter should help spot the misfits.

There are also those who use the OD label because it's now a good attention-getter and implies to many that the consultant has mysterious magical capabilities, when in fact the package offered is a direct-instruction course, therefore cannot provide the benefits of OD, Check it especially against the social change theory characteristic on page 957, the OD definition on page 978, and the action research characteristics on pages 983-984.

These two points are plainly acts of verifying integrity as well as personal OD competence and program benefit .

(b) The building and sustaining by a consultant of a client's dependency is a serious violation of the OD goal to teach managers to solve their problems, social and technical, on their own. Although most of those who do it have their eyes on the fees, some are filling their own need to be needed, but the hiring executive is usually partly to blame for not being involved enough to recognize what's going on.

Another protection along with the necessary involvement: include conditions of phase-out in the consulting contract even though it has to be vague, and it does. A most important indicator is the observable and ratable process of training in-house HRD personnel by the consultant during the projects so they can eventually take over.

(c) Equally questionable has been the practice of some embarking on programs they don't intend seeing through to ·completion, leaving after they get bored or their peak income period has passed—an old consulting practice in all disciplines that reference checks should reveal. The damage could Mean the end of OD in the company.

Finally, there's the special problem of the relationship between managers and inside OD staff people, and it should be introduced by first answering the question, which is better, outside or inside specialists? In small firms inside OD staff naturally wouldn't have enough to do to be busy year-round unless willing to wear an HRD hat part-time, which, it has been shown can be made interesting work for them. But in those that are medium-size and up, it becomes a full-time function for several to many if the management is sold on OD and OD has been, or is to be, properly integrated into the management system.

In the beginning, the outside consultant usually recommends training an inside person after being sure OD will be made a permanent function.

The advantages to the organization of having one (or the number needed) are the constant availability of counsel to lower managers, getting the administrative work done at lower cost, and ensuring the continuity and maintenance of OD principles and applications from then on.

Deciding to have inside OD staff also aids the phase-out mentioned above: when the consultant feels that OD commitment, enthusiasm and competence is firmly embedded at the top, that it has been infused down the hierarchy among a majority of the managers, that the managers are learning to be change agents themselves for their units (having adopted OD values and principles), and that the internal staff is able to initiate new programs and continue on their own—the time has come. The consultant should be needed from then on only periodically for review, updating and counsel.

On the in-house line-staff relationship, however, top management can at no time count on executives to refrain from pressuring or coercing the staff to bend or violate the truth or to be unethical. If the firm wants to get what it's buying—the truth—

no less than the CEO has to promise the specialist autonomy and job security, and it will of course have added meaning if it's in a contract.

7. *The absence of direct integration,* as has been said, is a major defect of the OD currently practiced (along with inadequate values upgrading and no Stranger T-grouping). The definition of OD on page 978 and comment that followed it explained the total technical-social integration intent of the discipline, but there should be no doubt from the described OD training and intervention techniques that as now undertaken it can only achieve indirect integration, and only partially at that, because the direct integration and its prerequisites are missing.

Plainly, superiors must first integrate their subordinates' personal needs and aspirations with what the organization wants in regard to their jobs' characteristics, goals and plans before they can expect them to develop as effective collaborative team members. Subordinate managers who do not feel personal congruence on these matters can be counted on to have priorities inimical to the interests of the firm regardless of any seeming cooperativeness professed to the boss or under the social pressure of the group.

For OD just to get started, those to be involved must preliminarily undergo the Stranger T-grouping for values and behavior upgrading followed by training on the direct integration. The whole of HRD's educational responsibility can be tabulated as below, the Table also showing the necessary sequencing: I to II to III and #1 to #2 within the II and III.

And during the educational process, for OD to truly succeed HRD must be doing its best to make progress on the prerequisites and structuring toward building OD into the management system (pages 1017-1020).

The complaints above, incidentally, do not mean to suggest that significant improvements cannot be achieved by a strong effort on group OD as it is presently practiced. They can, at both the factory and management levels. The Doraville/Lakewood and Tarrytown cases (pages 576-582) illustrated the former, the Harwood-Weldon (pages 563-565) and Exhibit 6 (in the appendix) the latter.

OD	Activities	Techniques
I Social education	Seminars, courses	Direct instruction: knowledge, skills, ethics
II Direct integration	1 Values & behavior change	"Social change" by • Stranger T-grouping[n]
	2 Technical-social integration (a) congruence development (b) technical development or change	• McGregor's direct integration process (in ch. 20)
III Indirect integration	1 Values & behavior change	"Social change" by • Stranger T-grouping[n]
	2 Technical-social integration (a) congruence development (b) technical development or change	• OD Group techniques

However, in each instance the write-ups either admitted or implied that the improvements, though considerable, did not reflect the full potential of OD, and on the Harwood-Weldon we do not know the staying power of what was done, because the recording was too soon after project completion. Indeed, in no published case of OD other than the high-tech ones cited has there been a follow-up two or three years later showing successful maintenance of initial glowing reports about the progress (virtually all of them experimental small-scale projects), and checks that have been made have shown either serious regression (e.g., the GM example per pages 582-583) or the CEOs lost interest, dropped them or let them fade away.

To sum up, start any organization change programs with (a) the comprehensive social education needed and Stranger T-grouping, (b) the installation of and education of a top management steering committee (with research to determine the organization's problems), to manage, monitor, coach, and support the activity, (c) the application by OD professionals of OD interventions found by the committee to be needed, (d) training on direct integration, (e) followed by the setting up of task forces on the major problems ... all with good professional assistance in the beginning. For the long-range, the Grid OD structure on pages 1012-1014 might be a helpful guide.

8. *The ethics of OD*. Some people have questioned the ethics of OD, that it may not be consistent with our highest principles by being (they believe) manipulative or coercive.

The goals of OD are clearly ethical—universal trust, openness, participation, teamwork and the collaborative solving of problems—so anything unethical has to be in how people use OD or use each other through it. Nevertheless the criticisms persist, the chief ones being:

a. The application of OD techniques to increase profits, where profit is the goal, at the expense of employees.

b. Manipulation for more control, manipulation being unethical by definition.

c. The coercion of subordinate managers to change their "styles" (purported to be fundamental to their personalities).

(a) Assuming the acceptance of the necessity of profit in commerce and industry, the crux of this complaint is certainly in what is meant by *at the expense of*. Objections are surely justified if OD techniques are used to induce or persuade unethical conduct or overwork employees without fair pay.

On the latter though, what is overworking? a matter of hours worked, output, quality, a standard, a mix? It brings to mind the Beckhard case in Exhibit 6 in which the happy complacent management objected to the professionalization planned by Mr. A and the consultant as the solution to the declining market share. The implication to the team: changing the comfortable status quo (if it works why fix it?) and pressure to be overworked at the same pay.

Apparently only Mr. A and Beckhard were aware that the organization might not be around for long to be happy about if the firm's profit health were not put ahead of their complacent satisfaction. The team was being asked to accept the social exchange of performance and behavior change for the survival of their jobs.

(b) The exoneration of operant conditioning on pages 89-90 from the charge of manipulation applies equally and by the same criteria to OD. OD is moral in accordance with all the definitions there of persuasion, influence and good, thus embraces too all personal rights. Indeed it's the key process (as proposed herein) by which organizations can eliminate all the manipulation, oppression, distrust and complaints so well described in the two publications referred to in Chapter 1, the HBR "Moral Mazes" by Jackall (pages 6-8) and "The Oppressed Middle" by Shorris (page 21, reference h).

(c) On the subject of coercing a change of "style," if the CEO of the three Theory X executives described in 4(a) on page 1020 *ordered* them to participate in a discussion of management philosophy, group processes and personal feelings, would it be coercion?

Coercion is in fact not even relevant. The subject is adequate training to do the leadership job. There's no difference to insisting that salesmen study and learn the sales manual and the products. Managers simply have additional texts for the social and team development side. Those who are not interested or refuse to learn are attitudinally unfit to manage people. Their technical talents should be redirected to jobs that don't require it.

The issue therefore is the legitimate authority to insist on competent job performance, to require the training needed for it and to introduce OD for that purpose. The three contrary executives were being allowed by their superior to usurp his authority and block the team, possibly the rest of the organization also, from the benefits of OD. Granted, fear of rebellion and loss of team members are potent CEO restraints, but perhaps the CEO should consider their actual flexibility motivated by *their* fear of having to find other jobs at their level.

These remarks on ethics are not in the least intended to deny the potential of OD for exploitation or violation of personal rights, but when they occur, they cannot help but be either the result of inept application or deliberate misuse.

As for OD ethics per se, the most elementary of remedies would naturally be a written code of ethics compiled by the leaders of the OD profession as soon as possible. Further, in contrast to technical management consulting, OD's theater of operation—human beings and their behavior—would seem to demand spelled-out minimum standards of education and internship before being permitted to claim to be an OD consultant; the same would be true for T-group trainers.

OD's strengths and future

The benefits of OD have been conclusively proven, and there is no longer any doubt that the discipline can be a major means toward the elimination of the wrong values, distrust, dishonest relationships, alienation, dysfunctional behavior and irresponsibility that plague organizations, the extent of the condition leading some analyses, as said, to conclude the theory of entropy.

We now know that none of, and no mix of, the basic characteristics of an organization (page 458) will inevitably produce inflexibility, mediocrity and all of Weber's evils, that the ecological cycle of birth-growth-decay-death is no more inevitable for an organization than for a society with vitality, high values and high moral standards. The theory, it seems, needs to be reexamined for its validity.

By vitality is meant health, commitment, adaptation and self-renewal. Organization development supplies the essential structures, processes and standards to make possible its presence and exercise, and, understandably, the values, attitudes and aspirations associated with OD carry over into the community with the potential for multiplying the vitality of all institutions.

That organizations have been major mechanisms for the advance of the species goes without saying, but with a great deal of suffering, drag and waste in the process, waste in the sense of the organizational decline and deaths that prompted the entropy myth. OD is proof that entropy is not inherently applicable to human organizations; in fact OD seems not only to be the missing ingredient that will allow organizations to stay alive and flourish, but to be a catalyst that can greatly accelerate their contributions to all of societal and cultural progress.

The way it can do so might best be seen in the results OD when effectively installed obtains for the organizations themselves, the employees, leaders, and society as a whole—keeping in mind the inevitable overlap of contributions to one which also accrue to all the others.

For organizations. Only a decade or two ago advanced business managements were confident that the key to generating and sustaining this vitality was the long-range corporate planning with annual updating described in Chapter 15. The discipline was without question a major step forward toward managing the destiny of the organization rather than leaving it to chance and fire-fighting.

However, it proved to have some traits of a fair-weather friend. In hard times, the advantages it gave over no corporate planning at all were marginal, or non-existent. The concept and its great directive value were irrefutable, but its predictive value (over-and-above economic forecasting difficulties) and the cost-effectiveness of its technical detail (with its lack of technical-social integration) have appeared to be very dubious.

The mistake, it's now evident, was in assuming that corporate planning was any more than a tool of management to manage its technology whether the organization was sick or healthy. It was an important previously missing tool, but the character, quality, health, commitment, motivation and leadership style of management remained untouched.

OD as recommended is transparently a major missing essential for the total planning needed, and adding human resources planning would complete the necessary planning package, one that would give a CEO the systems required to truly plan the control of the organization's destiny, its three parts being:

1. *Corporate planning* for the technical (Chapters 15 and 16),
2. *Human resources planning* for the social (Chapter 17),
3. *Organization development* as proposed for the technical-social (Chapter 18 and 19).

The remaining management ingredient for implementing it all is of course *organizational leadership* to combine them and act on their combination.

The overall pervasive characteristic of all three is plainly *change*, but only the proposed OD can achieve the behavior change essential for significant performance change within the other two. Of course much of traditional management *attempts* behavior change by targeting performance change through such processes as:

management by objectives	task forces
management development (current)	meetings
structural changes	personnel changes
process changes	pep talks

Except for the last, it has been shown that each plays an important part in effective management, but we now realize the changes that occur are essentially limited to technical performance, any small behavior change that might occur being unplanned consequences that have as much chance of being bad as good.

OD institutionalized moreover fills the dire need for built-in processes to help organizations cope continuously with all the internal social changes and external environmental changes going on all the time, the latter demanding the mediative and proactive management described on pages 913-915. It does so via three unique abilities, the abilities to:

1. (to repeat) effect *both* technical and social change and integrate them;
2. provide effective problem-solving techniques throughout an organization for internal problems of any nature (except pure high technology) including those caused by such changes;
3. provide a built-in system of organizational "values clarification" for the maintenance of beneficial behavior changes made and for continuous organizational self-renewal.

Some of the outstanding points about these previously stated or implied, are worth emphasizing. On #1, the ability of certain OD techniques to identify and resolve social dysfunction and of others to bring to the surface and make needed corrections of technical structures and processes, any of which may be contributing to poor performance or dysfunctional behavior, has been illustrated. By the use of the two capabilities and adding direct integration, OD can improve structures, processes, performance, and satisfaction in terms of organizational needs, team needs and individual needs— a process of *participation technical-social integration* that optimize the utilization of the organization's human and technical resources.

Re #2, only OD among the change options provides a total organization-wide system that makes possible the complete solution of virtually any organizational problem except pure high technology ones. The very nature of its processes, given the necessary climate and technical competence, ensures identification of the true issues, technical or social, and the integration of the technical and social. If then the system incorporates the linking-pin function for the whole organization, complications of authority differentials are minimized, and solutions will account for all influences at all levels.

However, because of today's rapidly changing societal goals, values and expectations, there is also a need for a way to apprise upper executives of the changes as they happen, preferably in advance, a continuous process of "values clarification" (#3), if the directives and policies of those executives are to motivate full employee collaboration and commitment continuously.

Building the OD techniques and linking-pin function into the management system as on-going parts of it fills the need through the feedback they get as they participate in the techniques.

In sum, for several decades the seers have been predicting the coming of a new organizational form that will remove the aversivness of organizational life and foster the pursuit of excellence. Perhaps they're gun-shy after mistakenly heralding the limited-purpose matrix forms as a panacea, or perhaps it's hard to accept that no archetypal all-purpose one is possible for such complexity. But the answer *does* seem to have been found on a higher level—a philosophy and system combination in the shape of the advocated OD that can be super-imposed on any and all forms—profit, non-profit, hierarchical, freeform, etc. The diagram

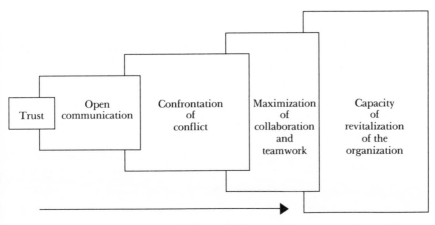

Figure 19.7

above pictures the end-result of what is superimposed, a sequential interlocked set of conditions that will produce the desired excellence and maintain the excellence in perpetuity.[24]

For employees. The humanist values underpinning of OD naturally pre-determines positive benefits for all employees at all levels when the management becomes committed to them. The consequences are impressive. Besides receiving systematic attention to the fulfillment of all psychological needs in column 3 on page 143 each individual gains significantly as to:

- truth and reality replacing many of his or her value misconceptions as both superior and subordinate
- maximized meaningfulness of one's work
- interpersonal skills
- improved personal performance and job success
- greater social success
- character improvement
- a say in planning both one's own future and that of the organization
- intrinsic satisfaction
- trustful relationships
- a motivating environment
- a rewarding quality of work life.

For leaders. Abraham Maslow once commented that "if the only tool you have is a hammer, you tend to treat everything as if it were a nail." Executives who end their educational effort at the undergraduate college graduation exercise naturally invite such a predicament. Whether too busy making a living or adequately successful as a result of sweat or personality, its simply a failure to keep the self and the organization managerially up to date and competitive.

OD education (regardless of how acquired) not only advances one well beyond the elementary undergraduate level of understanding people, processes, structures, and their relationships, but teaches how to maximize the effectiveness of the relationships, bringing gains of major importance to both the organization and its leaders jointly; outstanding among them:

- valid information for decisions,
- the cohesion, commitment and high regard of one's team and mutual trust allowing all wide behavioral flexibility to fit the situation,
- a productive, respectful and fulfilling human organization for all its members, and
- performance leadership of the organization in the industry for a CEO and for unit managers within the organization.

And a ticking off of the personal gains solely to leaders themselves should be the most compelling reasons of all for them to become committed to the whole idea, particularly:

- new learning toward better performance of specific managerial tasks,
- better communication and cooperation needed from others on the team to perform one's own job,
- better problem-solving of one's own personal organizational problems,
- better resolutions of conflicts with others,
- increased opportunity for personal growth and self-fulfillment,

- an increased say in one's own destiny as well as the organization's.

Not to be overlooked too is a singular latent effect on both the leader and subordinates, a gain of a more abstract nature, an intellectual and emotional consequence that is an eloquent commentary on both humans and OD. Argyris explained it in this oblique way.[25]

> Are managers aware that once begun, organization development is difficult to stop? Individual aspirations are raised and their hopes kindled when they believe that the quality of their life within the organization may he bettered. To call a halt to such a program would be to run the risk of confirming to everyone—especially the young and those of any age who are most involved—that the organization is unable or unwilling to find ways of making organization life more meaningful.

Moreover, the results are so intrinsically satisfying that efforts to suppress the changed thinking and behavior pattern do not succeed; "at best" he found and reported, "the pattern is suppressed until individuals can create conditions under which the pattern can (again) be surfaced."

For society. Need more be said? Anything that can bring about long-range improvement of all of organizational performance, individual returns, and personal intrinsic satisfaction injects new energy and endurance in society as a whole, and OD does all three, truly making possible Fromm's concept of *the good Life*: love and work under conditions of freedom and growth (pages 167-168 and 222).

NOTES

a. Current OD neglects direct integration.

b. It is with regard to this step that the comment was made in Chapter 15 that when an important structure or process change is under discussion, the staff organization planner (if there is one) should be present or be consulted.

c. An evaluation of the readiness of the team members should be made too; if the client is ready, this is less of a problem, but the results are still needed to guide educational planning that prepares them for the OD technique to be applied. An example is given ahead.

d.   Some consultants with an interpersonal skill technique for sale have incorrectly used the OD label because of its marketing appeal, perhaps under the claim that any performance change can be called OD change. The requisite as said is *behavior* change by a procedure that depends on social change theory. This is not to discount bona fide OD packages for sale; they will be reviewed ahead.

e.   Subgroups prepare glue-on/drawing collages of themes, e.g., "What is happening to the team?", then describe them before the whole team.

f.   An important rule: no attempt should be made to ferret out the author of any individual score card, though members may volunteer comments on their own ratings. The leader on the other hand is advised to wait for fairly high mutual trust before discussing his or her own ratings or behavior.

g.   One organization, Ebasco Services, Inc., has used the technique in a modified way to identify technical problem areas only, proceeding then right into problem solving. A corporate OD facilitator periodically interviews some 12 members of the senior staff to find out what needs improvement, then coordinates a 2-day meeting to discuss the subjects and plan actions. The approach was originally intended to educate top management on personnel issues, but the urgency of a new technological commitment temporarily sidetracked it to the technical after observing the technical payoff.[3]

h.   Two cautions from Fordyce and Weil: don't use a team-building meeting to deal with a hot one-to-one issue with one member. Don't conduct a meeting if about to fire a member; others will probably relate the dismissal to the meeting discussions.

i.   "Sensing" in the Figure refers to a way a consultant, staff person or a top manager can get a feel of the organization—that is, find out attitudes, concerns and needs—by listening to a cross-section of it through sample groups (about 12 each) in different functions, at different levels or diagonally, groups of employees with whom the managers normally have limited or no contact. It is an information-gathering technique in which the person mostly listens; it is quick and much less expensive than the interview approach (and less efficient), especially if the organization is large.

j.   Note that both the intergroup and total organization development techniques include skills of managing/leading interdepartment conflict, the A3 dimension on page 507 that is covered in Chapter 20.

k.   For a total organization change effort of any type to succeed it is critical that at least the top two levels have a clear understanding and consensus about where it's heading and what it takes to get there. It behooves top management therefore to precede any such efforts with a preliminary off-site confrontation-type meeting of these two levels, supplied by the needed prior research, to ascertain and achieve it. See "Senior management program" ahead on how.

l.   A question that comes to mind: is Harvard presenting this to students as representative of all OD, all OD team development, or a wrong specific approach?

m.   The opinions of the three men from interviews: participation is nonsense and Theory Y is neither action-oriented nor profit conscious. The Theory Y focuses too much on process and feelings, probes issues that are embarrassing, legitimizes the asking for help, and encourages subordinates to confront superiors; these are all signs of weakness. Leaders should be strong; management's job is to rule.

n.   Only the superior needing the Stranger T-grouping for the direct, but the team also needs it for the indirect OD team development techniques; of course the best solution is to do it for all involved at the start of their OD indoctrination.

REFERENCES

1.   Marrow, A. J., D. G. Bowers and S. E. Seashore, *Management by Participation* (New York: Harper & Row, 1967).

2.   Beckhard, R., *Organization Development: Strategies and Models* (Reading, Mass.: Addison-Wesley, 1969), pp. 16-19.

3.   French, W. L, and C. H. Bell, Jr., *Organizational Development* (Englewood Cliffs, N.J.: Prentice-Hall, 1973), pp. 99-101, abridged.

4.   McGregor, D., *The Professional Manager* (New York: McGraw-Hill, 1967), p. 173.

5.   *Business Week*, June 15, 1982, p. 126.

6.   McGregor, D., op. cit. (1967), p. 171.

7.   Fordyce, J. L and R. Weil, *Managing With People* (Reading, Mass.: Addison-Wesley, 1971), pp. 124-130.

8.   Ibid., p. 104.

9.   Ibid., p. 103.

10.   Beckhard, R., "The Confrontation Meeting," *Harvard Business Review*, March-April, 1967.

11.   Bolt, J. F., *Executive Development* (New York: Harper Business, 1989), pp. 55-68.

12.   Schein, E. H., "How Can Organizations Learn Faster?" *Sloan Management Review/Winter* 1993.

13.   Beckhard, R., *Organization Development* (Reading, Mass.: Addison-Wesley, 1969), pp. 45-56.

14.   Lippitt, G., *Organizational Renewal* (New York: Appleton-Century-Croft, 1969).

15.   Blake, R. R. and J. S. Mouton, *The New Managerial Grid* (Houston, Texas: Gulf Publishing Co., 1978), page 11.

16.   "Simonds Precision Products," in *Organizational Change and Development*, op. cit. (1970), pp. 82-103.

17.   Argyris, C., *Management and Organizational Development* (New York: McGraw-Hill, 1971), pp. 187 and 191.

18.   Argyris, C., *Increasing Leadership Effectiveness* (New York: Wiley, 1976).

19.   Argyris, C., *Interpersonal Competence and Organizational Effectiveness* (Homewood, Ill.: Irwin-Dorsey, 1962).

20.   Zand, D., "Trust and Managerial Problem Solving." *Administrative Science Quality*, June 1972; a validation: Boss, R. W., "Trust and Managerial

Problem Solving Revisited," *Group and Organizational Studies*, Sept. 1978, p. 331.

21.   Bennis, W. G., *Organization Development: Its Nature, Origin and Prospects.* (Reading, Mass.: Addison-Wesley, 1969), pp. 78-79. Abridged.

22.   Argyris, op. cit. (1971A). pp. 66-70.

23.   French and Bell, op. cit., p. 172.

24.   Porter, L. W., E. E. Lawler and J. R. Hackman, *Behavior in Organizations* (New York: McGraw-Hill, 1975), p. 497.

25.   Agyris, op. cit. (1971A), p. 153.

Chapter 20

Organizational Leadership

The indiscriminate use of the word leadership at times leads to wrong assumptions or expectations and misunderstandings. There are at least four basic applications of it that need differentiating for an unambiguous discussion of the subject:

a. The leadership of people sans resources—sports captains, senators, drill sergeants, social group leaders.

b. Leadership of people in organizations—also called human resources leadership—as defined on page 631: (i) initiating, directing, guiding, or controlling and/or influencing the activities, behavior, performance, attitudes and opinions of those people with their consent; (ii) incorporating the qualities of personality and training that make the effort successful (making it evident that the success is due to the leader's qualities and skills, not position power, sanctions, coercion or extrinsic rewards).

c. Organizational leadership—as on page 630: the art-science of managing the material resources and technologies, leading the people, and melding the three in such a way as to synthesize organizational and individual ends and means that will optimize their utilization toward the organization's purpose.

d. Entrepreneurial leadership: exercised by a person, one commonly very independent and strong willed, who initiates and organizes a new business or project, inspiring a motivated cohesive subordinate group in the early stages but usually parochially pushing his or her own goals and ignoring important peers and superiors (thus a poor fit for organizational leadership as defined above).

In progressive firms the importance of (b) and (c) at all levels is certainly universally appreciated now, but many managements are apparently still unable to recognize the presence or absence of either, attested by the amount of poor to mediocre performances that abound. Yet there are a number of criteria for judging competent leadership in general, and J.P. Kotter's book *The Leadership Factor* does a superior job of presenting them, describing the programs and practices of the successful and weaknesses of the others, the criteria an appropriate introduction to what should be done to develop effective leaders, the purpose of this chapter being to review, summarize, add to, and go deeper into key points covered in prior chapters of this text. The criteria:

1. *Sophisticated recruiting of leadership potential—*
   - Line management drives it—the CEO has made clear they're fully responsible—staff role is secondary, up to 1/2 of CEO's time on it (he knows best what is needed).
   - Candidates brought to Hq. to meet senior executives, seeking good interpersonal competence and common sense not just smart technicians.
   - Aggressive follow-up of college interviews with letters, interviews, offer.
   - Recruiting program results evaluated at least once a year with ratios of acceptances and who went to competitors.
   - Degree of potential of new hires rated on their annual appraisals.

2. *Ensuring an Attractive work environment* (essential to good retention)—
   - Volunteered quotes: "Great place to work," "Fun," "People are treated well."
   - Lack of politics and bureaucracy.
   - People try to help each other.
   - Honesty and high ethical standards in firm's credo.
   - Informal, friendly environment.
   - Quality of fellow workers.
   - Internal open market (selection) with lateral movement made easy.

3. *Challenging opportunities—*
   - Making entry-level job challenging.
   - Promotion opportunities are made challenging.
   - Stretching the potential ones early with exercises in leadership, e.g., assigning temporary supervision jobs.
   - Using positions of "assistant," "assistant to," "executive assistant" for development.
4. *Early identification potential—*
   - Making the promising visible in one way or another to senior management, e.g., special projects with final report to them— situations that put them "on stage."
   - Key functional executives asked to bring along high potential subordinates to executive lunches.
   - Formal meetings of senior executives once a month for 2 hours to review a percent of the high potentials and their progress—with pictures and biographies in advance.
5. *Planned development—*
   - Formal training (as in Chapter 17 and ahead).
   - Lateral moves for broadening and promotions.
   - Task force, project and/or committee assignments.
   - Coaching.
   - Assistant positions as listed above.
6. *The essentials for attracting, retaining and motivating good potential—*
   - Quality career planning (Chapter 17).
   - Developmental job opportunities.
   - Incentive compensation plans.
   - CEO attention to succession candidates.
   - Feedback from superiors and from and to the organization.

The evidence of poor leadership could be summarized as the opposite or absence of all the above, but certain characteristics of poorly led organizations stand out—

7. *Hiring policies:* no criteria except get lower cost; no university recruiting, hiring only for entry level jobs and for

technical competence, not leadership potential—managers competitively fear hiring superior competence; top officers only want obedient subordinates who are not threatening; when they must hire outside to fill important vacancies, the good new people are frustrated, stay only a short time.

8. *No management development* at lower levels, little above, no lateral transfers (check by counting how many each year); career paths only vertical and narrow resulting in promoting unprepared people; no performance reviews for managers thus no feedback, a basic principle of learning. The culture and practice: develop few if any leaders.

9. *Short-term business pressures and politics dominate:* Those promoted are those who get short-term results, are politically astute, are good at parochial infighting (see Chapter 1's "moral maze" example).

Knowledgeable executives may say this is all obvious, but a survey by Kotter of 900 responding executives in 100 large firms decidedly indicated the needs for effective leadership are apparently not obvious to a large majority. Asked to rate how well their own organization is doing on each of the following, their answers were:

- On recruiting and hiring a sufficient number with the potential to be leaders:
Very good to excellent	27%
Poor or fair	30%
- On how good your firm is doing developing high potential employees:
Very good to excellent	19%
Poor or fair	42%
- On how good at retaining and motivating high potential people:
Very good to excellent	20%
Poor or fair	43%

And these were firms with the resources to do the jobs well. One can imagine the ratings if the survey had been for all of the other some 2000 corporations of the nation.

Needless to say, the successful characteristics above were instituted by effective leaders, and to produce them there are certain prerequisites of a development program that need to be taught and to be learned by those it's applied to: research concepts developed in the past now held to be valuable to being good at it, basic principles that have evolved, and consequent role responsibilities. For the first—

Developed research concepts. Philosophers, theorists and researchers have produced a somewhat zig-zag path of ideas to follow for those attempting to lead organizations, a path that seemed at times to be little better than guesswork. Particular events that made some learning contributions were as listed below, complementing Figures IIa and IIb on pages 438-439:

Highlights of early organizational theory and research

B.C. - 1940s	Trait theorists
1909	The bureaucratic model
1920s-30s	Situation theorists
1927	Psychology and participation—Mary Parker Follett
1927-32	Hawthorne studies $\left.\right\}$ —Elton Mayo
1930-50s	Human relations school
1939	Authoritarian / Democratic / Laissez-faire $\left.\right\}$ —Kurt Lewin, R. Lippitt and R. K. White[a]
1940s	Leadership theorists' model / Start of organization behavior school and OD
1945	Initiating structure / Consideration $\left.\right\}$ —Bureau of Bus. Research Ohio State Univ.
1940s-50s	Interaction theory
1960	Theory X & Y and direct integration—Douglas McGregor
1961	Systems model of organizational leadership $\left.\right\}$ —Rensis Likert

Briefly as a refresher on what has already been covered, from B.C. to around 1940 the universal view of leadership competence was the "great man" theory described on page 344, an idea propounded even as recently as 1933 by Carl Jung and in 1937 by Gordon Allport, an opinion that conveniently complemented the authoritarian model passed down with it. The 1907 bureaucratic model of Weber but institutionalized the authoritarian one, a view unfortunately still dominant in most organizations. Put inelegantly, leaders are born, not made.

Then along the road from the authoritarian model to the humanistic (page 168) emerged the simplistic situation theory, that a person's leadership success was determined primarily by the situation,[b] which was followed by an awakening by Elton Mayo and Kurt Lewin, et al to the importance of human relations to leadership. This was expanded on by the research at Ohio State University, producing the two basic elements "initiating structure" and "consideration":[c]

> *Initiating structure* (accounting for about 1/3 of the common-factor variance)—the leader is production-oriented, giving primary attention to the planning of goals, programming, scheduling, and evaluating results.
>
> *Consideration* (accounting for about 1/2 of the common-factor variance)— the leader is employee-oriented, gives primary attention to developing relationships of trust and rapport with good two-way communication, is friendly and considerate of subordinates needs and ideas.

But the most progressive thinking about the specifics or leadership came from Douglas McGregor in the 50s and 60s— his **interaction theory** followed by his Theory X, Theory Y, and "direct integration" in his 1961 book, *The Human Side of Management.*[5] The interaction theory combined the realization that traits are important with the conclusions of the emerging organization behavior school that personality, interpersonal skills, behavior, and the environment are also key parts of it; the theory: leadership is a relationship of (1) personality, (2) the followers, (3) the organization and (4) the environment... in which 2, 3 and 4 are considered the elements of the situation. Put in terms of leadership in action—that is, leadership style— it would result in a chart like this:

Traits[d]		The Situation	
Personality		(a) Structures & Processes	
Assumptions	Applied to	(the mgmt. system)	Org'l
Skills		(b) Interpersonal relations	= Leadership
Behavior		(leadership behavior)	Style

Recall that Theories X and Y were described on page 16, and the direct integration is so significant to success that, as said earlier, it is on the level of a basic principle and will be described ahead with the others.

As for the style equation, it's certainly an oversimplification (as with any model), because each factor is of course a situation variable, each with a wide range of possibilities that can swing the style radically. The most potent variables:

- The organization's culture, climate and norms
- The environment: economic, social, political, the market, competition, government, laws
- Organization goals, structures, processes, technology, policies, bureaucracy, internal politics
- Demands on the individual, destructive ones illustrated in the Chapter I "moral maze"
- Believed expectations of superiors, peers, and subordinates
- Competence and quality of superiors, peers and subordinates
- The leader's philosophy of "the nature of man" (pp. 150-156)
- Upbringing treatment of the leader—authoritarian, democratic, participative, abusive, uncaring neglect.
- Past leadership attempts, successes, failures in the unit being led.

Furthermore, the text has presented enough convincing research and evidence, it seems, to make clear that for optimum results one aspect of leadership behavior must remain constant, regardless of overt behavior changes believed necessary by a leader, for the organization to cope and prevail in any environment or growth stage. That aspect: the person's philosophy as to individuals' rights and self-respect and concern for their wants and needs. Applying such, a leader will not only be more likely to gain trust, high regard and cooperation but be better able to handle the needs of adverse circumstances that require unilateral directives because the leader will at the same time still honor these concerns.

Thus the ideal organizational leadership style for the preponderance of circumstances would be the consequence of

Theory Y philosophy, superior social and technical skills, and a pattern of integrating them effectively. However, what the discipline still needed along with McGregor's contributions was a complete picture of what should be targeted, an overarching one that in general accounts for all the forces and needs, a model an organization leader should try to follow.

Organizational leadership models. The outstanding models over the years have of course mirrored the managerial thinking of their time, and a knowledge of them, even cursory, can help leaders and managers develop their own ideas and discard the flawed and illogical.

First, note the thinking behind the now-rejected authoritarian model. It assumed the interests and goals of the individual and organization to be irreconcilably in conflict, so the leadership principles propounded were concerned with the modes of unilateral control. The superior-subordinate relationship was considered little better than a master-servant one in which dealings should be made as impersonal as possible by the use of structures, processes and rules; job execution and compliance was believed obtainable only with a punitive authoritarian climate.

(The word "principle" was of course used by these proponents the way philosophers have used it: apply it to any event or pattern they believed had universal applications. Philosophers and theorists alike often found to have been wrong. In the management of people some license tends to be accepted in its use when the statement is true the preponderance of the time, or it is better than a rule-of-thumb...which would be considered heresy by purist.)

Then around 1927 an appreciation of psychology and participation emerged, and along with the Hawthorne studies *the human relations school* blossomed. But its precepts unfortunately went too far in the other direction: "be nice," on the theory that good performance is a natural corollary of job satisfaction, one that failed to account for the importance of commitment to goals and what it takes to develop it.

A few years of sad experience with it in the field sent the theorists back to the drawing boards, and some of them produced a new one that became quite popular because it was easy for practicing managers to accept, *the leadership theorists'* model that attempted to reconcile their authoritarian philosophy with the new appreciation of individual needs. They accepted the discrepancies between individual and organizational goals, but saw the problem only as one of satisfying the organization's needs and therefore one of bringing the individual around to accepting the organization's goals. The principles recommended were to reduce the person's autonomy and increase dependence, using the superior-subordinate personal relationship to persuade, and to increase subordinates' personal involvement. The consequence understandably was subordinate frustration and interpersonal conflict.

But at about the same time the *organization behavior school*—Lewin, Argyris, McGregor, Bennis, Likert et al.—was beginning to make itself felt, and as we know, it divided the weight of importance between the individual and organization fairly evenly. Warren Bennis went so far as to say that "leadership is the fulcrum on which the demands of the individual and the demands of the organization are balanced."[6]

It is also pragmatic and in accordance with the new conclusions of organization behavior research: the purpose of an organization is not primarily social (unless it's the planned objective) or technical, but both (per the explanation on page 459). In the end, if anything has to give it's the individual for the welfare of the group, but it should seldom have to come to that, especially in the mind of the individual whose main ego need is to have a fair hearing, a feeling that what is being asked or required is objective, just, and functionally reasonable, a feeling that is induced when the superior follows the above principles and those described in the next section.

These organization behaviorists however naturally appreciated that each of their valuable theories only provided part of the picture; not only did they themselves need a full systems model of organizational leadership, especially to guide their organization development work, but CEOs were rarely buying their theories for lack of persuasive detailed backup and logical integration.

Fortunately, the U.S. Office of Naval Research contracted Rensis Likert and his team at the Survey Research Center of the University of Michigan (in 1947) for a project that made it possible for him to verify unequivocally the model he proposed in his 1961 book.[7]

Five findings that those who want to master leadership need to be familiar with form the core of this important research:

1. All the principal organizational systems variations in the country with respect to their management philosophies were found to be classifiable into roughly four types, the headings in Figure 20.1, that were also labeled for easier reference as Systems 1, 2, 3 and 4.

2. Six major functions common to the system were studied and were discovered to be, within each system, closely tied to its leadership policies and behaviorally interrelated with each other. The functions were:[c]

Motivation	Decision making
Communication	Goal setting
Interaction influence	Control

3. The performance and satisfaction levels within the four systems formed a continuum from System 1 to System 4 and from low to high.

4. In each of the systems the optimum performance of the system as a whole was found to be achieved when all the parts of the system reflect the same philosophy; individual behaviors out of balance detracted from the total results. (This naturally is not intended to suggest the accommodation of the people to the system meant they produced at their best or were satisfied.)

5. Each system tends to require, attract and produce people suited to the system; e.g. an authoritarian one (Systems 1 and 2) requires, attracts and tends to develop dependent personalities on the part of all except those in control at the top, and consequently it does not develop leaders. Participative organizations require, attract and tend to develop emotionally and socially mature people capable of effective interaction, initiative and leadership. Systems between these two extremes would do similarly, proportional to their location on the continuum.

Profile of Organizational characteristics

	Exploitive authoritative System 1	Benevolent authoritative System 2	Consultative System 3	Participative group System 4
1. Leadership processes used				
a. Extent to which superiors have confidence and trust in *subordinates*	Have no confidence and trust in subordinates	Have condescending confidence and trust, such as master has in servant	Substantial but not complete confidence and trust; still wishes to keep control of decisions	Complete confidence and trust in all matters
b. Extent to which subordinates, in turn, have confidence and trust in superiors	Have no confidence and trust in superiors	Have subservient confidence and trust, such as servant has to master	Substantial but not complete confidence and trust	Complete confidence and trust
c. Extent to which superiors display supportive behavior toward others	Display no supportive behavior or virtually none	Display supportive behavior in condescending manner and situations only	Display supportive behavior quite generally	Display supportive behavior fully and in all situations
d. Extent to which superiors behave so that subordinates feel free to discuss important things about their jobs with their immediate superior	Subordinates do not feel at all free to discuss things about the job with their superior	Subordinates do not feel very free to discuss things about the job with their superior	Subordinates feel rather free to discuss things about the job with their superior	Subordinates feel completely free to discuss things about the job with their superior
e. Extent to which immediate superior in solving job problems generally tries to get subordinates' ideas and opinions and make constructive use of them	Seldom gets ideas and opinions of subordinates in solving job problems	Sometimes gets ideas and opinions of subordinates in solving job problems	Usually gets ideas and opinions to make constructive use of them	Always gets ideas and opinions and always tries to make constructive use of them

Figure 20.1

Particularly valuable is that the total systems concept applied to each of the four in the Figure, that like all biological and ecological systems, all the parts of socio-technical systems are also heavily interacting and interdependent. True, simple observation tells one this, but besides being verified here scientifically, Likert also convincingly demonstrated the significance to management: performance *at all levels* is closely linked to the character of organizational leadership in whole and all its functional parts. The knowledge payoff of the research: a total-organization leadership model to guide all top managements, a complete set of interrelated goals for OD, and a valuable predictive tool for organization behaviorists as illustrated in the System 4 case in Chapter 13.

But recall that in each of the examples in the text, including the one in Chapter 13, of successfully improving organizational leadership and performance that have been described (and the most successful were selected), the professional experts guiding their implementation admitted that the results were always short of goals, to which one can reliably add that durability was also open to question for lack of longitudinal study.

Given the dedication of the leaders behind them, one has to conclude that either something must have been still missing in the leadership, or the OD techniques were not sufficiently adequate, or both. Of course we now know it's both—for OD, the inadequate job on values change within its power (caused in large measure by eliminating Stranger T-grouping), its inability to affect the deep-seated values (page 191), and its failure to teach direct integration.

And on the leadership, one should not be surprised. Business schools themselves are only now beginning to take the subject seriously, so it's the rare current top leader, including those with MBAs, who is familiar with even the basic principles and role responsibilities essential to success.

The principles

There are eight, clearly all collectively essential to optimizing voluntary compliance, collaboration and commitment. That the first four are fundamental must be evident at this point if it wasn't already:

1. Building mutual trust
2. Social exchange
3. Participation
4. Supportiveness...

and any lengthy comment on them would be repetitive. But one matter about the first is especially relevant about today's corporate leaders and should be added: plainly, there can be no genuine leadership without trust, and within the factors of integrity, morality and fairness that are obviously essential to it is the assumption of a reasonable restraint on greed (definition on page 120) regarding the use and abuse of power as well as acquisitiveness. Top executives of large corporations, it seems, generally fail to see the effect (or don't give a damn) that bloated compensation for themselves has throughout the organization, that obscenely high compensation, especially without commensurate performance (their pay now averaging 85 times the level of the lowest employees vs. 17 times in Japan), gains only deep distrust and disgust.

It's commonly known that those who are so overpaid control their boards and dictate what they want and get, often upping it into millions while demanding cost cutting and layoffs. They're obviously robbing the company. Who is going to be committed and follow let alone respect thieves (calling a spade a spade)? A solution to produce board and management accountability on the subject is given in Chapter 22.

It's worth noting too that job satisfaction, which is so important to commitment, is determined more by the degree that trust is characteristic of the climate than by the degree to which participation is practiced.[9]

On the other principles, of course the heavy interdependence of superiors and subordinates described on page 472 makes the "social exchange" obviously necessary, and "participation," besides filling important ego needs, is the most potent general motivator (contrasted with delegation that is specific to a task), "supportiveness" being a companion principle necessary to build self-regard and a desire to collaborate. One may recall that #3 and #4 are also Likert's interaction-influence subprinciples #1 and #2 on pages 569 and 571.

Douglas McGregor delineated the other four in his *The Human Side of Management,* four that have already been probed abstractly in previous sections but need some added comment concerning particularly their importance to leadership as principles: authority, interdependence, self-management and integration.

5. *Authority.* McGregor pointed out that down through history there have been two major transitions with regard to authority, which he called "the central means of controlling human behavior in organizational settings." The first was the one that occurred thousands of years ago, the change from sheer physical force to a reliance on formal authority, and the second, still underway, has been from full reliance on legal authority (also called position authority) to a means that, he commented, is not yet clear to most as to either its goal or direction, the change from legal authority to the psychological authority defined on page 469.

But, it's quite evident that, though the legal is the current predominant approach, progressive companies and managers are now at least on the road to the psychological with a good idea of both direction and goal, thanks to the more recent teaching progress of the behaviorists and OD developers.

Those interested in joining them have first to think through (a) the nature of authority, (b) the dynamics of the requirements of leadership, and (c) how knowledge of the nature and dynamics can be fitted together for a set of guidelines on the application of authority.

(a) The nature of authority has already been treated at length in Chapter 11, so here are just major points for review.

The *legal authority* (or position or formal) of managers was described as based on the power to punish, which in turn relies on material dependency; but it was reminded that the changed status of individuals (as subordinates) and increasing restraints on applying punishment has resulted in:

- little ability left to punish;
- a wholly insufficient amount of dependency upward remaining as a basis of unilateral authority for it to gain compliance reliably let alone regularly;

- a potent counterability of subordinates to punish superiors;
- a relationship that is now one of the almost complete interdependence rather than dependence.

Furthermore, managers are beginning to recognize, even if only intuitively, the negative character of position authority unless it's an emergency, that it cannot motivate, only coerce. All together, legal authority has become a double-edged sword of dubious value as a regular recourse: if applied as a standard practice or inappropriately, it's apt to backfire, or you may have no one left to do the job.

Conversely, the employment of **psychological authority** seems to have all the opposite consequences. Along with the widely felt human need for it and admiration of it, its use is able to:

- motivate intrinsically
- integrate individual and organizational goals directly and indirectly, and
- get the work done while providing job satisfaction for both superiors and subordinates.

A complication is the values, perceptions, talents and training it takes to apply it consistently compared to the simplicity of ordering "do it."

Nevertheless, legal authority as said in Chapter 11 is still indispensable to management for selected situations of urgency or crisis and in the event that psychological authority fails.

(b) The dynamics of leadership refers particularly to **the five different kinds of variability** leaders have to be able to manage listed on page 349; to repeat:

- the functional and behavior variations required of them to be effective in the role responsibilities; motivating, directing, coordinating, controlling, teaching, changing, and representing (p.631), including the range from supporting to disciplining and discharging;
- the differences of leadership necessary for different subordinate personalities;

- the variety of behavior changes to be elicited from subordinates;
- the differences due to different echelons, functions, and external contacts a leader must work with;
- the differences of situations, including the different requirements at different management levels.

(c) In order to fit these simple facts of nature and dynamics together for guidelines on the use of authority, one has to first look a little closer again at one fundamental use of it: *influence.*

Influence in this the leadership context is the gaining of voluntary acceptance, collaboration and/or compliance on orders, requests or suggestions (that may be but hints), a definition that appears to be similar to the one for the leadership of people at the beginning of the chapter. But of course influence—assuming it's non-coercive like Lewin's approach on page 97 is only one form of "motivation" which is itself but one of the seven leadership role responsibilities (in the first dot) and, influence can get degrees of compliance short of commitment.

There are four ways we know to make the influence effort: overt threat of punishment, legal authority (its power being in an implicit threat), a carrot, or the psychological authority of technical or social skills, Lewin's recommendation being an example of the social.

Certainly the overt threat type needs no comments, and the limitations of the legal or position authority have been described, but one important qualification about the legal should be added. Over and above the usual absence of volition and the problems reviewed in (a) above, it has but one dimension, *power*; you can only administer more or less to get results in the immense range of circumstances that occur, and that's it. Leaders who restrict themselves to it bring to mind Maslow's statement quoted earlier that "if the only tool you have is a hammer, you tend to treat everything as if it were a nail."

It is not always appreciated, incidentally, that the traditional influence technique for what we call *persuasion* is a form of legal authority. Regrettably, most managers lose sight of the basic idea that should be behind persuasion (the voluntary acceptance) when they try to apply it. As has been noted, the recipient is somehow subtly, though perhaps unintentionally, informed or knows that legal authority will be administered if the persuasion doesn't work; it's really manipulation and coercion.

In fact, because of the authoritarian nature of the conventional climate, all persuasion is generally assumed to be authority-based. Even in a System 4 setup, one application of power is all that's needed and a threat will from then on be perceived as behind the kindest request, until a significant change occurs that justifies the necessary trust to accept future persuasion attempts as genuine. Given a good climate, the key to bona fide persuasion is the maturity of openness to alternative suggestions, the willingness to admit one is not always right, and accepting the failure to persuade when not successful.

A problem with the carrot as a standard policy to be applied to managers is also one of limitation. First, repeated offers of one in task after task become an insult to their intelligence and self-respect; second, the combination of circumstances necessary for extrinsic rewards to be effective are rarely present:

- each task has to be identified and clearly linked to the reward—and, there are far too many tasks;
- each task has to be measurable, which is most often not possible in management;
- the carrot has to be big enough and important enough to the subordinate to influence—a difficult calculation for any of the tasks let alone so many of them.

Behaviorists have found out too that emphasizing extrinsic reward for doing a job (the way authoritarians do) is an excellent way to make the job boring and invite repeated requests for more of the reward (especially pay). The person comes to see the rewards as the dominant reason for working, doesn't identity with the job or its goals.

Knowing now the pros and cons of legal and psychological authority, the demanding dynamics of leadership, and the requisites of influence, one can assemble a set of guidelines for best results through the years by simply stating clearly when the legal and psychological should be applied, applied in conjunction with the philosophy or authority developed by Fromm (pages 167-169) and McGregor (especially his Theory Y):

Legal (position or formal) authority—
is conferred by society, which is manifested through its laws creating, condoning and/or supporting organizations;
is neither bad nor good in and of itself;
is only one form of influence with the sole dimension, power, of more or less for getting results;
is positively effective (sometimes negatively) only in certain urgent situations (crises, time constraints, misbehavior);
is not able to motivate, can only coerce;
is ineffective without upward dependence;
is nevertheless essential to managing an organization toward its goals, but only because of its emergency or last-resort power.

Psychological authority—
is the most powerful leadership influence on performance and behavior;
is possible through a wide variety of leadership techniques;
is the only authority capable of intrinsic motivation;
is the only authority that can integrate individual and organization goals;
can be a vehicle toward job satisfaction for both superiors and subordinates;
is essential to effective organizational leadership of people as defined.

Clearly it's a matter of selecting to fit the situation, and one should never forget the "technical skills" part of psychological basis of authority (p.469), for example, the importance to success of strategy as shown in Chapters 15.

It might be well to tick off here the coverage to this point of the consequences of the misuse of authority, that is, authoritarian conduct: the effects of "structuring" it on page 278; the effect of authoritarian goal setting and appraising on 403-404; the norms and fears it instills on 485-486; information manipulation on 547;

and the indirect consequences through "bureaucracy" on pages 448-453.

6. *Interdependence.* The importance of keeping this in mind as a principle becomes more clearly apparent when one reminds oneself that a constant appreciation of it is necessary to apply successfully over time all the other seven principles and all interpersonal skills.

Surely no additional elaboration beyond the discourse on it in Chapters 8 and 11 need be given. Keeping aware of it in all interpersonal relations with subordinates should significantly improve the outcome for those who've neglected it; and for the particular occasions when orders are necessary, developing an intuitive habit of determining beforehand into which of Barnard's three categories on page 496 they fit should be a big help in handling orders effectively.

But there is one generally ignored aspect of interdependence that superiors should also keep in mind and understand in detail. The leadership goal is plain enough: voluntary committed collaboration; but as virtually all managers know, collaboration comes in different grades from the commitment to subservience, the various shades of the latter called by traditional managers *loyalty*, sorely twisting the value of loyalty's true meaning. Because it can block or seriously distort truthful communication, one had better understand what is involved and how to manage it.

Webster's defines loyalty as "fidelity; the careful observance of duty or discharge of obligation." The social exchange is transparent, but there seems to be considerably more to it; moreover, there are important differences between loyalty to a person and loyalty to a group.

Loyalty to a person, we all know, is similar to friendship but stronger, coming from an accumulation of feelings due to any or a mix of companionship, admiration, intellectual agreement, common interests, passion, spiritual conviction, common values or goals, personal need; and an emotional "personal contact" seems to have been made in each instance. It is also a consequence of charisma (page 350), but generally, references to loyalty are when it is independent of charisma.

In organizational life the personal need is the most frequent basis, usually overlapping other causes, and a biting description of its functioning (in all these instances) drives home an important feature of its character: "Loyalty persists while the bond exists, and the bond exists while the need persists." One simply has to face up to the fact that, regardless of the cause, both friendship and personal loyalty are unstable intangibles subject to decay and evaporation. Personalties change, interests diverge, pleasures peter out, needs degenerate into dependence, new relationships conflict, interpersonal competition emerges.

And clearly, in the unequal superior-subordinate relationship, the need, whether or not mutual, especially the upward need is most often the *only* bond, and under an authoritarian superior it's easy for any subordinate to contrive *peon* loyalty, a pure servitude from fear of economic punishment or losing one's job—the kind of loyalty many managers demand, as Warren Bennis commented, "to muffle dissent."[10]

Certainly the only thing that can minimize the subservience and develop (that is, start) the loyalty wanted is consideration, respect for rights, and honoring the ineluctable fact that loyalty up requires loyalty down (e.g., sharing both cutbacks and benefits), which will lead to openness and trust. There's plenty of evidence of honorable subordinate loyalty. Adding humanism, honesty and technical effectiveness will reliably evoke it.

Still, no one needs to be told that in any power-differential set-up some pragmatic deference will always be present affecting the information feed-upward. All experienced executives know that getting the unvarnished truth from below is one of their most difficult jobs. Even the most highly regarded humanist has to make a positive constant effort to obtain it, realizing they're always being watched for contradictory signs.

Three rules-of-thumb for guarding against both peon loyalty and pragmatic bending: don't rely on subordinates for all the truth, particularly on crucial issues; circulate—"wander around" quite frequently (page 494) to see, hear and feel a lot of the truth yourself; build OD techniques into the management system—they produce and sustain trust, and truth comes more easily for both subordinates and superiors.

Needless to say, performance and behavior of this sort by managers at this interpersonal level is cumulatively at the heart of subordinates' loyalty to their group and larger organization. In the smaller group or department a principal manifestation as explained in Chapter 3 is cohesion, an identification with and internalization of the group's goals, and it was shown that leadership made it happen.

Indeed, the way for a leader to gain the loyalty of subordinates to his or her group or to the larger organization is basically the same—all that has been recommended herein for effective leadership. For a brief review: it starts with the philosophy that people are fundamentally good, not evil, and the introspective approach to subordinates' performance and behavior described on page 155, which shows the leader's trust, sensitivity, consideration, responsiveness, and concern for their needs (page 97).

If the leader feels this way, giving participation to subordinates in making or influencing the decisions that affect them comes naturally, and from it the subordinates develop a sense of ownership of the decisions, commitment to make them succeed, and a "vision" of the group or organization to their liking.

But there is of course a need for the vision of subordinates to be also a long-range perspective as well as an opinion of the present, which raises the issue of the *leader's* vision so important to the board and stockholders that also answers the two concerns of all thinking subordinates: where is the organization headed down the road, followed closely by the one of how they themselves will be treated. J.P. Kotter nicely portrayed the "big picture" in a tabulation of the requisites as follows, much of it applicable to leaders at all levels (all medium size and large organizations today being complex; read "strategy" where applicable to people as policies):[11]

Effective Leadership in Complex Organizations

I. *Creating an Agenda for Change*
   a. Which includes a vision of what can and should be
   b. A vision that takes into account the legitimate long-term interests of the parties involved

   c. Which includes a strategy for achieving that vision
   d. A strategy that takes into account all the relevant organizational and environmental forces.
II. *Building a Strong Implementation Network*
   a. That includes supportive relationships with the key sources of power needed to implement the strategy
   b. Relationships strong enough to elicit cooperation, compliance, and (where necessary) teamwork
   c. Which includes a highly motivated core group of people
   d. A core group committed to make the vision a reality.

Part II of this work obviously describes the art-skill, "the parties involved" in Ib above being all others in the unit, loyalty developments a consequence of the art-skill.

7. Self-management. McGregor used the term "self-control," but self-management is being substituted here to avoid confusing his intention with the personality trait of self-control described in Chapter 3 (pages 63-65).

Remember that he made his concept of it proposition #2 in Theory Y on page 16.

> Man will exercise self-direction and self-control in the service of objectives to which he is committed.

In other words, there's a close linkage between objectives, commitment, and self-management, a truth that in the saying reminds one of the inverse: a person who doesn't like and hasn't accepted the objectives will not be committed and will not exercise self-direction toward attaining them.

The proposition was of course not just a sudden flash of brilliance out of thin air. It was his summary conclusion combining earlier thinking, particularly the MBO idea (promoted by Drucker six years before in *The Practice of Management*), his work with Lewin on group dynamics, and his years of consulting experience.

The basic idea of MBO, we know, was the use of participation that Follett, Coch, French and others had been urging, because all their study and research seemed to prove that it motivated commitment and self-management. But, as explained at the start of Chapter 10, psychologist McGregor saw that participation was in fact only a climate determinant that opened the door to commitment and self-management; it didn't produce them; the participation could just as well result in unacceptable goals or solutions producing the opposite outcome. It but fostered a readiness to comply and collaborate *if* the deal made in the participation was acceptable.

Thus participation is a basic *general* purpose motivation technique. It's crucial to a wide variety of individual and group tasks producing a long list of motivation and morale benefits, but in any that involves the planning of a task, job, goal or solution to be carried out by a subordinate, something else has to be added; as in selling, the sale has to be closed. McGregor may have been the first to call it "integration."

8. *Integration*. Clearly, achieving this is closing the sale, the activity having the two parts, direct and indirect, defined in Chapter 2 (page 32) the two inextricably interdependent; one simply cannot be fully achieved in the organizational context without the other.

A tabulation of them in terms of the three determinants of climate:

Integrative systems, techniques and skills
for gaining voluntary collaboration and commitment

Climate determinants	Principal systems, techniques and skills	Leadership approach
Structures } Processes }	Management System 4 OD built into the management system Open personnel system; pay, selection, appraisal, files Cybernetics, where needed, including linking-pin function	Indirect Integration
Leadership	Participation Job-designing Goal setting Control planning Career/devel. planning Counseling	Direct Integration
	The indirect techniques above	Indirect Integration

However, only the coverage of the indirect has been completed in the text (culminating in Chapter 19's OD) and the functional (the "what") side of the direct; to succeed on the direct one of course also has to learn the "how," the psychology and skill that are not being taught.

How, for instance, can you be sure to keep the subordinate from feeling manipulated or coerced when participatively job planning, goal setting or programming each time they have to be done? McGregor illustrated with a superb description of how to do the job planning process, one that made indisputably clear that the idea—integration—is not celestial theory, but down to earth practical logic:[12]

> The central principle which derives from Theory Y is that of integration: the creation of conditions such that the members of the organization can achieve their own goals *best* by directing their efforts toward the success of the enterprise.
>
> Perfect integration of organizational requirements and individual goals and needs is, of course, not a realistic objective, In adopting this principle, we seek that degree of integration in which the individual can achieve his goals *best* by directing his efforts toward the success of the organization. "Best" means that this alternative will be more attractive than the many others available to him: indifference, irresponsibility, minimal compliance, hostility, sabotage.
>
> It is a deliberate attempt to link improvement in managerial competence with the satisfaction of higher-level ego and self-actualization needs.

The illustration was a hypothetical scenario of a v.p. of staff services helping his new manager of personnel develop the position's design and goals, using the four steps of MBO:

1. The clarification of the broad requirements of the job.
2. The establishment of specific "targets" for a limited time period.
3. The self-management process during the target period.
4. Appraisal of results.

A reading in the book of the v.p.'s skill in handling the project is a cogent lesson not only in doing it and in managing subordinates but also in teaching subordinates how to manage their own subordinates. It is strongly recommended, and here is some of the intelligence presented that deserves particular note:[13]

1. **Job designing**: The manager of personnel had received at induction a formal description of the position's general expectations, one without any detail as to specific responsibilities, and was given about 8 months to get a feel for the job (a little longer, it seems, than necessary), after which "integration" meetings were to be held by the v.p. to firm up the job's characteristics and goals in a tactful and patient negotiating process.

The eight months of observing by the v.p., however, led him to believe he may have chosen a poor manager. The man seemed to have an inadequate conception of the position's responsibilities, be unable to utilize the department's resources of professional knowledge, and done nothing to upgrade other top executives' naive views of the personnel function, becoming their errand boy in his over anxiousness to impress them; in time he used his own subordinates as errand boys.

It was clear that the manager's most fundamental need was a broadening of his own view of the function in order to see the department's purpose and place in the organization; only then would he correctly conceive the desirable specifics for his own planning and managing.

In the first meeting therefore the superior asked, after a friendly review of the problems and progress of the 8 months, for a simple easy initial step: that he give some thought to, and list for a second meeting, what he felt were the position's major responsibilities, not limiting his thinking to the constraints of the formal description. The vice president only contributed a verbal depiction in broad terms of the company and its situations as he himself saw them.

2. **The subordinate's perception of the superior.** In this first meeting, the v.p. made a point of trying to get the manager to see him as a colleague and aide on the project, not as a traditional boss. Only then, he felt, would the person begin to think creatively on his own and not just try to please his superior.

An equally important goal was to help him develop in his mind through the process the full role he himself wanted to occupy as the personnel executive, and in doing so to clarify his own responsibilities as a subordinate.

3. **The superior's attitude.** Underlying the whole approach was the superior's sincere desire for the subordinate to grow in competence, and therefore a desire for him to build a job within the formal description that would require the challenge necessary for growth.

Their discussion in the second meeting of the crude list submitted was therefore principally a drawing out, probing the "restraining forces" that may be present (p. 97), listening and guiding toward this end with the principles of enrichment on page 300 in mind.

4. **Self-management.** Then to motivate self-management the manager was asked in the third meeting to prepare goals, programs and measurements for himself and his department, based on the new description and discussions to date, which they would go over together and come to an agreement on in the fourth meeting.[f]

Notably, the personnel manager began to treat his own subordinates similarly, asking their views and working together to clarify the department's mission, then its goals and programs, probably stimulated by the v.p.'s inquiries in each of these meeting about subordinates' opinions.

5. **The process of integration.** Note that the superior applied the best activators of responsibility and commitment by both what was asked and how it was asked. The subordinate filled in the design of his own job, planned his goals, programs and measurements, learned how to manage subordinates, engage participation, and operated his department all with minimal supervision from above, yet aware of the distinct concern, encouragement, guidance and monitoring of his superior. In the process the manager came to see that what he wanted and what the v.p. wanted were congruent, the result being goal internalization and commitment.

The idea of letting a subordinate write his own job ticket, or almost, undoubtedly raises some eyebrows. The top organization planning staff must naturally supply the basic elements of job descriptions down the line to tie all the work together, be sure there are no gaps, and clarify who's responsible for what. The formal description mentioned was one of these.

In traditional firms that are not interested in "integration" the descriptions may contain considerable detail both to teach the jobs and hold the incumbents accountable for all identifiable tasks. In advanced integrative firms, they are relatively vague so the incumbent can be asked to do as above. At the same time, a new superior, who is interested in integration but unfamiliar with his or her subordinate positions, might request both a detailed and general one from staff, retaining the former for his or her own education.

Thus some design vagueness should be built into many if not most manager descriptions, especially jobs that require a substantial amount of unique decision-making, problem-solving or innovative creativity. Additionally, an amount of ambiguity and uncertainty will motivate as well as allow a competent enterprising manager to take on responsibilities where needed to "get the job done" even if the authority doesn't seem to have been clearly conferred. Recall too the comments on page 314.

Of course the principal point of the participation is the integration of individual and organizational goals can only occur when the subordinate thinks through and negotiates what is needed to evolve a fit. Further, the thinking through in this manner, whether planning the position, goals or programs, is essential for the development of confidence in them and the sense of ownership that generates commitment.

In sum, what is involved is elementary: cost-effectively, the organization will suffer seriously if the personal goals and needs of its managers are ignored; it will gain if they are integrated. Integration is very pro performance; its not social charity as some hard-nosed executives still believe.

There is, of course, the subtle inexorable catch mentioned before, that the technique only works with a sincere Theory Y concern for the dignity, welfare and development of people, all people, a regard that also supplies the patience to apply the much greater time and the devotion needed to do it well. And McGregor added:

> This approach does not tack a new set of duties on top of the existing managerial load. It is, rather, a different way of fulfilling existing responsibilities—of "running the job." I have yet to meet a manager who has made effective time of this managerial strategy who is critical of the time required. Several have said, "if this isn't the primary job of the manager, what is?"

A point all would-be leaders might particularly note too about direct integration is that it is not only the skill of integrating individual and organization interests and goals, it is an integration of all 8 principles of leadership: it's a participative technique of making a social exchange in which psychological authority is used in a situation of interdependence to motivate self-management toward an agreed-upon common goal, mutual trust and supportiveness being necessary parts of the psychology. Depicted in a flow chart:

Mutual Trust
social exchange ⎫
participation ⎬   + integration ⟶ Goal internalization ⟶
supportiveness ⎭

Commitment ⟶ Self-management ⟶

Better performance.

...clearly the ultimate demonstration of competence in the leadership of human resources.

The leadership role

Some years ago an organizational psychologist described the way many people view the executive job as follows:[14]

> As nearly everyone knows, an executive has practically nothing to do except decide what is to be done; to tell somebody to do it; to listen to reasons why it should not be done, why it should be done by someone else, or why it should be done in a different way; to follow up to see if the thing has been done; to discover that it has been done incorrectly; to point out how it should have been done; to conclude that as long as it has been done, it may as well be the way it is; to wonder if it is not time to get rid of a person who cannot do a thing right; to reflect that he probably has a wife and a large family, and that genuinely any successor would be just as bad and maybe worse; to consider how much simpler and better the thing would have been done if one had done it oneself in the first place, to reflect sadly that one could have done it in 20 minutes, and, as things timed out, one has to spend two days to find out why it has taken three weeks for someone else to do it wrong!

Though a tongue-in-cheek description, there are many untrained managers, especially in bureaucracies, who would characterize their jobs that way, managers trying to "get things done through others" without any conception of the nature of the leadership role, therefore why this sort of aggravation truly can occur.

The text has been developing the basic elements of the role to this point, and now they may be assembled and organized for a coherent conception that should guide them out of their ignorance.

Keeping in mind that leading-managing has 2 parts, the technical and the social, and a "role" is what one does contrasted with how one does it, recall that in Chapter 14 it was summed up in five words under the text's preliminary definition of organizational leadership (page 630):

Analyzing + Planning + Decision making + Managing + Leading.

Then on page 631 the people part of the leadership role was described as consisting of six directly interpersonal role responsibilities and an intermediary less direct one (the last) that determine the level of leadership effectiveness:

Motivating	Controlling
Directing	Teaching
Coordinating	Changing
	Representing

But before going into the seven, one should appreciate that, although these role responsibilities are basic to good leadership across all managerial jobs, what a manager does on each of them and the emphasis varies somewhat-to-a-great-deal depending on certain key conditions of the situation, factors that should therefore be reviewed first. Lumping them under "key conditions" ...

Key conditions. Five in particular have a major influence, the first, purely descriptive on how the philosophy variable influences decisions, the others on how relevant decisions *should* be made:

a. The leader's own philosophy—the Theory X to Theory Y continuum
b. Organizational level of the leader
c. When dealing with a group, the type of group being led

  d. When dealing with a group, the group's basic function
  e. Basic organization structure—mechanistic to organic.

  a. **Leadership philosophy**. A contrasting of the way a Theory Y manager would define the six direct interpersonal role responsibilities compared to the opinions of a Theory X person would supply sufficient evidence of the importance of philosophy. For Theory Y definitions:

  1. *Motivating*—inspiring, modeling, supporting, rewarding, reinforcing, delegating, giving participation, power sharing, integrating directly and indirectly.
  2. *Directing*—initiating, activating, supervising, commanding, regulating, conducting; a major constraint under normal conditions: invite subordinates to participate in decision making that affects them, mutual agreement being the goal (see page 567 on other than normal conditions of participation and the details ahead).
  3. *Coordinating*—interrelating and synchronizing people and their activities by communicating all relevant information, mediating, encouraging mutual adjustment, power balancing, good administration.
  4. *Controlling*—applying structures and processes for the guidance of performance and measuring in order to fill the organization's homeostatic and mediative needs (pages 913-915), and for subordinates' self-control, engaging them in the design of the controls affecting them and in their use to evaluate, not to find fault or to blame.
  5. *Teaching*—training, educating, developing, coaching and counseling all subordinates on both the technical and social requisites of job competence and helping them grow toward advancement.
  6. *Changing*—Acting as a change agent to one's subordinates for better performance, behavior and satisfaction and to fill all of the group's task and maintenance needs.

The Theory X manager, on the other hand, disagrees with these definitions in the way they're to be executed, and on some, that they're even responsibilities:

- *Motivating* is a role responsibility, but because individual and organizational goals will always be incompatible, it can only be induced by fear, extrinsic rewards and interpersonal competition; technical-social integration is impossible and intrinsic satisfaction is irrelevant; participation and power-sharing are abdications of responsibility and signs of weakness.
- *Directing, coordinating and controlling* are the chief responsibilities, but the execution must be unilateral, unequivocal, and firm.
- *Teaching* need only be technical to cover how to do the current job; a favorite subordinate can be taught your own job when, and only when, you've been told you've been promoted or are to be promoted.
- *Changing* behavior and/or attitude is most unlikely and shouldn't be a concern of a leader; the leader can in fact only change technical competence (by training), the work conditions, and bodies (move or remove and replace personnel).

b. **Organization level of the leader.** It was pointed out on pages 907-909 that each of the three major levels of management requires a managerial emphasis in order that the total organization survive and prevail in its environment:

Lower management	— homeostatic
Middle management	— mediative
Upper management	— proactive

...each step up the ladder retaining the prior responsibility along with the added emphasized one.

Additionally, there are role differences due to the differences of particularly *motivational* problems commonly found among subordinates at each level. When they are in:

- *Lower management*—overcome apathy, alienation, resistance to instructions, hostility toward authority; motivate effort and performance above minimum standards.

- *Middle management*—motivate to stay in the organization; overcome apathy (the "indifferents" are usually the large majority), motivate innovation, high standards, "professional" pride, self-development, subordinate development. (There is much less a problem here of motivating to work hard, which even the apathetic usually do.. while there's life there's hope, even in the "moral mazes" in Chapter 1).
- *Upper management* (including headquarters staff executives)—motivate to stay in the organization, cooperate (not compete) with the other top management team members, make decisions for the long-range welfare of the organization in effective balance with the short-range, be innovative, develop subordinates for top management continuity.

These of course have to be emphasized within the six interpersonal role responsibilities, and plainly, the best ways to motivate managers to stay are to create an inspiring, promising climate, to pay in proportion to performance, and to succeed on technical-social integration. (Also see research on pages 624-628).

c. **When dealing with a group, the type of group being led.** Being reminded of the differences between interacting groups (interdependent members), coacting groups (independent members) and counteracting groups (members in conflict, e.g, labor negotiations) also reminds one that the leader role is apt to be different in each. One can succinctly summarize it as:

In an interacting group:
- The standard leader role of all seven responsibilities: motivating, directing, coordinating, controlling, teaching, changing, representing.
- The emphasis on team development and the motivation of group as well as individual performance.

In a coacting group:
- The standard role but with emphasis on individual development and individual motivation.
- Usually a greater need for supportive attention and anxiety reduction.
- Low requirement for team development and coordination, but—
- Keep interpersonal competition from being damaging to either the organization or individuals.

In counteracting groups:
- Maintain the group.

- Facilitate communication and understanding.
- Establish a climate conducive to problem-solving.

At the same time, a group, though solidly in one category, may contain some characteristics of others, so a group leader has to be sensitive to and ready to respond to not only the current dominant group needs but to a variety of others simultaneously.

d. *When dealing with a group, the group's basic function.* Managers have to fall back on their general knowledge and experience to weigh leadership role responsibilities for specific group functions, because there is no research on it to give any help. One can see, for example, that the nearest thing to it, the ten elements in Figure 8.8a (page 305) tell nothing about even the importance of leadership among the five functions shown there let alone its roles.

It's well known, however, that significant variations are required of the roles due to the functional differences. A supervisor of basic R&D knows that directing and controlling has to be downplayed, motivating and coordinating stressed; one in manufacturing knows that it's often the reverse, and so on. Four important criteria are the intellectual level of the people attracted to that kind of function, the unique vs. routine nature of the function's work, the degree of uncertainty inherent in the function, and its relative rapidity of change vs. stability.

e. *Basic organization structure.* This is with regard to Woodward, Burns and Stalker's revelation that stable technologies tend to have mechanistic structures according to the chart on page 446 and dynamic technologies organic ones. The role responsibilities of an organizational leader remain the same in all, but, short of project management and free-form organizations, *more* or *less* direct effort has to be devoted to most of the six interpersonal ones because of the differences of both industrial dynamics and of coordination and control techniques used (page 460):

	In organic	In mechanistic
Motivating	— same —	
Directing	less	more
Coordinating	more	less
Controlling	less	more
Teaching	— same —	
Changing	more	less

In the project management and freeform organizations (818-826), however, the subject gets quite complex, and principles are involved that all managers should be familiar with for those dynamic or special situations in which they may find themselves (e.g., product, market or project management). Here, too, the level of management is significant.

The chart below shows the structuring, the project or business managers located on the same status level as the functional specialty supervisors to the subordinate managers, all four reporting to the shared top leader, the general manager. Now that there are two reporting arrows for each two-boss subordinate manager.

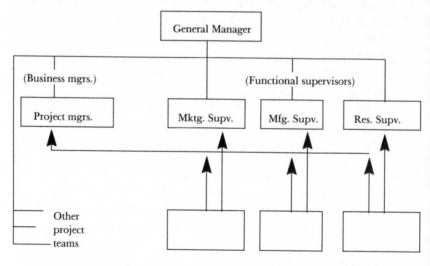

(Two-boss subordinate mgrs.)

For *general managers* to be effective, they must stress (1) power balancing (under "coordinating" in the list of six), (2) managing the context (under "motivating"), and (3) standard setting (under "controlling").[15]

For the *project managers* or business managers their emphasis has to be on selected aspects of motivation and coordination due to the limitations of sharing authority over their subordinates, their leadership deriving mainly from psychology and technical competence made necessary even more so by the generally high intellectual level of the subordinates. A useful insight from the cited article to keep in mind: "success flows from *facilitating* decisions more than it does from making them."

For the *functional supervisors* to be suitably effective, the leadership emphasis has to be on coordinating and teaching (also see the goals on page 820).

And for the *subordinate managers* who must function as a process team, when they themselves have subordinates, their performance of the role responsibilities follows the standard guidelines for all managers in general, some of the major concerns reviewed ahead.

In sum, all four types of managers are highly trained professional technical problem-solvers who are nevertheless expected to solve also some very complex social ones for which they are universally not trained. It must be evident that all firms with such a structure had better make a point of it.

Role responsibilities

The contrast between Theory X and Theory Y views of the six interpersonal role responsibilities of leadership on pages 1074-1075 demonstrates well enough the breadth of interpretation possible, and needless to say, the Theory Y interpretations are those that advanced leadership education must promote. A reading of the text this far would supply enough information to fill in most of the requirements listed in the six Theory Y sketches and the "representing" role as well; the following is intended only to aid a review and add some points of value that have not been covered.

1. Motivating. Perhaps the most important overall information on this subject for some has been the ranking of methods of motivation as to their strength in regard to what each technique can and cannot do—broadly for example, that extrinsic rewards, though fundamental, are limited in many regards (Chapter 8); intrinsic ones have deeper and lasting effect; conducive design of structures and processes is indispensable to motivating effectively; and culture and climate management are at the top of the list with consistent leadership success on the technical-social integration a most important element. of major climate importance also are the numerous techniques and systems of human resources management (e.g., Chapter 17).

And one should of course keep in mind the power of an exciting statement of organizational purpose—the vision as described by Kotter on pages 1065-1066—conveying an organizational future worth striving toward. Chapter 8 covered the subject at the job level ("meaningful work"—p. 300), but equally important is employee faith in the big picture they see themselves part of and contributing to. CEOs must be sure they articulate one clearly, incorporating the two parts on pages 1065-1066, periodically repeating the first at all levels of the firm. Waterman gave a memorable example in his book *The Renewal Factor* to illustrate the impact an understood vision can have and the probable result of its absence. Quoting a vignette given him by the CEO of Porsche:[16] "Three at work on a construction site were all doing similar jobs, but when each was asked what his job was, the answers varied.

"Breaking rocks," the first replied. "Earning my living," said the second. "Helping build a cathedral," said the third... a view a leader can inspire.

2. Directing. Since the primary function of a manager is to get the job done effectively, directing does appear to be the most important of the role responsibilities, so some managers have tended to overlook the other six, the tandem nature of directing and motivating, and the interdependencies of this and the other five interpersonal ones.

Functionally speaking, it is primary, but that its success is so heavily dependent on how it is done is the reason why "motivation" was put at the top of the list.

It takes one back to the philosophy and nature of authority described on pages 1058-1063. A Theory X manager stresses legal authority, fear and punishment, a Theory Y one psychological authority, competence, and need congruence. Take your choice and reap the social exchange.

Still, plenty of managers have been turned off about Theory Y directing by the writings of behaviorists who've said it should always be in terms of individual needs, which is very confusing because it gives no indication of what has to precede it, what else is involved, and that there are important exceptions.

The Theory X inclined person is, we now realize, unable to go directly to motivating direction; acceptance and adoption of

Theory Y as a philosophy and some training are prerequisites. Additionally, the functional purpose of the organization—performance—must always be dominant, and if in its pursuit the leader is sincere about Theory Y, the directing will give due weight to the needs at the appropriate times. Subordinates will appreciate the effort even if it's a bit clumsy in the beginning and will be favorably inclined toward compliance because of it. Then in these circumstances when, as explained, candid commands may be necessary:

- misbehavior,
- emergencies,
- time is of the essence,
- stalemate situations,
- poor judgment of a subordinate or group has to be overridden,
- an intrinsically hostile, power-struggle or conflictful climate/environment—

firm direction will be readily accepted, at least by the majority, as an essential part of leadership.

One other point to consider: the primary position in leadership of directing is of course evident to subordinates also, and it has an interesting psychological effect on many of them: the superior's power and authority to back it up leads them to relate it to the father/son relationship, to see the person as a father figure.

Freud believed that all leaders are father figures to those they lead, the led transferring their childhood feelings of love, fear and respect, and we know the feelings can easily flip over to contempt and hate. It seems that we all do transfer some measure of our childhood desire for security and freedom from responsibility.

The ethical smart executive will not try to target it to better use subordinates, but he'll also not ignore the phenomenon and will recognize it as one of those deep-seated needs that ethical supportive treatment will satisfy, and it will honorably improve performance accordingly.

The happening brings to mind another enigma of leadership: just as a father asks himself, can a father be a duly inspiring model to a youngster and also a buddy, so does the buddy question commonly occur about the superior-subordinate relationship. A prominent World War II general recommended an answer for organizations: a superior should know all his men extremely well and at the same time maintain "an indefinable reserve."[8]

3. Coordinating. Usually a prime responsibility after directing that most thoughtful executives have been aware of has been this one, perhaps partly because they've read some past authorities who designated it "the final objective" but more likely because it's a major purposeful activity of directing a team; and, overall, things clearly do or don't happen to the extent that it's present.

That it is of special importance seems to have been confirmed by the position given it in organization design (page 458) and the traditional principles on pages 743-744.

Again, however, the stumbling block has been "how" the effort to coordinate has been made. After stating the goals and giving the orders on what to do, commonly if inadequate coordination occurs, it's successively followed by first more orders, then rigid rules, then the enforcement of the rules with rewards or punishment. The consequence: both coordination and performance are mediocre at best.

Granted, a large part of coordinating is good planning for the five "means" on page 459, well designed incentives to reduce interpersonal competition, and the compatibility of the parties involved, but, even if one assumes the request asks for the right action, the coordination response still depends on substantial acceptance of the decision and command, the lack of which is the principal hangup in the above paragraph sequence.

Proof of what the first step must be: research has shown that poor acceptance of decisions has been due to no participation in making the decisions far more than poor decision quality.

4. Controlling. Chapter 11, the comments on pages 458-462 the warnings about the effects of too-close control of subordinates, and the importance of participation in controls design and performance evaluation have together covered the subject fairly comprehensively. But an aspect of the more general meaning of control needs to be added, is becoming a growing problem, and warrants serious consideration especially by upper executives.

Although much of the growing popularity of delegation and decentralization across commerce and industry seems to have been made possible by and been a result of the new wealth of information at headquarters from computerized information systems, installation of the systems, as observing managers know, have been commonly followed by the opposite.

Two things have been going on. While the centralized information greatly improves top management's own decisions as the ability at headquarters to digest and analyze it increased, so has the temptation to make or dictate the decisions that belong down the line.

Second, upper executives have often not limited the mechanization of decisions to the repetitive routine; increasingly, computer models are being created that incorporate all the key variables for many unique decisions of middle management, such that either the best answer or the two or three best alternatives are clearly evident to them. The specious reasoning that may be used to excuse calling all those shots at the top is hard for some top executives to resist.

If one speculates on the effect of going all the way on the expropriation of these decisions for maximum "efficiency," some disturbing questions arise. Will not the excessive (in the sense of imprudent) use of tangible mechanization (the MIS) result in excessive intangible mechanization producing the effects of bureaucracy described on pages 447-450? Will not the stature of middle management suffer? To what extent would (or is) their creative potential being forfeited? Will its changed character no longer appeal to potential leaders of the future and attract instead only mediocrity in search of security?

We must, and will, never throw out the electronic marvels, but what can be done to prevent these events? Hopefully the text made the solution apparent. If top management decides on a System 1 or 2 organization the odds are high for the worst, while targeting a System 4 will open minds to seeing the social as well as technical gains of genuinely following Principle IX on decision delegation. Moreover, regardless of believed increased capabilities at headquarters, a little creativity at the top can work out ways to engage and make the most of the creativity down below, inspiring the needed sense of belonging and commitment. A careful study of Chapter 14 on making decisions and information technology should lead to some good ideas and solutions.

5. Teaching. Fifty years ago teaching a subordinate to be competent in management was simply a one-shot instruction on the technical requirements of the specific position; the congeniality that got the person the job was expected to take care of the social. The educational requirements today: obviously much in the outline on pages 1090-1091, a lot of it provided by professional training—which has unfortunately led many superiors to assume erroneously that they've been relieved of their teaching obligations.

It's advantageous of course to hire personnel for management positions or as trainees who've had some prior, experience or courses in the function, and the . firm's own training and development courses can fill in to some degree, but all still have to learn a great deal from the superior for fit to the job assigned (e.g., the teaching in the "direct integration" on pp. 1067-1069), also what is needed, including the subtleties, of each new position as they move up the ladder.

Because there is a different and significant educational need in each position of the hierarchy, one can in fact visualize the necessity of a *managerial teaching hierarchy* in every organization. The effectiveness of such a structure would of course be a product of the teaching performance standards and procedures of evaluation set up and modeled by the top team. Top management must further make a major issue of periodically checking the linkage, especially in the key-position ladder, to see that it is not broken increasing the likelihood of incompetencies being promoted.

The gravest problem in the older organizations today is the fact that the teaching by undeveloped superiors at this advanced time cannot be more than trivial. But also, there are in all organizations plenty of good managers who haven't the temperament or interpersonal skills to teach. The educable must not only be taught—by development programs—but taught how to teach subordinates. Decisions on the uneducable are of course for the top and not easy.

6. Changing. A while back the responsibility of a leader to "change" people was always interpreted, if the word was used, as meaning only the technical performance for better results through training and incentives, and traditionalists still hold to the same view. But since then the behaviorists have made us realize why training and incentives can only go so far, that wherever unsatisfactory performance is present any behavior that may be causing it also has to be changed if there is to be any improvement. Further, as stressed throughout, wherever structures or processes impact on behavior, they generally have to be changed as well so that they can accommodate the behavior change in order to avoid extinction, and coworkers must be changed for the same reason.

We know that three other issues are involved also: (a) along with the need to change both the technical and social, the changing is not a one-shot proposition, has to be done again and again, (b) who does it is crucial, and (c) how the change effort is made is equally crucial.

There are many reasons for the continuing need (a), the most obvious ones being personnel change, institutional growth, the stream of specific new problems constantly arising in every unit that require change, the handling of all participative situations that commonly entail some, and the dynamic change of the environment that always goes on, all requiring at one time or another some change of behavior, structures, and processes.

The volume in itself tells who should do it (b)—the leaders-superiors themselves. Plainly, trying to have OD specialists in attendance for even half the changes would bankrupt the organization, aside from raise doubts in the minds of subordinates about the superior's leadership competence.

A second important reason for the leader doing it is that performance (and therefore behavior too) is, after all, the most fundamental responsibility of every superior, one that only the superior should tinker with whether directly or through behavior change, though staff help may certainly be used, is often necessary.

Third, there is the obvious advantage of a superior's authority to get attention and results compared to the lack of authority of a consultant or staff person, once the superior has learned the skills of bringing about behavior change.

And fourth, the structure or process change that may be necessary to make them fit behavior change or achieve goal congruence can only come through the superior; indeed the person had better be intimately involved in any tradeoffs made in the negotiations with subordinates. Making the line manager do it all is not only practical but essential.

Finally, Chapters 18 and 19 supplied the solutions on "how" (c): OD specialists teaching the managers in the process of an organization change or upgrading program and withdrawing on completion of the teaching.

7. Representing. It certainly goes without saying that every manager is obligated to represent the organization and management above to the subordinates and unit and to any job-related outside contacts, and also to represent the subordinates to management above, the two functions being the representational aspects of the "communication direction" issues described on pages 546-549 that made evident how badly they're commonly carried out in both directions.

Any organization would virtually grind to a halt if its managers badly neglected these responsibilities, especially representing *downward* with communication directives, policies and plans from above, and *upward* with operating information, major problems, feedback on directives and policies (*all* the consequences) from below—to which should be added what is rarely passed upward: formal periodic communication of employee needs expectations and values (within the cybernetics described on pages 485-488).

And there's the confrontational side of it, the task referred to earlier of "mediating between the individual and the organization," or as some have referred to it "being in the middle," in instances where superiors want more performance than is possible or fair and/or those below want more compensation, considerations, resources, etc. than reasonable or feasible.

Naturally, the principal recourse in either direction in such instances is a matter of managerial judgment, doing the best one can on the justifiable and equitable (and making them aware you have) and candidly saying no on the unreasonable. Of course in some situations a no upward can be hazardous and acquiescence is prudent, for example:[17]

- where the boss is insecure and/or despotic,
- in highly political situations, where threats abound, or where loyalty per se is all-important.

Normally however, reconciliation is not a passive process; at times some attempts are necessary to modify or reinterpret demands from above, subordinates need defending, or resources have to be obtained either from superiors or laterally, in which cases *advocacy* is essential. Done adroitly, those above see commitment to the job and group, those below see also that you're interested in their welfare.

Motivating role performance

Though the ego-satisfaction of leading may seem on its own to generate enough self-motivation, it's plainly only a general emotion for the job as a whole with no thought of the specific role responsibilities. The descriptions presented should make it clear that if they're not taught and stressed there's going to be a lot of omissions resulting in mediocre to poor leadership.

Assuming the teaching is well indoctrinated through HRD development programs, carrying them out as recommended on first learning them is admittedly quite demanding, and there's the difficulty of making them habit.

Any CEO dedicated to organizational excellence certainly must plan a system of motivation and monitoring giving it personal attention, and some thoughts on what is psychologically involved will help the planning.

Probably, the most crucial factors are the complex ways each person totes up the reward/risk/cost equation and determines his or her individual degree of commitment, ambivalence or indifference about the leadership job and these responsibilities. The equation thoughts they are inclined to have in mind about leadership that must be considered:

Rewards: higher pay, recognition, status, prestige, peer regard, autonomy, power, control.

Risks: failure and its economic and social consequence, e.g., losing the job, demotion, difficulty in getting the next job, the lost reputation, humiliation, lower family regard, shattered self-regard.

Costs: responsibility-loading, anxieties, criticism and blame, the excessive
time and effort required, loneliness, the self-respect cost of such "rules of
success" in environments like the Chapter 1 "moral maze."

For each as well as the mix there are personal go-no-go points
based on individual values and "utility" over which management
has no direct control; but it can do a lot to enlarge the "rewards"
perception toward commitment: leadership development that
teaches the roles thoroughly plus periodic refresher seminars, a
climate of growth and supportiveness, conducive structures and
processes (especially the Chapter 17 human resources ones), OD
built into the management system (pages 1017-1020), and the
incorporation in managers' incentive plans of specific role
activities for both themselves and their leader subordinates—and
of course competent training and promotion of the leadership
skills described ahead.

Parenthetically, all managers had better keep in mind also the
essential fillip to the performance of role responsibilities, that
leadership of people itself, like all human processes, does take
maintenance, and that there is an ever-present threat about it to
less than attentive leaders: in addition to the lax superior getting
lower group performance, the group very often confers (usually
unconsciously) informal leadership on whoever in the group fills
the vacuum. A traumatic event to find out about, especially if the
boss find out too—or first.

Executive training and development[h]

(As stated in Chapter 17, the executive training and development
proposal of this text is for an in-house program though it may
be partly or largely assigned to vendors or expected from college
programs, and HRD must plan it to fit into the organization's
budget and specific needs at each level.)

McGregor's "Interaction Theory" on p. 345 gave the basics of
the organizational leadership definition on page 630 that are the
major concerns in designing an effective program. One had to take
into consideration each of, and the interaction of, the four
components; briefly on what they entail:

1. *The leader's personality*—philosophy traits, skills, behavior, assumptions, temperament, attitudes, goals, and see the high probability model on page 348.
2. *The followers*—their needs, goals, personalities, attitudes, expectations, and so on.
3. *The organization*—its purpose, strategies, goals, policies, technology, structure, processes, practices, culture, climate, norms, morale, politics.
4. *The environment*—economic, social, political, stability, complexity, laws, the competition, markets.

(...to which should be added the impact of superiors and peers— their expectations of the leader (as he/she perceives them to be), their competence, their helpfulness or not or their obstructive competitiveness.

Part I went through considerable detail on #1, #2 and the culture and climate of #3. Part II supplied much of the balance of #3, the organizational matters that have to be put in good shape if the training and development program is to be truly effective, Part III's chapter 18 and 19 showed how to change #1 and #3, and this chapter has given to this point the foundation of effective leadership learning: the principles, role responsibilities and integration skills.[i]

Chapter 17, recall had an outline of how to pull it all together in a program, the outline of it repeated below for reading convenience (the word "executive" in the title refers to all in management—see the GE model in Chapter 17 on how to handle the different levels), followed there by a list of important program *purposes* and planning *policies*.

A chart of ten major program *objectives* (stated by executives in a broad survey) for the achievement of the purposes was present by Bolt in his excellent book on executive development,[18] all the objectives are expected by the respondents to be even more important in years ahead; the ten in general in the order of very important to important:

Program Objectives

1. Key business issues
2. Gen. mgmt. perspective
3. Critical knowl. & skills
4. Shared vision & purpose
5. Managing the culture

6. Increase "bench strength"
7. Communicate/implement strategy
8. Build teamwork & networks
9. Forum for idea interchange
10. Estab. the firm's identity

But what to cover and stress for a particular company still requires a needs analysis, and the two believed most important sources of what is needed Bolt found was:

- suggestions and requests from top managers, who are these days becoming more knowledgeable and vocal about their operating needs.
- surveys and/or interviews with prospective program participants to elicit what they want and don't want.

Additionally, an emerging trend has been the interview also of subordinates, along with the surveys mentioned earlier, on the development needs of their bosses and sometimes a cross-section of employees or management in general. HRD then combines it all in a report to the top executives and, with their leadership, builds the solutions to the needs into the program. Here is some important elaboration on selected subjects in the outline to complete what has been presented in the text to this point, information that should round out the total picture for the design and implementation of what is required.

Executive Training and Development Outline

1. *Cognitive training and development*
    a. Knowledge (the technical and the social)—
        philos., values and ethics
        org'l. psychology
        group dynamics
        motivation and climate
            mgmt. (Ch. 7 & 8 for intro).

        leadership education
        the science technology
        the industry(ies)
        the functional specialties

    b. Management technology skills—e.g.
        corp. & orgn. plan'g.
        human resources plan'g.

        quantitative analysis
        problem-solving

operations plan'g.   MIS & Computer techniques
and mgmt.   improving the situation

   c. Managerial judgment—
relational and integrative thinking; concept formation and their
diagnostic use in pattern identification for decisions and actions.

2. *Personal and interpersonal development*
   a. Personal self-knowledge and development
   b. Interpersonal skills
   c. Team development and team leadership

3. *Organizational leadership development*
   a. The basic knowledge of principles, roles, obligations
   b. Upgrading the organizational culture and climate
   c. Technical-social integration skills
   d. Organizational leadership
   e. Leading/managing conflict
4. *Motivational training and development*
   a. Organizational policies, standards and norms
   b. Development of the individual's attitudes, goals and values to congruence with
the organization's and a commitment to its strategies, goals and policies.

Cognitive training and development (#1). Part I attempted to supply much of what is needed for the left side of the outline list under *knowledge* (#1a), but constant updating should be made available to employees for both sides, which can be aided by having an accessible library in every medium-size and large unit plus a periodically issued list from HRD of recommended reading and recommended supplemental courses or seminars. Particularly important:

In-house orientation for new members (should be required)
In-house periodic refreshers on the organization's objectives, strategies, values, and ethics policies (also required)
Industry updating at convention seminars
College seminars on current philosophy, psychology, group dynamics, the changing expectations of society on ideology and ethics
Courses on relevant science and functional specialties.

Then to keep their knowledge current to be operationally effective (for instance, the employees' values today, not 5 or 10 years ago) they need to be supplied or know how to get:

- the available purely factual on the environment for both the technical and social;
- feedback on the effectiveness of one's own decisions and actions including how they can be improved;
- feedback on how well the organization (or unit) as a whole is identifying and solving its technical, social and technical-social problems.

The periodicals, the MIS, and "environmental scanning" (footnote a, page 764) are, needless to say, the principal answer to the first, and for the second and third to be achieved requires not only a good MIS and conducive superior-subordinate interpersonal relations and skills but systems that foster the two as described in Chapter 4 on feedback and Chapter 11 on the social system along with the feedback from genuine participation and teamwork.

For the *management technology skills (#1b)*, while there is no substitute for learning these on the job, many courses can supply valuable information and insight that the job experience may not be clear enough to reveal or extensive enough to cover adequately, the good ones will speed up the learning. On some, like business games, there's still much subjective controversy as to whether they contribute anything to their basic goal—improved managerial performance. A rule of thumb: if a manager has a need and sincere desire for the relevant decision-making skills, assign a course with a good reputation or reputed instructor; something may be gained, possibly a lot, and the organization will be ahead.

Managerial judgement (#1c): the importance of this crucial capability for middle and upper management increases in proportion to the industry's dynamism, complexity, uncertainty and unpredictability. Horizontal job rotation across the organization and across functions, as said a number of times, is most important (see "key-position" ladder on p. 874). For supplemental courses: (a) the case method when from real-world research should nudge some holistic growth while increasing familiarity with all the variables involved; (b) computer simulations can be helpful for combining the linear and holistic in complex "what-if" analyses.

Personal and interpersonal development (#2). On the subject of *personal self-knowledge and development (#2a)*, although traditionalists still question any effort of an organization on this, the extent to which a good program by the individual and organization together can pay in all of higher competence, productivity, and commitment should be apparent from reading the text's attempt to help toward it, the sections on:

- Evaluating one's own normality, maturity and self-control and directing development toward the criteria of maturity on page 63 (Chapter 3).
- Learning how to learn and teach (Chapter 4).
- Examining one's philosophy, ideology, values and ethics (Chapter 5).
- The most damaging management value misconceptions that must be upgraded (p.118 in Chapter 5 and Chapter 6).
- Specific self-evaluation and development including one's frame of reference (pp.180-181 in Chapter 5).
- Emotions (Chapter 7).
- Individual change (the OD in Chapter 18).

And unquestionably the last, by showing how the individual can in fact change or upgrade the values misconceptions, demonstrates also how the person can be freed up to fully understand and undertake satisfactorily the other six (in the above list).

Two cautions however. First, in many instances of value change there's a "no-man's land" between the learning and doing, a chasm between theory and action, such that after changing to Theory Y, managers are commonly erratic for some time, relapsing to Theory X behavior out of anxieties related to giving up old values and assumptions and out of fears of appearing weak, of blundering, of confusing subordinates. The managers themselves have to be prime movers in bridging it.

The second is only a reminder: the organization that's been smart enough to help with Stranger T-grouping of course has to be smart enough also to avoid the mistake of changing only the behavior of the manager (away from the workplace) without making changes in those he or she will work with.

Interpersonal skills (2b). The purpose here as in the last subsection is only to review what has been presented on the subject, comment, and supplement as believed helpful, starting with the list below of the skills required either directly or indirectly to improve employee performance, each learned through one or a combination of seminars, courses, on-the-job experience, superior's teaching and guidance, and/or self-development reading:

a. Ethics (see Index)
b. Climate development (Ch 8)
c. Interpersonal and interdependency relations (Ch 8,11)
d. Performance review (Ch 9).
e. MBO, counseling, coaching, goal-setting (Ch 10)
f. Political skills (ethical - Ch 11)
g. Info technology skills (Ch 14)
h. Gaining compliance (Ch 11, 18)
i. Leading/managing conflict (Ch 11, 18 and ahead)
j. Problem-solving (Ch 14, 19)
k. Customer & supplier relations (Ch 15)
l. The HR planning (17)
m. Indirect integration (Parts I and II)
n. Direct integration (this chapter)
o. Leadership style (this chapter).

All have been duly covered in the chapters indicated, but a few additional comments on a, b, c and o seem warranted.

A basic point on the first (a): *all skills that involve people must avoid unethical behavior for the skills to work more than once.* To repeat from "the requisite skills" section in Chapter 8 (p. 286), allow a little immorality in and you get little-to-no motivation, indeed over time the reverse: indifference, low morale, alienation, contempt.

For the climate development (b): the extent to which it is crucial to all of motivation, job satisfaction, performance and even personality was demonstrated by the research in Figure 8.3d of Chapter 8's "Developing the climate" section; and on page 282 it was explained that a leader can substantially advance the development by promoting 8 norms across the organization, the skills for doing so described there.

On the interpersonal and interdependency relations (c), one should keep in mind, along with the discourses on them in Chapter 8 and 11, the 24 "Common behavioral requirements in management" on page 303, which are in fact a combination and overlapping of traits and skills. And most HRD professionals are well aware of the Modeling" technique for developing the skills needed to handle a variety of interpersonal events: class instruction on the psychology involved in each event, a video tape showing a professional handling it correctly, followed by individual role-playing doing it that way. Some comments about it published in a Business Week article:[20]

- "This modeling" technique shouldn't be confused with behavior modification in which the managers' behavior would be changed by praise, reward or withholding reward. It is imitative learning of how to use psychology, and it can be applied to a variety of interpersonal situation, a class usually targeting one. (see p. 93 on limitations of imitative learning).

- Some basic psychology principles taught: make the employee or other person feel at ease, maintain and enhance the other's self-esteem, be friendly, listen and respond with sympathy, ask for his or her ideas in solving the problem, and so on, all obvious but ordinarily not done because of value misconceptions, self-consciousness, the desire to appear "strong." The role-playing starts the change process through had observed good results.

- Over 300 corporations are now using the approach: GE had trained to May 1978 over 6000 with it, Xerox over 2000, Ford has made it mandatory for all new supervisors, "Lukens Steel has credited it with more than $1 million a year in productivity savings."

- It is particularly effective for lower level managers up through middle management; top managers will not sit still for it. The role-playing is new to most, and at first it's embarrassing, but the classes only have peers, they come out "unscathed," and they develop a greater openness to each other and greater mutual respect.

● An outside consulting firm can provide either packaged or tailored services. One firm that trains over 35,000 managers a year has a $7,500 package (in 1978) that will provide training for 24 first and second line supervisors and 6 higher level managers in 10 different problem areas. It has 20 such "kits" that include orienting new employees, reducing tardiness, disciplining workers, setting goals, and motivating lackluster employees. Examples of other courses: appraisal sessions, labor relations, dealing with co-workers, handling complaints, responding to peer pressure, staff relations with line managers, interfunctional relations."

Finally, leadership style (o) is in essence but how a leader does all of (a) to (n), a simplified model of it pictured on page 1050 where the ideal leader for the preponderance of circumstances was summarized as one who adhered to and applied Theory Y philosophy (implicitly covering the personality, assumptions and behavior "traits") to produce superior social and technical skill in implementing the a to l ... to which one should add behaving more a facilitator than "boss."

Team development and team leadership (2c). In the "Team philosophy" section of Chapter 13 (pages 584-599), teams were classified as (1) top management teams, (2) management teams below the top, and (3) blue-collar ones. The concern here is on the first two, both needing a bit more explanation; the development of blue-collar teams there would seem to have been informative enough.

Top management teams (1). Top managements are one of the first two types of work groups described on page 1076: a coacting group (the members are essentially independent) or an interacting one (they're interdependents); and a CEO should be careful to keep in mind the type he or she is attempting to lead, and adhere to the roles described there for that type.

The coacting generally applies to conglomerate or diversified firms in which the CEO's direct subordinates are accountable for only their own divisions, do not engage in "collective work-products" and thus feel no responsibility for group results. That's the CEO's responsibility—along with his/her standard responsibilities of motivating, directing, coordinating, controlling, teaching, changing, and representing—and his development role is essentially their individual development (as at GE's Crotonville on pages 923-925) and keeping down anxiety and damaging competition for succession.

A CEO with an interacting group naturally has to deal even more so with the complications described in Chapter 13 as to forces and pressures on the team, the group tasks, and the members' unique traits; and certainly he also has to have the same fifteen skill requirements (above) plus team development, the motivation effort being on both the group and individuals, with the basic team "teaching" (at this level largely refreshers, refinements, subtle hints) including external boundary management, prime underlying goals being mutual trust, mutual sense of accountability, and commitment.

Management teams below the top (2). As said previously, a work group is not a team just because someone called it a team, a claim one might expect from a traditionalist executive who has no understanding of team dynamics and wants to appear progressively up to date, so sets up a "team" to get a job done and walks away without giving it the necessary guidance, support, resources or incentive to work as a team.

Even for a work group (compared to teams on page 587) the superior setting one up must take the time to convey clearly its mission, goals, standards, processes, constraints and how they tie into and support those of the larger organization. For a team, along with the superior's guidance and support, the selected team leader's philosophy, values and behavior are particularly crucial and their caliber are naturally a matter initially of leader selection. Comments on these points, including criteria for selection, were given on page 590, so won't be repeated here.

Indeed, for any executive or intended team leader, traditionalist or not, it would pay the firm well to send them to a team development workshop administered by experts or one like those at NTL to learn team dynamics and thinking, techniques and skills, and group roles (pages 539-541) before promoting team philosophy down the line.

Some essential knowledge on *the dynamics*. McGregor again supplied the basics, a group behavior model. Expanding on Kurt Lewin's individual behavior model on page 26, $B = f(P,E)$, he produced the equation below.[21]

$$B_{group} = f(M_{a,b,c} \ldots T_{f,g,h}, \ldots O_{m,n,o} \ldots L_{q,r,s} \ldots E_{u,v,w} \ldots)$$

where M includes the attitudes, knowledge, skills and capabilities of the members; T includes the characteristics of the primary task of the group; O includes the structures and internal controls of the subsystem; L includes the skills, capabilities and other characteristics of the leader; and E includes the large number of variables in the larger organizational system and in society.

Part II attempted to guide leaders on how to make the "O" motivating, and considerable detail is given at the end of this chapter on how to manage the principal situations of "E."

Assuming then that the leader "L" has done a fair job of personal development (section #2a above) and has group members that are reasonably intelligent and stable, the initial concerns about "M" that can be quickly influenced by the leader should probably be their "sentiments," a factor that Homans highlighted, the 5 types listed in Chapter 12 (p.530): (1) attitudes and feelings, (2) perceived progress, (3) identification with the group (do I belong and am I seen as belonging?), (4) ranking (status, e.g., does Joe have more prestige than Al or myself?), and 5. evaluation of behavior.

Especially for a new team the leader should move directly to the "identification" (#3) and attempt to make each feel he/she belongs and is a valued member, then make some observations about feelings of status (#4), noting who talks to whom and not to whom during discussions and how the quiet ones are treated, whether or not they are in fact viewed as "outsiders" and being intimidated, or are indifferent, are low on the totem pole, or are in fact "independents," points raised under "group roles" in Chapter 12 that should lead one's thoughts throughout the life of the team to evaluating members' role behavior and how to manage it by means of the suggestions given there (pp. 541-542). Quoting McGregor again, "Skillful and sensitive membership behavior is the real clue to effective group operation," and members must be educated as to what that entails, particularly their role performance obligations. "Perhaps it is now clear why an effective managerial team seldom just happens. It is a complex and delicate system the building and maintenance of which requires such time and attention."[22]

Underlying these concerns should be a gestalt picture in the leader's mind of the whole process of developing and sustaining a team like the one in Figure 20.2[23] One can see how the effort above on "identification" fits into Stage #1 where the questions members have are not only "why am I here?" but "why a team?" It's obviously also the location where three OD interventions should be seriously considered: stranger T-grouping for each individual followed by the OD family team diagnostic meeting (page 994) and family group team building (page 997).

Then in Stage #2 each member at least subconsciously asks not just of the others "Who are you?" but of the leader "What are you going to ask of me?" And in Stage #3 the goal should be spelled out with the clarity described on pages 524-525 and cover the role education mentioned. Finally, it would hardly be necessary to tell the reader at this point how the leader inspires the commitment of Stage #4, but briefly for a mental review: as said in the comment on "style" (the "o" in the list of skill), being more a facilitator than boss, engaging collaborative decision-making on all team issues like who does what, standards, rules, scheduling, team boundaries and intergroup activities—which participation helps build mutual trust and a safe climate, drawing out the best in each member and bringing the team to life. The notation #5, #6 and #7 are enough to suggest the rest.

Still, one of course cannot assume constant idealistic harmony among the members or with others affected, each having different assumptions, opinions and traits that will at times cause negative behavior that may be difficult to discern or politics. Here are some common situations to be on guard about with ways to alleviate the problems:

- *On task forces, committees and sometimes new teams*—(a) members less informed on subjects to be covered can feel embarrassed and forced in ignorance to support decisions

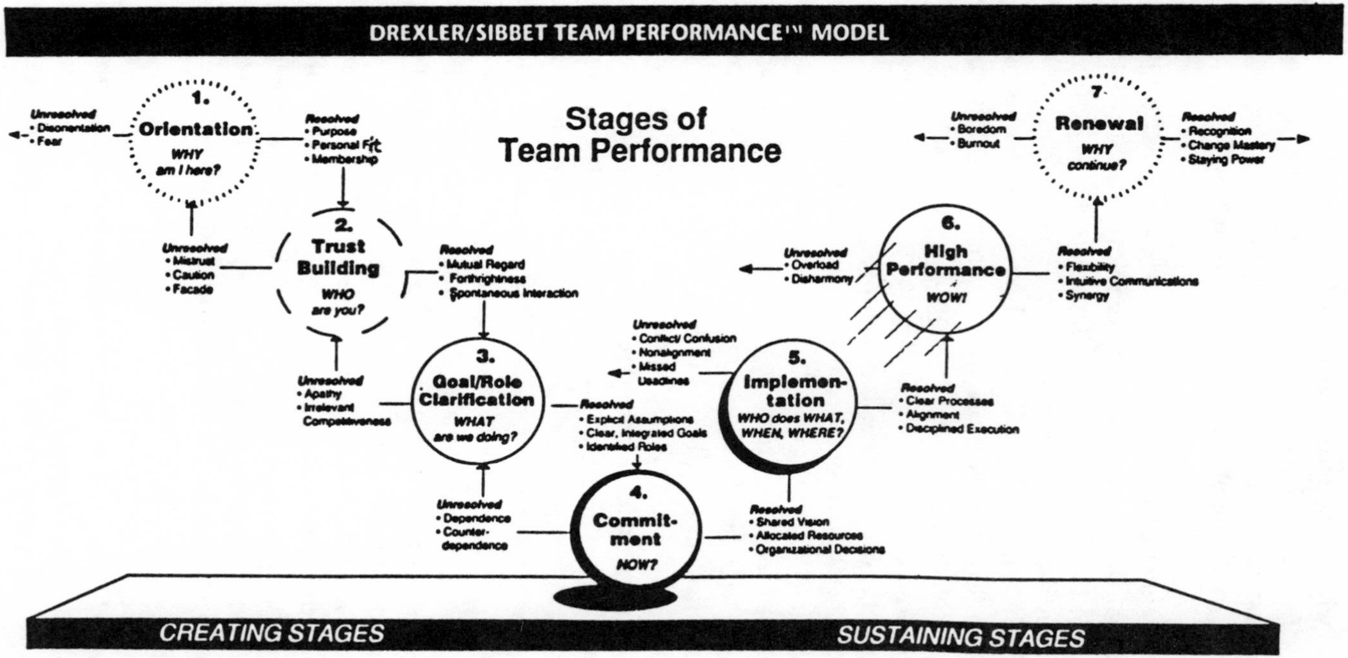

DREXLER/SIBBET TEAM PERFORMANCE™ MODEL

Stages of Team Performance

1. Orientation — WHY am I here?
- Unresolved: Disorientation, Fear
- Resolved: Purpose, Personal Fit, Membership

2. Trust Building — WHO are you?
- Unresolved: Mistrust, Caution, Facade
- Resolved: Mutual Regard, Forthrightness, Spontaneous Interaction

3. Goal/Role Clarification — WHAT are we doing?
- Unresolved: Apathy, Irrelevant Competitiveness
- Resolved: Explicit Assumptions, Clear, Integrated Goals, Shared Roles

4. Commitment — HOW?
- Unresolved: Dependence, Counterdependence
- Resolved: Shared Vision, Allocated Resources, Organizational Decisions

5. Implementation — WHO does WHAT, WHEN, WHERE?
- Unresolved: Conflict/Confusion, Nonalignment, Missed Deadlines
- Resolved: Clear Processes, Alignment, Disciplined Execution

6. High Performance — WOW!
- Unresolved: Overload, Disharmony
- Resolved: Flexibility, Intuitive Communications, Synergy

7. Renewal — WHY continue?
- Unresolved: Boredom, Burnout
- Resolved: Recognition, Change Mastery, Staying Power

CREATING STAGES

SUSTAINING STAGES

Figure 20.2

they may later regret; give them special briefings on the needed information before meetings; (b) attend to the political necessities of gaining-effectiveness; e.g., diplomatically keep peers and superiors in the larger organization informed about decisions that affect or interest them, especially about those that may make them feel threatened— get their opinions, involvement, support.

- *On teams composed of different functions or levels*—there's generally a problem with regard to deference, lower level or status members feeling obliged to agree with higher ones in fear of retribution or refusal to cooperate at a later time; informally encourage the higher ones to try to prevent it by being supportive of the efforts and suggestions of the lower ones.
- *On all teams*—natural defensiveness and fear of idea rejection inevitably results in some reluctance to express one's opinions and ideas; discuss openly in the first meeting, and occasionally again the value of, and a genuine desire for, different opinions as essential to problem solving, the creative process and best operating effectiveness.

Also, be aware of and ready to manage different types of covert dysfunctional behavior that can occur, for instance:

- when a member is blocking progress with emotional stubbornness, drop the psychological leadership and be tactfully directive;
- not mistaking "individual role" playing for functional differentiation and dealing with it adroitly (page 539);
- sensing when the whole group may be taking advantage of leniency or humanism and firmly clarify "the rules," perhaps a little more skillfully than King Arthur in the cartoon,[24] which suggests a "group arrangement" as one temporary (or permanent) solution;
- calling a halt and reviewing processes at any sign that only superficial information is being generated on major problems instead of valid information;
- going back to square one on members who are still allowing interpersonal competitiveness to interfere with collaboration.[j]

The mature team (in 2) To repeat for reading convenience the definition from page 532, it is a team in which the members:

- have overcome their obstacles to valid communication,
- can resolve their internal conflicts,
- feel and transmit mutual trust,
- cooperate with little to no interpersonal competition where collaboration is needed,
- can discuss both ideas and feelings openly,
- feel free to be innovative,
- are mutually supportive,
- work hard with commitment to the goals,
- can mobilize their collective resources and take intelligent action,
- and as a consequence have high productivity.

"You're all probably wondering what's become of the round table. Very simple. Some people began to forget just who the hell's in charge here!"

This doesn't mean they're all bosom friends or in total agreement by any means. In the first place, members of management or task teams usually do not have close social relationships after hours, if not because of residential distance because of different life styles; but also there may be deep differences of opinion, like those that are common between highly differentiated specialties. But there's not only a mature acceptance of the differences and recognition of their value, all the elements of an integrative climate are present without which the team development would be negligible.

And of course the degree of success in achieving such maturity is mainly the outcome of superior leadership, the result of a superior job a pleasure to behold or be a part of. A composite of such a group from the author's personal experience and research would by and large look like this, a recognizable description to anyone who has ever been a member of a truly effective team or committee:

- There's an informal, friendly, comfortable feeling and the pleasant tension of goal-oriented achievers who expect to make progress, but not at the expense of another's self-respect or dignity.
- The group purpose is well-known by all, and subgoals are set in open free discussion that makes it easy for each member to accept them and become committed.
- Consensus is sought on decisions, but disagreement or constructive conflict are not avoided.
- Members expect a respectful hearing when they do differ; the logic is thoughtfully discussed and resolution attempted; unresolved differences are accepted and are not allowed to block the continuation of progress.
- Decisions are never made by majority vote, which is recognized as a mode of compromise.
- Criticism is low-key, frank, constructive, non-personal, and accepted because of trust.
- The leader doesn't dominate, allows others to take the lead in instances of demonstrated superior knowledge or competence; there are no injections of power struggle.

- The members are sensitive to and reasonable about interpersonal competition, confront it openly when it becomes dysfunctional.
- The group is conscious of and pleased with its problem-solving process, periodically assesses it, and always stops for such an evaluation at any time the group begins to bog down on a topic.

A McGregor insight in his own discussion of the subject seems especially revealing. As we know, groups customarily undergo at least some changes of membership from time to time; commenting on new members entering mature groups, he observed that "within minutes of the start of the meeting, they are as much a part of the group as if they had been members for years."[25]

Organizational leadership development (#3). Given that the 3a, 3b, and 3c in the page 1091 chart have been detailed in the text, no more has to be added here, but it might be helpful to pull together and summarize the 3d with the key issues and factors that underlie the subject, the subject of the total three-volume work (also, the 3e, though discoursed in Chapters 11 and 18, needs the additional explication that follows):

Organizational leadership (3d)
- A top concerns here should be the overall culture, climate and norms and a System 4 operating system, the means described where each is discoursed; aid them with OD interventions, and incorporate a comprehensive long-range program like the GE's Management Development Institute at Crotonville.
  (1) *Culture*: one that helps the organization anticipate and adapt to environmental changes; the ideal: "that managers throughout the hierarchy should provide leadership to initiate change in strategies and tactics whenever necessary to satisfy the legitimate interests of not just the stockholders or customers or employees, but all three."[26]
  (2) *Climate*: analyze the "Operating characteristics"
  (Figure 13.4, p. 570), then work on the "Climate dimensions"

(Figure 8.2, p. 277) to move the characteristics toward System 4.

(3) *Norms*: leaders should try to induce or encourage the 8 desirable norms on p.282 that foster favorable opinions of the 9 climate dimensions, the "how" described on pages 282-289.

(4) *The basic human resources policy*—in Chapter 21.

● General basic leadership education needed—on:

(1) *The social*: Part 1, the social knowledge. The skills, and the "awareness learning" (see Foreword, p. xxi)

(2) *The technical*: Part II on control, processes operations planning and structure building with due concern for the general social considerations (p. 264)

(3) *Organization and behavior change*: utilizing OD interventions to develop the specific social considerations.

(4) *Technical-social integration*: (a) the indirect—non-participative building-in of the general social considerations in planning the organization. (b) the direct—participatively making congruent the organization's needs and goals with the needs and aspirations of the individuals.

(5) Strategy planning: goals—optimum utilization of organizational resources for competitive advantage, long-term maximization of stockholder value, return, MVA and EVA, employee satisfaction and customer satisfaction, the underlying processes for achieving the goals being the 10 major options on page 742.

Leading/managing conflict (3e)—addendum. The constant potential for and presence of dysfunctional conflict in all interpersonal events make evident enough that handling it is an essential skill, both to become aware of it when it happens and deal with it effectively. To cover it, one may recall, the subject was divided on pages 504-505 into the three parties that can be involved, listing them as A1 the interpersonal, A2 intragroup, and A3 intergroup—the foundation of A1 supplied in Chapter 11 (pp. 492-513), the psychology of conflict regarding both individuals and groups in Chapter 18 (pp. 951-956), and an OD treatment for the intergroup in Chapter 19.

This addendum is more on A3, put here in this chapter because a mastery of the leadership training and development just covered can importantly increase the prospects of successful resolution of intergroup conflicts that are generally much more complex than the A1 and A2.

Executives with two or more substantial subordinate departments don't need to be told that conflicts between them occasionally, sometimes often, arise. And the most reliable solution to handling them is to develop a habit of tackling them systematically: go through the following thinking steps, most of which can be done very quickly after applying them a few times, doing it carefully too prior to an interdepartmental OD intervention to help insure harmony as well as handle the dysfunctional conflicts that may arise.

The steps:

1. Define the conflict problem.
2. Analyze the problem context.
3. Appraise the parties—personality, job competence, strengths, weaknesses—and their interpersonal relationship(s).
4. Determine the relevant resources of each and the strategies they're using or are apt to use.
5. Review in your mind your own goals.
6. Plan your approach, and proceed.

1. Typical questions for defining the problem: is it a competition for limited corporate (or state) resources or over turf, power or prestige, a conflict due to competing constituency or coalition demands? Is it due to different opinions or vested interests on planned top management changes of policies, programs, structures, processes, and so on? Is it a matter of (to repeat for convenience from page 507) ignorance, misunderstanding, mistrust, insensitivity, different values, philosophy, assumptions, goals, or job differentiation?

If you can, along with the answers concluded, find out how the problem developed over time and also how each of the parties themselves define it, you will have collected important building blocks in the set of 6 steps toward effective conflict leadership.

2. By knowing the problem context you can gauge the effect it has (and it will) on the parties' performance, behavior, opinions and judgments, which will help you determine how to lead them to the best mutually acceptable solution. The principle context components:

- the units' institutional differences: technology, professionalism, management system (1-4, therefore leadership style), incentive systems (and their pressure to "win");
- climate (the definitions on page 27 or their opposites);
- norms (the range of ideal on page 282 to bad on pages 6-8);
- formal goals and plans of each unit;
- the relative importance of each unit to the larger organization (and as perceived), tending to indicate a dominant position of one (or a believed one) or a ranking among several.

3. Needless to say, your understanding of the parties is vital to leading them in any situation, helping you judge behavior, anticipate in advance their reactions to viewpoints and alternatives, and make your own decision choices. Consider writing down the key points, a sheet for each person, as a memory and gestalt aid and for review at future times as may be useful.

Recall that the chief factors to examine were reviewed on pages 491 and 507. Add the critical events in their past and current relationships, disputes if any with causes (could they be due to goals or structures set up by top management)?, the degree of mutual respect, indifference or hostility, any deference that may be accorded and why, the interdependencies and degree of collaboration in the past. Also, contrast the differences of the parties on attitude, values, ethics, management philosophy, motivation, energy (or apathy) interests, stakes, job differentiation. And what will each gain by winning, lose by losing?

4. Their resources that are relevant to the conflict plainly spell out the power of each to win, the support they're likely to gain from coworkers and onlookers, and the probabilities of who's apt to come out on top if left to their own devices. A review of what

each has can be invaluable to your leadership for a final solution that's in the best interest of the whole organization. How does each stack up on and then compare on—

position authority	financial control
intelligence and alertness	personnel control
persuasiveness	importance of the unit to the org.
expertise on the subject	centrality of the individuals
personal power (p.467)	power to "punish" the other(s)
reputation for judgment	a coalition on the issue
control of a relevant asset	relationship with the CEO
information control	other important relationships

Naturally, all of these afford "strategy" opportunities to the parties, and if you discern the use of one, there's a good chance that deceptive politics is at work given current corporate mores. But remember from the discourse on strategy and politics in Chapter 11 (pp. 505-513) that there's no reason why an ethical person should eschew a logical ethical strategy in a political struggle to achieve what is believed best for his/her unit and the larger organization. For example, a divisional manager, aware of his or her unit's dominant importance to the organization would raise doubts about initiative, intellect or debating competence if the person failed to use it subtly (and ethically) in such a situation.

To get the best for the organization, the effective leader will certainly give due recognition to individual subordinates' superior intelligence, judgment and expertise in given areas, but counter applied irrelevant imbalances of position authority and personal power, and check the pressure of aggressive energy or a coalition that's in reality a dysfunctional clique. And if either or any are complacently sitting on the duff, they sometimes can be jarred into contributing to the discussion by reducing a bit their feeling of security—not to confuse them with the laconic or quiet types who may need tactful drawing out.

5. With this foundation (#1 to #4) for leading the conflict, it's a good precaution to review quietly to yourself your goals—that you're going to try to get the parties to:

    a.   engage in a constructive dialogue and avoid dysfunctional behavior;

b.   contribute all the relevant information they have on the subjects;
c.   give their best thinking and be committed to produce the best alternatives and make the best choice;
d.   agree on a win-win solution, leaving no bad side effects;
e.   agree on a solution that's best for the larger organization.

6. To those who accept the leadership precepts of the text given to this point, it's undoubtedly apparent that the best way to achieve (a), (b) and (c) is climate development (in Chapter 8), team development (this chapter), and building leadership development and OD into the management system. Recognizing that they all take time, a review of those pages will still tell you what can be done immediately to improve your odds. The achievement of (d) and (e) would be but matters of leader guidance.

Of course only a few organizations have made any significant progress on those developments; nevertheless, a well regarded leader who has read it all carefully can do fairly well on all five goals in many interdepartmental conflicts, the initial move being to put together the components of an appropriate approach. To get the thinking going...

First, which of the four on pages 507-508 is best for the situation: smooth over, compromise, force, or confront, given the consequence of each stated there? As said, the best the preponderance of the time is confrontation. Assuming that's the choice, would one of the intra- or inter-group OD interventions listed on pages 993-1002, all confrontational, be advisable?

Don't force a choice to fit if it's not right for the situation (your HRD should be helpful), but don't hesitate to adapt OD concepts and methods to a simple meeting of subordinate managers with a conflict to resolve; e.g., having a preliminary diagnostic meeting to clarify the problem, identify assumptions, and list points of agreement and disagreement, all for a cool, organized start on the problem. Consider too the use of a facilitator who has a repertory of methods to help it along (pages 994-995).

Another option is "The Interaction Method" described on pages 604-605, an effective feasible method for even traditionalists as long as they're somewhat open to the idea of power sharing. And note there the "incentive" suggested to motivate movement toward an agreement the superior says, "If there's no consensus, I'll make the final decision myself"—implication to the parties: get involved and produce one if you want a decision that contains your point of view.

Then there are times when the nature of the context considerably complicates the choice of approach. For examples (that incorporate some points from a new book on interdepartmental conflict.[27]):

- Consider a conflict in which the leader is faced with one or more units that, with powerful political resources, adamantly oppose a policy change. You have a zero-sum situation in which any of smoothing over, compromising, persuasion, mediating, negotiating or a confrontational debate will most likely accomplish nothing. Goals (a) to (d) become irrelevant. Forcing with position authority is the only way to achieve (e).... after listening and being open to modification.

- Suppose a leader has two units with relatively equal resources stalemated on a decision important to both and to their relationship. Forcing with position authority risks an inferior decision for lack of all the information they have, poor implementation for lack of participation, and a bad "aftermath" (p. 952) for the relationship and with the leader. An open honest debate is best, supervised by a trusted "honest broker" leader (hopefully the way they perceive you) who may add some guidance toward a preference if believed important to both and the organization.

- The same recourse for the same reasons is generally best when both are vying for scarce resources, say in budget planning. The leader needs all the facts, pros and cons, that only a truthful confrontational debate can bring out, not only for the allocation but to avoid making it a win-lose event?

- On the other hand, consider the situation in which the leader must get two or more units to cut costs, which usually arouses conflicts among them as well as with the leader.

Plainly, a debate would be fruitless, the best approach being one-to-one meetings for all the facts and opinions followed by integration planning and the "force" of directives to achieve (e).

And check again the "conventional solutions" on pages 998-999 to be sure you appreciate the probable consequences before resorting to one.

The amount of small detail within any approach that a mind well imbued with sophisticated leadership development takes into account is certainly myriad and too much to try to describe. For a brief indication, consider what four of the leadership principles can and should suggest what for action and/or fulfilling the expectations of the other(s):

Building mutual trust (the other(s) with you): since the degree is heavily dependent on the climate you've developed, work on the dimensions (page 277) over time, but if you haven't started, check them for what can be done on short notice. A major underpinning of the climate perception and your conflict leadership is being seen as an open, ready-to-listen, fair-minded judge, objective, dedicated to reason, willing to admit being wrong and yield, and volunteering any relevant information about the organization needed. What is done about the following three principles are plainly also critical contributions to trust.

Supportiveness: performing the task and maintenance roles on page 540 in the meeting, building their sense of personal worth and importance (page 571), and guiding the solution to a win-win outcome if possible; at least avoid a winner-take-all result, which means not necessarily an equal division but some satisfaction for each, preventing loser emotions and damaging aftermath. In a group, pay subtle attention to "interaction facilitation," the creating and maintaining of good relations among the members.[28]

Participation: knowing all the benefits described in Chapter 13 this principle should recommend every effort to engage it at appropriate opportunities, including "The Interaction Method" (page 604) and the OD interventions of Chapter 19, along with the conflict techniques given above.

Authority: psychological authority should be the immediate thought (vs. position authority), demonstrating leadership through competence and "personal power" (that include interpersonal skills), for example:
   —leading a high quality debate, establishing and insisting on norms of
      civil behavior (no shouting or abusive language) and mutual respect;

—removing politics by quickly exposing deceptions, misinformation, dissembling and lies, and stopping "games" that bureaucrats play, like prolonging a discussion to talk it to death;

—preventing intimidation and coercion by the powerful and establishing power equality for the discussion;

—requiring systematic problem-solving, the process accounting for opinions, feelings and diversity as in OD interventions;

—listing all the conflicts between the parties or with yourself and starting on the easy ones to solve, developing a pattern of success on the move toward the tough ones;

—perhaps using an incremental approach for a big problem: breaking it up into small digestible parts that are easy to solve, require small commitment, and entail small potential loss;

—for a group discussion-and-planning meeting, designing the membership in the first place for the optimum combination of *creative* conflict (debate), diversity and cross-fertilization.

Summing up some key points on organizational leadership

Having now completed all the parts of the formal investigation (in Parts I, II and III), the problem-solving executive had a strong premonition, especially from the findings of this chapter, that the principal cause of his organization's unsatisfactory performance was the failure of its manager at each level to learn all the requisites of and for effective organizational leadership, the most obvious underlying causes broadly: the authoritarian culture and climate the leadership had induced or permitted down through the organization, the failure to build in a problem-solving and vitalizing process like OD, the lack of an on-going leadership development program, and the failure to establish sound criteria for management hiring and promotion, a combination of omissions that his research had told him was quite common across commerce and industry.

The enduring solution, as he saw it, would be to start with a comprehensive organization change effort like Exhibit 6 in the appendix. In brief, employ a consultant like Beckhard, the author, to sell the change to the management team and oversee the procedure described in the exhibit; begin the building-in of the OD process and the leadership development program after the change starts to take hold, and set goal dates for the completion of each structure and process planned.

Then for the hiring and promotion criteria, start with the interaction theory equation on page 1050; "traits" + the situation = organizational leadership style (good or bad); fill in what it takes to produce the most desirable results, and make leadership potential for the desired style a dominant criterion. Admittedly, the meaning of each word in the equation is so large and complicated, the filling in can be a bit confusing. Some thoughts on simplification that should help:

The "traits," as said on page 1050, include all of personality and its consequent behavior, assumptions, and skills, and "the situation" covers all of the followers, the organization, and the environment (McGregor on 1050... the intricacies of the two suggested by Figure 20.3 designed to help behavioral scientists in their thinking through the improvement of leadership effectiveness, the three boxes on the upper left being the "traits," those on the right the situation.[29]

Extracting the "skills" from the "traits" and describing them separately because they are both crucial ....

"Traits." We now know there is one absolute essential to leadership effectiveness, the motivation to manage. The three requirements on page 275, and the page 348 model described all the desirable that will provide a high probability of effectiveness, assuming technical competence.

Given that the model is an unattainable ideal, it was well qualified there that, for example, plenty of successful leaders have very mediocre profiles, have only average intelligence but have high motivation and ability to learn from experience, compensate for weaknesses with strong points, or competently use the strengths of others on the team.

So one is inclined to ask what in the model, along with the motivation to manage, is most important in the search for leadership potential? What should one particularly look for in hiring and placement? There are eight characteristics; the absence of any will importantly detract from the caliber needed:

- Maturity
- The "strong personality" traits: dominant, social, outgoing, self-accepting

Integrating Framework for Research on Leadership Effectiveness

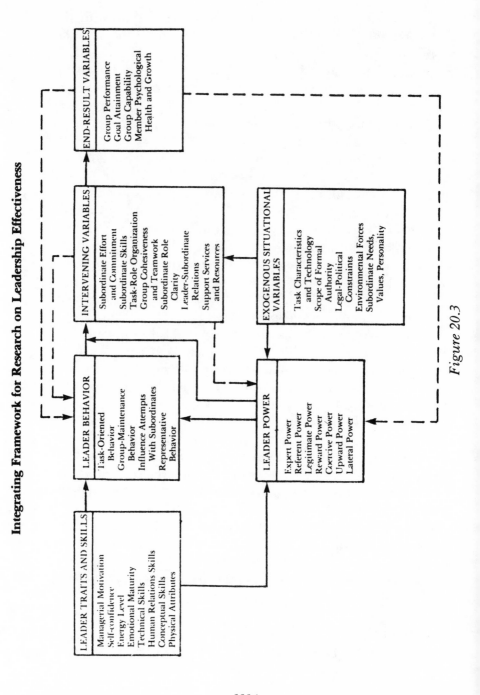

Figure 20.3

- High achievement drive
- High on energy and stamina
- Good managerial judgment
- Commitment to humanistic values (e.g., page 118)
- A substantial repertory of interpersonal skills
- Superior technical knowledge.

The order does not signify importance, but note that the first four have to be brought to the organization by the individual; very little if anything can be done about them after entry except to aid or block the motivation to pursue achievement and the development of maturity over time. On the second four, however, it's obvious that much can be done by good leadership of the superior and the development program of a quality HRD.

At the same time, the "absolute essential" (the motivation to manage) of course remains uppermost, and the best choice will have a combination and optimum balance of *thinker* (analyze, plan), *doer* (initiate) and *feeler* (the sensitivity to succeed on the social and technical-social integration)—to which virtually every superior leader adds the capacity and spontaneity to *improvise* which requires imagination and flexibility along with the good judgment and initiative. Indeed, without it the odds of exceeding mediocrity are low.

Skills. On this subject too, one understandably wonders, given a manager or candidate with the eight basic traits above, which of all the skills on page 1094 are really fundamentally necessary, even while knowing they're all important? The answers can be summarized as follows (certainly incorporate also for individual positions the specific technical requirements and behavioral fit described in Chapter 8):

- Demonstration of, or a record that shows potential for, the knowledge and skills of leadership role responsibilities (on pages 1073-1088) and that they would be based on theory Y requisites (page 16).
- Evidence, record or high potential for in-house development as needed of #1, 2 and 3 on pages 1090-1091, especially the

interpersonal skills of motivating, counselling, coaching and empowering.

- Communication skills—persuasiveness (non-coercive), tact, presentation competence, writing that manifests clear thinking.

- Political skills, or potential for them, those applicable up and down the hierarchy for the benefit of one's unit toward its services to the larger organization (pp. 509-513)—usually discernible from the "traits" and communication skills.

- And additionally for top management: (a) a record of organizing and decision-making skills guided by a preponderance of values on page 118; (b) at least an open mind about OD if ignorant of it or not already committed to it; (c) demonstrated ability to develop a mature team (1002-1004) that can achieve the organization's dual purpose of success on the functional activity and intrinsic satisfaction for the members and other constituencies.

At the same time, recognizing that, as pointed out in the Forward, many important leadership skills within these subjects are too complex to teach, it is still essential for a training and development program to induce an *awareness of the unteachable* in the hope that the participants will be inspired to developed them over time on the job.

The greatly over simplified comparative chart below published in the 2/22/93 *Fortune* may nevertheless be a useful mind-jogger to start a little thought in the "old," still the vast majority, the article pointing out that the "new" won't be seen in great numbers for another 5 to 10 years.

The situation. As described earlier, this includes both the internal and external, and here is what leadership can do about the former, the latter being limited largely to proactive activities. But because the internal has such a myriad of variables, the leadership effort has to be restricted to the major ones, those with the most leverage on results. Leadership can do little about some but much about most.

Dividing the organizational levels into three—the top management one of the larger organization, the smaller

WHICH KIND ARE YOU?

OLD MANAGER	NEW MANAGER
■ Thinks of self as a manager or boss	■ Thinks of self as a sponsor, team leader, or internal consultant
■ Follows the chain of command	■ Deals with anyone necessary to get the job done
■ Works within a set organizational structure	■ Changes organizational structures in response to market change
■ Makes most decisions alone	■ Invites others to join in decision making
■ Hoards information	■ Shares information
■ Tries to master one major discipline, such as marketing or finance	■ Tries to master a broad array of managerial disciplines
■ Demands long hours	■ Demands results

organization or unit of a division or department, and the job of the subordinate manager—what with respect to the situation in each can a leader having a commendable portion of the "traits" and "skills" listed above do to improve performance?

The larger organization. This list of variables and the opportunities they afford would be for both medium and large entities; only parts will be applicable to small ones and those be subject to differences in character (e.g. the style apparel industry with its unpredictable personal nature vs. steel):

The major internal situation variables of the larger organization

1. The organization's purpose, goals, and resources: material (money, plant, supply, product) human (personnel, competencies, the social system); its products and services.

2. The management technology requirements of the organization necessary to optimize "the industry-organization match" and maximize operational effectiveness.

3. Top management philosophy, values and HR policies, the underlying determinants of the management system (system 1, 2, 3 or 4).

4. Management of the top management team.
5. Size of the organization.
6. The 14 structure characteristics on page 446, and the location of the organization in those respects on the mechanistic-organic continuum.
7. Extent and types of staff services.
8. Extent and sophistication of MIS.
9. Past history of success and failure.
10. The present overall culture and climate.

One can tick off the possibilities for top management as:

- #1 and #5 would be considered fixed for this analysis, though they're not always, for example, mergers or acquisitions can make quick changes in either.
- On #2, there are of course plenty of management technology opportunities for performance improvement and gaining competitive advantages through changes of strategy structures or processes (Chapters 11 to 16).
- #3 is clearly the principal opportunity because of the scope and depth of changes it can cause throughout the organization, changing the management system, culture, climate, selected items in #6 and many aspects of #7; particularly important, check the consequences of the present philosophy with periodic opinion and climate surveys (that will tell you what it really is). Don't overlook this major technique for knowing your organization so you can act effectively.
- For the top management team members, #4, the discourses on its development in Chapter 13 (p. 588).
- Given in #6 that the optimum point on the mechanistic-organic continuum cannot be a goal, is a result, all 14 have to be analyzed for best design to produce the best location for the organization.
- On what staff services (#7) can do for an organization and what might be needed, see Chapter 16 and comments on top management neglect, and Chapter 17 for the many ways a superior HRD staff alone can improve performance.

- Improving the MIS, #8, can naturally upgrade significantly all decision-making (see especially the information technology subsection in Chapter 14.
- While each failure in #9 is an opportunity for improvement, a bad overall record, we know, generally requires a new CEO who has the added problem of low morale; a "confrontation meeting" by the *new* CEO will probably provide the best start if the top team has the prerequisites, an overall approach outlined on page 1006.
- The importance of the culture and climate (#10) is attested to by its status as a major general target of organization-wide OD; discourses on this in Chapters 8, 18 and 19.

The smaller organization or unit. Lest the use of the word be misunderstood, the "variables" of the organization, unit, or job may be so (or not so) from one organization, unit or job to the next, but not be variables for the best results of an established purpose and set of goals. The major variables in this situation:

**The major internal situation variables
of the smaller organization or unit**

1. The purpose, goals, resources and output of the unit (as in the larger organization's #1).
2. The management technology requirements of the unit's jobs necessary to maximize operational effectiveness.
3. The present climate of the unit.
4. The group's dynamics and processes.
5. Subordinates' characteristics: job-knowledge, intelligence, maturity, traits, experience, age (aver. and range), training.
6. Importance of the unit in the larger organization and the hierarchical level of the leader.
7. The actual authority delegated to the leader.
8. The subordinates' leadership expectations re mechanistic to organic and the leader's personality style (position authority, competence, psychological leadership—page 000).

9. Quality of the leader-member relationships.
10. Recency and record of the previous leader.
11. The unit's past history of success and failure.

However, when a leader can do something about any one of them to improve performance, it is variable for the leader. The best opportunities to do so in your own unit or those of subordinate managers are apt to be as follows:

- Although the purpose in #1 is a given, is there a full superior-subordinate understanding and agreement on the goals, should improvements be made in the resources (perhaps via the political skills on pp. 509-513), does the product need redesigning?
- Chapters 11 through 16 might suggest improvements for #2 and a good MBA or "Executive" education can be a decisive help to subordinates who haven't had one.
- Given that climate (#3) is a prime leadership consideration, have climate surveys, the principle tools of analysis, been made a standard periodic activity? Assuming yes, does your latest one indicate that any characteristics of "an effective group" (p. 532) are missing? Review this chapter's "team development" for leads to how shortcoming might be corrected.
- Chapters 12 and 19 provide solutions for group dynamics problems (#4), all of Part II for processes and for OD where dynamics, structures or processes impact directly or indirectly on people.
- Although the subordinates' characteristics as a group in #5 may have to be considered a given in the short run, the superior must certainly make a point of understanding them to carry out effectively on their behalf the 7 leadership roles (that include control, planning, development, motivation, compensation): also a review of them may suggest structural changes (page 446) for better fit to their nature... or personnel changes.
- On #6, if your unit's value is being underrated by upper management it may be losing out in many subtle ways.

Consider applying your political Skills to ensure recognition of its due status (pages 509-513). Of course unit leadership and unit success are major factors in their rating.

- Though #7 may be a given for you yourself, do you know for sure what your delegated authority is? be certain you and your superior agree (keeping in mind the need for a little chutzpah in its application, p. 501) and that your subordinates do regarding your authority over them. Note that if subordinates doubt you have enough to satisfy their extrinsic and intrinsic needs it can affect performance and order-compliance adversely. The same would naturally be true for subordinate managers' subordinates. Superior must subtly ensure the desired perceptions.

- The climate survey should tell much indirectly about the group's leadership expectations, #8, and so should your relationships with your own group.

- Again the climate survey will reveal much about the quality of the relationships (#9) whether it's a subordinate manager's unit or your own. If unsatisfactory, check the whole of the organization's leadership development section (pp. 1088-1105) for clues.

- For one's subordinates' departments, the most important initial issue in #10 is the selection of new managers, especially not to put an authoritarian in after the prior superior got them used to participative management (or at any time!). Any new manager nevertheless will, we know, be compared to the departing one, and whether a hard act to follow or not, help the person with a personal complimentary introduction expressing strong support. The potential consequences of forgetting to should be evident.

- On #11, consider a policy of thorough reports to new subordinate managers of their units' strengths and weaknesses to give them a fast start, and an opportunity to undertake, a staff or consultant-aided OD team diagnostic meeting (pp. 994-997).

The job (of each subordinate manager—and check the possibilities on your own). One might think at first glance at the list below that all are givens, but consider the comments that follow it:

The major situation variables of the job

1. The job's purpose, goals, resources (provided), and product.
2. The job's technical difficulty.
3. The importance of the job (e.g., is it on the key position ladder?).
4. The cognitive, interpersonal, behavioral, and motivational requirements of the job (Chapter 8).
5. The information uncertainty and its ambiguity.
6. The nature of the required decisions.
7. Interdependencies with, dependence on, or obligations to other parties or units.
8. The quality of the superior/subordinate relationships.
9. The higher-order motivation fulfillment potential of the job.
10. The job urgency, pace, and pace consistency.
11. The population familiarity (contact with outside pop.).

Comments:

1. Has the purpose been well defined for the subordinate, were the goals and job characteristics set in a way that motivated commitment, is there a clear agreement on what they are? It's never too late for direct integration as a mutual clarification process (pages 1068-1072). Also, have needed resources been supplied?
2. Does the person's record or performance recommend more training or development?
3. On the ladder or not, be sure the incumbent feels it's important.
4. Is the incumbent a good fit in these regards, and if so, would more development help, a job change if not?
5. Is the right type, quantity and quality of information needed being provided? If not, should any changes be

made? Is the person up to it? Does he or she have, or should have, a computer, or be on a network?

6. Check the types involved and the planning (pages 631-634); is the planning best for the job and person's capabilities up to desired performance.
7. Spell them out, include in performance reviews; see Chapter 16 for structural improvement possibilities.
8. Need more be said.
9. Can performance be improved by enrichment (pages 299-304)?
10. Can more resources, more information or faster information help?
11. Can the information or communication systems be improved for better understanding and responsiveness to markets and community?

Summary comment. Four important ones. First, to sum up from the text, the ideal organization every advanced top executive should want internally:

A participative System 4 organization with minimal direct supervision and rules appropriate to the location on the mechanistic-organic continuum and to what employees require to be proficient, norms of communication in any direction as needed, the practice of "mutual adjustment" for coordination wherever feasible, and all teams mature and effective, resulting in a freed-up integrative climate of trust, commitment, and intrinsic satisfaction.

And the reason why it's desirable is not just for morality, though it's one essential ingredient; such characteristics will yield the highest productivity and performance possible...and it's the easiest kind of organization to lead toward those ends.

Understandably now, to get it all four key management skills described have to be developed to a high degree of excellence; the four: the three on page 1036 plus the leadership development just presented:

1. *Corporate planning* (management technology, operations, strategies and policies) for the technical

2. *Human resources planning* for the social
3. *Organization development* for technical-social integration
4. *Leadership development* for the implementation.

Outstanding organizational success would be inevitable.

Second, a question that leadership theorists and behaviorists have argued about for decades can now be answered with assurance: "Can a truly capable leader be universally effective in any organizational situation?"

Recognizing that three fundamental skills are involved-technical, social and technical-social integration—it's easy to see that, since the social is applicable universally, if it and the technical-social integration skills have been learned, the answer is "yes" wherever the technical skills have been mastered adequately (e.g., the example on page 563).

Naturally, one must be practical. The quintessential leader will always be only a hope for as long as we can imagine; we seek but *effective* leaders, and all of them will have their flaws. Maturity alone tells us to eschew the romantic idealism of youth of settling only for perfection. As quoted earlier, Abraham Maslow once said, "If you demand a perfect leader or a perfect society, you thereby give up choosing between better and worse. If the imperfect is defined as evil, then everything becomes evil, since everything is imperfect."

Such unrealistic expectations could perhaps be considered one reason for the present low regard for business and government authority and leadership, but it's most unlikely on such a large scale; and, recall Chapter I showed that the low regard is present in the internal attitude of employees as well as the external. The fact is, our leaders currently measure up so seldom to *realistic* expectations of leadership.

Of course the finger of blame once again has to be pointed mainly to where the buck stops, to those executives at the top, especially the CEOs, all admittedly overloaded but paid well enough to take the heat and to do better. There seems to be little actual awareness there, in spite of all the literature on it, of the importance of the top management model, that all those up-from-the-ranks managers promoted from within learn their leadership style from their immediate bosses who also look to their superiors on up to their own CEO leadership.

And the model commonly found at the top? The extensive research on CEOs has shown that many still hold to the following operating rules and behavior:

- designing and managing the environment unilaterally (vs. participation);
- maximizing winning and minimizing losing (vs. collaboration);
- deliberately selecting mediocre immediate subordinates;
- setting "satisficing" goals (page 621);
- manipulating human relations—the way most of them got to the top;
- not tolerating truths that will rock the boat;
- bristling at any suggestion of limiting their believed right to be arbitrary.

The prospects for the immediate future in most organizations therefore are depressing, the best hope being the younger generations moving up and a few rare senior executives who do not flag in their pursuit of excellence.

For the third observation, there is a pervasive problem in our society implied throughout of low social responsibility,[1] the poor job that's been done getting it *internalized* in the individual and *institutionalized* in the organization, the failure of which the author of one commendable recent book holds is the cause of our inability to achieve a humane society and dooms it to eventual fragmentation.[31]

But the knowledge herein, the new and the reviewed, gives good reason for hope in that much can be done on both via organizational leadership.

At the national level, responsibility has been institutionalized, we know, in the "justice of enough" (page 161), though we're still quite delinquent on it, and in the giving of international assistance of many kinds including our efforts to keep world peace. And for the individual, education must be capable of doing something right to be able to develop the responsible leaders we do have (e.g., those with "socialized power," page 272).

Moreover, the standards and requisites for individual internalizing have been well delineated: we've made responsibility a criterion of maturity (page 63); it's the fundamental idea of justice (the "don'ts" though, not the "dos"); most of the "Criteria for Moral Decisions" assembled on page 176 have been urged for a very long time; and thoughtful people know at least intuitively that, as Fromm explained, it's an essential ingredient of morality and love (page 222).

The problem has been the failure to spread the news about all that and to sell it, even sell the simple realization of the mutuality of responsibility within every community and organization. And of course the major obstacles have been ignorance and deep-seated value misconceptions like those on power and individualism, the latter used also as a convenient excuse for the rampant "me first, the hell with you."

Education's job ahead of teaching and removing the misconceptions is plainly monumental, and some ideas for doing it are presented in the last chapter. But the obligation of organizational leadership to promote responsibility would seem to be considerable by its position in society alone, and given the fact that the overwhelming proportion of the populace spends a third of its life in work organizations, the opportunity for it to make a major impact is enormous, the magnitude amplified by the direct psychological authority it has compared to that of the state or Education. Much is achievable in a comparatively short time. How? Picking it out from what has been said, by organizational leaders:

- instituting Leadership development programs that teach and indoctrinate interpersonal ethics, the Leadership principles and the role responsibilities, provide the leadership development described, and produce managerial judgments that include consideration of justice and the human consequences of decisions;

- building OD into the management system as presented in Chapter 19, thereby institutionalizing an integrative climate, making participation and technical-social integration standard operating procedures;
- planning and institutionalizing a humanistic social policy statement as given in the next chapter;
- modeling the responsibility propounded in the programs and policies.

A strong sense of interdependence and responsibility would inevitably evolve down through the organization, maximizing its effectiveness, and could not help but carry over to the outside community and nation .

Finally, the fourth observation is with regard to the widespread inadequacy of formal top management *basic human resources policies* (the #4 "Top concern" on page 1105) that includes the social policy mentioned above. As constructs of all that's been given to this point, it's now possible to assemble them into coherent statements in the next chapter and demonstrate their importance.

NOTES

a.   One behaviorist labeled and described the three in this vivid and rememberable way.[3]

- Autocrat: a.   Dictator—absolute ruler, despot
  - b.   Bureaucrat—rule by rules; efficiency replaces productivity
  - c.   Neurocrat—workaholic, which results in domination for productivity
  - d.   Benevolent autocrat—Theory X with some concessions to humanism
- Democrat: participative and humanistic
- Abdicrat: laissez-faire

b.   One still encounters modified theories, for example, Hersey and Blanchard's "Situational Leadership Theory" based on their definition of "task relevant maturity" of subordinates (page 73, footnote n), the subordinates postulated as the situation; the theory: when a Leader should increase or decrease each of task behavior (initiating structure) and relationship behavior (consideration). Blanchard has attempted to simplify it (though already too simplified) in his "One Minute Manager" books, his latest being *Leadership and the One Minute Manager*,[4] that's on the level of an "executive coloring book"—fill in the behaviors (that he mislabels as styles) by the numbers. Shallow short-cuts for the short-range, but might be helpful to beginners before going into true organizational leadership.

c.   Two still-popular questionnaires that were developed illustrate: The Ohio state Leader Behavior Description Questionnaire (LBDQ) given to subordinates and the Leadership Opinion Questionnaire (LOQ) answered by the leaders themselves. The former has now been expanded to include ten additional scales and is called the LBDQ-XII; the scales in total: consideration, initiating structure, representation, demand reconciliation, tolerance of uncertainty, persuasiveness, tolerance of freedom, role retention, predictive accuracy, production emphasis, integration, influence with superiors.

d.   In traits/situation discourses, traits are generally given a broad meaning (designated here by quotes) that includes the ten components of personality on page 00, behavior, assumptions, and all the learned technical, interpersonal and leadership skills.

e.   Figure 12.7 on page 552 for the one on communications and Figure 13.4 on page 570 for interaction-influence. It is probable that he did not include leadership among the functions because the project was with respect to the consequences of types of leadership; however, he added it in the form shown in Figure 20.1[8] to his 1967 book in conjunction with developing a climate survey questionnaire. Likert explained, incidentally, that the charts are only simplified illustrations from which one has to interpolate other functions and extrapolate for detail.

f.   Consultants have repeatedly found that, when goal-setting delegated to subordinate managers is a new experience, they invariably set them too high for some time in their enthusiasm; it takes them a while to find out what they never knew before—their own and their department's true potential above the former low goals they formerly planned in defense.

g.   L.D. Clay.

h.   Some 25 percent of the nation's high schools now have "leadership" training classes on basic skills available to students covering such subjects as public speaking and collaborative planning for student organizations and social events. Similarly they are only on the technical and just scratch the surface of leadership. This is not to knock their value on task-specific skills; many have proven to be a helpful start.

i.   The OD program of TRW Systems has as its first step "Leadership Development Laboratories" that include T-grouping, and their experience led them to stress in them the evaluation of personal values.[19]

j.   Some aware CEOs prohibit the use of "I" in team meetings, make "we" mandatory.

k.   Quote from conclusions of 4,279 responses in an HBR survey (43% top mgmt., 30% upper middle, 14% lower middle): "Members of top management differ from executives at other levels mainly in their avoidance of the subordinate who falls in the "trouble maker" pattern (outspoken and independent) and their willingness to accept in his place a "dull, apathetic' and 'retiring' subordinate."[30]

One must ask therefore, aren't they really seeking servants to suit their personal drives and ego needs? The bent today is the same as in 1961, the date of the survey.

1.   Differentiated from the two other types of responsibility: the psychological need (page 143) as in the achievement oriented (page 241) and Principle #III.

REFERENCES

1.   Kotter, J.P., *The Leadership Factor* (New York: The Free Press, 1988), pp. 84-90.

2.   Ibid., p .66.

3.   Jennings, E.E., *The Executive* (New York: Harper & Row, 1962).

4.   Blanchard, K.H., P. Zigarmi and D. Zigarmi, *Leadership and the One Minute Manager* (New York: William Morrow, 1985).

5.   McGregor, D., *The Human Side of Enterprise* (New York: McGraw-Hill, 1961), pp. 180-182.

6.   Bennis, W.G., "Revisionist Theory of Leadership," *Harvard Business Review*, January-February, 1961.

7.   Likert, R. op. cit. (1961). Model on pages 223-233.

8.   Likert, R., *The Human Organization* (New York: McGraw-Hill, 1967), pp. 197-198.

9.   Driscoll, J.W., "Trust and Participation in Organizational Decision Making as Predictors of Satisfaction," *Academy of Management Journal*, 1973, Vol. 21, No. 1.

10.   Bennis, W.G., *The Unconscious Conspiracy* (New York: Amacon, 1976), p.52.

11.   Kotter, J.P., op. cit., p.20.

12.   McGregor, op. cit. (1961), pp. 62-76.

13.   Ibid., p.76.

14.   Levinson, H.

15.   Lawrence, P.R., H.F. Kolodny and S.M. Davis, "The Human Side of the Matrix," *Organizational Dynamics*, Summer 1977.

16.   Waterman, R.H., Jr., *The Renewal Factor* (New York: Bantem Books, 1987), p.283.

17.   Sayles, L.R., *Leadership* (New York: McGraw-Hill, 1979), p.117.

18.   Bolt, J.E., *Executive Development* (New York: Harper Business, 1989), p.13.

19.   Davis, S.A., "Building an Organization For the Future," in *The Failure of Success*, ed. A.J. Marrow (New York: Amacom, 1972), p.269-270.

20.   *Business Week*, May 8, 1978.

21.   McGregor, op. cit. (1967), p. 168.

22.   Ibid, p.239.

23.   Johansen, R., D. Sibbet, S. Benson, A. Martin, R. Mittman, and P. Saffo, *Leading Business Teams* (Reading, Mass.: Addison-Wesley, 1991), Sibbet p. 25. The model by Drexler, A.B., D. Sibbert, and R.H. Forrester in *Team Building Blueprints for Productivity* (NTL Institute, 1988).

24. Source: *Sales and Marketing Management* (magazine), copyright September 23, 1974.

25. McGregor, D., op. cit., p.236.

26. Kotter, J.P. and J.L. Heskett, *Corporate Culture and Performance* (New York: The Free Press, 1992), p.50.

27. Yates, Jr., D., *The Politics of Management* (San Francisco: Jossey-Bass, 1985). pp. 94-96.

28. Bowers, D.G., and S.E. Seashore, "Predicting organizational effectiveness with a four-factor theory of leadership," *Administrative Science Quarterly*, Sept. 1966, 10(2), 238-263.

29. Yukl, G.A., *Leadership in Organizations* (Englewood Cliffs, N.J.: Prentice-Hall, 1981), p.270.

30. L.B. Ward, "Do You Want a Weak Subordinate," *Harvard Business Review*, Sept. -Oct. 1961.

31. Vickers, G., *Human Systems are Different* (New York: Harper & Row, 1984).

Chapter 21

Leadership Policies

Policies were defined, it may be remembered, as "contingent decisions" made in advance to be implemented under certain conditions that either will occur or are probable. As a technique of precontrol to guide decisions by organizational members on recurrent events, they essentially reflect the "wisdom" and "morality" of the management. The "wisdom" type generally refers to the technical decision and the "morality" to the social.

In small organizations under one roof the frequent face-to-face contact of all managers certainly reduces the need for formalizing them, but even then it could be an expensive omission since newly hired managers usually learn them only after violations, and when non-management personnel are not informed of those relevant to them, it multiplies the risks. Progressive organizations, small and large, try to do a thorough job on both the technical and social.

The technical

The logic behind having formal technical policies is so evident competent managers would not expose themselves to the criticism of not having them. Their purpose, we know, is to give quality, consistency and predictability to the management of repetitive events. Because they are repetitive they need not be thought through for a decision each time as with unique events; one can capitalize on the wisdom gained from past experience.

Their value is in fact so widely recognized we see them planned for virtually the entire spectrum of organizational precontrols, all the way from board resolutions to standard operating procedures in a plant. If the use complies with the "contingent decision" definition, it qualifies.

The consolidated list below, all but a few essentially "technical," suggests the scope. It was obtained from a survey of large corporations made some 30 years ago in which at least 60% of the firms were found to have policies on all of them, 70% to 80% had them on most, and the percentages are certainly much higher today:[1,a]

General company
Public relations
Stockholder relations
Government relations
Competitive relations
Prod. scope of interest
Company size, growth
Delegation

Sales/marketing
Market coverage
Distribution channels
Brands
Product quality
Pricing/discounts
Customer service
Packaging
Ad and promotion

Procurement
Purchase vs. mfg.
Vendor relations
Vendors per item
Quality of purchase
Hq. vs. branch purch.
Lead time

R & D
Types of R & D projects
Project selection/approval
Patents, copyrights, royalties
Payout

Financial
Sources of funds
Use of funds
Valuation of assets
Change of assets
Depreciation of assets
Inventories
Receivables

Manufacturing
Production plan'g and control
Quality control
Equipment purchasing
Equipment maintenance
Methods improvement
Performance standards
Plant location
Warehousing

Personnel
Wages and salaries
Hiring
Placement
Training
Seniority
Working conditions
Working hours
Employee benefits
Safety
Mgmt. development
Mgmt. benefits
Mgmt. compensation

They're usually sorted out for formulation to top committees, headquarters staff, manager committees, and/or technical specialists, who recommend the policies they've planned either to the top or to a delegated top line executive. Or, the entire subject may be centralized in an executive committee that ensures appropriate coverage by the concerned level; for example:

Corporate: the organization manual on structures and processes; broad "do" or "don't" operating directives for both the corporate and division levels; policies for each staff department.

Divisional and department: functional policies, standards, procedures, methods, rules.

The degree of centralization and sophistication of planning understandably determine which policies should be where and how simple the statements can be or can turn out to be. For example, planning one for manufacturing in a large organization can be as intricate as in Figure 21.1.[2] Obviously, such a procedure requires sizable resources and specialized talent; smaller firms must settle for short-cuts and faith.

Finally, every management should attend to the task of regular periodic policy review on a rolling schedule though few do. The adage that "you can't argue with success" seems to obscure the fact that the success on which the policies are based is itself based on environmental conditions that almost always change in time, sometimes rapidly, changing many good policies to bad ones.

The social

Given that the social side of an organization has the two parts, individuals and the organization, Part I stressed principally the understanding and development of ethical behavior in the former, and the main concern here is the collective behavior of the latter that results in its ethics, standards, norms, climate and culture.

First, consider a frequently overlooked elementary organizational influence—pride. Anyone with some social education knows that people in general need to have pride in the organization they work for as a matter of self-respect and social acceptance, that the pride is based on a combination of their firm's success image and the community's regard for its managerial sophistication on management technology, employee concern and ethical behavior—for example, the reputations of Xerox and General Electric.

We know too that employees convert the pride into an increment of cohesion and motivation toward better performance, so common sense tells one that along with all the direct benefits of providing intrinsic satisfaction, participative management and

The process of manufacturing policy determination

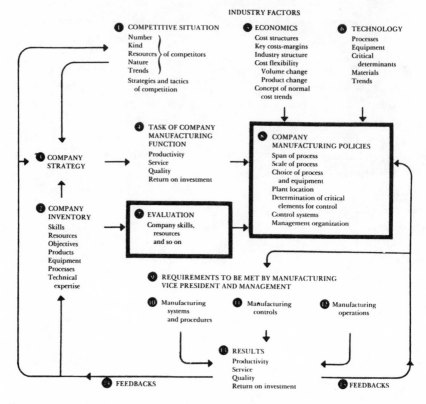

INDUSTRY FACTORS

❶ COMPETITIVE SITUATION
Number
Kind
Resources } of competitors
Nature
Trends
Strategies and tactics
of competition

❺ ECONOMICS
Cost structures
Key costs-margins
Industry structure
Cost flexibility
Volume change
Product change
Concept of normal
cost trends

❻ TECHNOLOGY
Processes
Equipment
Critical
determinants
Materials
Trends

**❹ TASK OF COMPANY
MANUFACTURING
FUNCTION**
Productivity
Service
Quality
Return on investment

**❽ COMPANY
MANUFACTURING POLICIES**
Span of process
Scale of process
Choice of process
and equipment
Plant location
Determination of critical
elements for control
Control systems
Management organization

**❸ COMPANY
STRATEGY**

**❷ COMPANY
INVENTORY**
Skills
Resources
Objectives
Products
Equipment
Processes
Technical
expertise

❼ EVALUATION
Company skills,
resources
and so on

**❾ REQUIREMENTS TO BE MET BY MANUFACTURING
VICE PRESIDENT AND MANAGEMENT**

**❿ Manufacturing
systems
and procedures**

**⓫ Manufacturing
controls**

**⓬ Manufacturing
operations**

⓭ RESULTS
Productivity
Service
Quality
Return on investment

⓮ FEEDBACKS

⓯ FEEDBACKS

Key

1. What the others are doing

2. What we have got or can get to compete with

3. How we can compete

4. What we must accomplish in manufacturing in order to compete

5. Economic constraints and opportunities common to the industry

6. Constraints and opportunities common to the technology

7. Our resources evaluated

8. How we should set ourselves up to match resources, economics, and technology to meet the tasks required by our competitive strategy

9. The implementation requirements of our manufacturing policies

10. Basic systems in manufacturing (e.g., production planning, use of inventories, use of standards, and wage systems)

11. Controls of cost, quality, flows, inventory, and time

12. Selection of operations or ingredients critical to success (e.g., labor skills, equipment utilization, and yields)

13. How we are performing

14. Changes in what we have not, effects on competitive situation, and review of strategy

15. Analysis and review of manufacturing operations and policies

Figure 21.1

technical-social integration, it also pays indirectly through employee pride to engage in enlightened social management in *all* regards, including and especially morality. And, taking the first step on morality doesn't cost an out-of-pocket cent: publish a statement of policy.

But the vast majority of organizations still don't even take the first step; indeed, many, seeing no relationship of these factors to employee performance don't give a damn about manager behavior itself let alone policies on it. One large firm recently illustrated the indifference by paying a $100,000 fine for an executive proven guilty of sexually harassing his secretary, refusing to reinstate the woman (he fired her for non-compliance), and continuing the executive in his six-figure position as if nothing had happened.

However, regardless of executive irresponsibility or abuse of rights, the policy statements in themselves give the troops some hope of the organization's moral intent, they constrain the less ethical somewhat because of their top management origin, they provide minimal moral guidelines, they reinforce the statement of organization purpose the CEO has (should have) articulated, and, there are external advantages.[b] C.D. Stone suggested as a starting point the general policies in Figure 21.2[3] to which specificity should be added to fill recognized needs. They in themselves collectively provide:

- A guide to managers and employees as to the organization's concept of minimum moral behavior;
- An appeal to some higher ideals of all organization members;
- A confirmation to them that a valuable "purpose" in life and contribution to the community can be filled by working for the company;
- An implied challenge to sublimate destructive competitiveness and greed to cooperative enterprise;
- A notice to the public and stockholders of the company's good and honest intentions and of its asset value to the community.

Indeed, ethics pays, and the unethical costs in profits, penalties, and crucial intangibles. On profits, a comparison of the change

the corporation as citizen

- to be concerned with obeying the laws (even if it can get away with law breaking profitably)
- to aid in the making of laws, as by volunteering information within its control regarding additional measures that may need to be imposed on industry
- to heed the fundamental moral rules of the society
- not to engage in deception, corruption, and the like
- as a citizen abroad, to act decently to host country citizens, and not inimically to U.S. foreign policy

the corporation as producer

- to aim for safe and reliable products at a fair price

the corporation as employer

- to be concerned with the safety of the work environment
- to be concerned with the emotional well-being of its workers
- not to discriminate

the corporation as resource manager

- not to contribute unduly to the depletion of resources
- to manifest some concern for the aesthetics of land management

the corporation as an investment

- to safeguard the interests of investors
- to make full and fair disclosures of its economic condition

the corporation as neighbor

- to be concerned with pollution
- to conduct safe and quiet operations

the corporation as competitor

- not to engage in unfair competition, on the one had, or cozy restrictions of competition. on the other

the corporation as social designer

- to be innovative and responsive in the introduction of new products and methods
- not to close its eyes to the fact that it's products, promotion and conduct of business have an impact on the quality of our lives, and to concern itself with that impact responsibly.

Figure 21.2

in market value over the last 10 years of a large number of major firms that have given it a lot of attention showed that their value increased by 11.3 percent vs. 6.2 percent for the Dow Jones.[4]

And the 1991 Federal Sentencing Guidelines succinctly spelled out the penalty costs, stating them in terms of the following minimum leadership and structural requirements:

- The establishment of formal compliance standards and procedures;
- High-level personnel designated to oversee compliance;
- Effective communication of the standards and procedures through training and publication;
- Responsible steps to achieve compliance through auditing, monitoring processes, and a system for employees to report criminal conduct without fear of retribution;
- Consistent enforcement of standards through appropriate disciplinary measures;
- Appropriate response when offenses are detected;
- Reasonable steps to prevent recurrence of similar offenses.

A program that (but) complies with these requirements is called "a compliance-based program"—to prevent, detect, and punish illegal conduct; and the material penalties by the courts for omissions depend on who is bilked (customers, employees, society) and by how much, the smallest amount being the dollars billed if all of these have been attended to; with only a program but no monitoring, reporting or high level attention and responsibility, substantially more; with not even a program it can skyrocket to 200% of the loss suffered, millions.

Other costs: the legal fees, lost sales, lost customer trust, lost market share, fired key executives, damaged relationships and reputation in the market; examples: total cost to Beechnut on fake baby food an estimated $25 million, to Sears on padded auto repair bills $60 million.

So a compliance-based program, though important, is far from enough, and to avoid such costs top managements have to first face up to the fact that "typically unethical business practices involve the tacit, if not explicit cooperation of others and reflect the values, attitudes, beliefs, language, and behavioral patterns that define an organization's culture.[c] Ethics then is as much an organizational as personal issue. Managers who fail to provide proper leadership and institute systems that facilitate ethical conduct share responsibility with those who conceive, execute, and knowingly benefit from corporate misdeeds."[5]

The United States Sentencing Commission was plainly attempting by the comprehensiveness of the guidelines to induce managements to make the needed culture and climate changes, to make evident (also by the sentences meted out) that managers who ignore ethics run the risk of severe penalties both personal and corporate, to compel them to tackle the problems *underlying* unlawful conduct, and to "manage for industrial integrity" in the words of L.S. Paine quoted above. (Webster's definition of integrity: firm adherence to a code of especially moral or artistic values; incorruptibility. Antonym: duplicity), who provided the comparison below of the organizational consequence of a compliance-based approach to one aimed at integrity (as stated earlier, when dealing with people the word policy should be used rather than strategy).

Characteristics of Compliance Strategy		**Characteristics of Integrity Strategy**	
Ethos	conformity with externally imposed standards	Ethos	self-governance according to chosen standards
Objective	prevent criminal misconduct	Objective	enable responsible conduct
Leadership	lawyer driven	Leadership	management driven with aid of lawyers, HR, others
Methods	education, reduced discretion, auditing and controls, penalties	Methods	education, leadership, accountability, organizational systems and decision processes, auditing and controls, penalties
Behavioral Assumptions	autonomous beings guided by material self-interest	Behavioral Assumptions	social beings guided by material self-interest, values, ideals, peers

The sequence of steps to make the changes are obvious: (a) formalize the desired organizational values and standards and draw up the code with the participation of a representative group of organizational personnel (for their commitment and ownership); (b) set up the systems and procedures for auditing, monitoring, reporting violations, penalties, and periodic review of methods of prevention; (c) plan and implement an effective training program.

Recall that substantial material was supplied by Chapter 5 for (a) with its "Criteria for Moral Decisions" on page 176 and for (b) the Toffler advice on page 177 followed by the Gellermann et al. "Five-Step Model for Ethical Thought (p. 186, w)." Also, it has been found that (b) is best achieved by setting up an ethics officer to manage the program and act as an ombudsperson, a steering committee of top executives and rotating middle managers to oversee the ethics office, and the very conscientious have a board ethics committee overseeing the steering committee.

One ethicist packaged it all in three parts this way back in 1984:[6]

1. **The code development**: have a committee of representative members in each major unit prepare a code of ethics for the unit based on its own operating needs; integrate them for the larger organization by a participative process that will produce a code all personnel will support.
2. **Undertake training activities** that will establish, without preaching, the acceptability of moral discourse at work to aid clear thinking about principles and their application to problems encountered; for example, roundtable discussions at all levels with top management and professional visits to discuss values, current dilemmas, options, guidelines.
3. Set up a **permanent policy or steering committee** in each major unit that rotates membership among mature managers and non-managers (functioning as sub-committee to the HR Management Committee); its responsibilities:
    a. managing the training program and ensuring maintenance by periodic discussion groups mixing organizational levels (administered by HRD);
    b. monitoring code compliance (with enforcement authority);
    c. acting as appeals board (in the absence of a "Due Process" described ahead).

d. institute a "hot line" for advice and complaints of questionable behavior (Raytheon Corporation's receives some 100 calls a month).

Interestingly, General Dynamics planned and implemented a complete program along these lines shortly after its debacle with DOD on ethics in 1984, the plan requiring seminars for all of its 100,000 employees, an headquarters steering committee headed by two VPs to oversee the program, an ethics program director at each GD division whom employees were encouraged to contact on violations, plus a committee of outside directors to oversee the whole process. Three provisions in the ethics code: managers cannot give or accept gifts however small, whistle blowers are guaranteed protection and rewarded, violators are guaranteed sanctions up to discharge and referral for criminal prosecution.[7] Paine's 1994 article quoted described an identical program that was set up subsequently by Martin Marietta after its billing troubles with DOD.

And in spite of the pessimism in footnote b there's been commendable progress across industry among at least the majors. Quoting the Fortune in reference #4, a 1992 survey of the Fortune 1000 showed that over 40 percent hold ethics workshops and seminars and some 200 have appointed vice-president ethics officers; and the article summed up the motivation with: "Successful enterprises are inevitably based on a network of trust binding management, employees, shareholders, lenders, suppliers and customers... When companies slip into shoddy practices these crucial relationships start to deteriorate. Eventually a kind of moral rot can set in which stifles even innovation throughout the company."[8]

Needless to say at this point however, even the most comprehensive of programs designed like the General Dynamics one will not significantly improve the culture, the assumptions and associated behavior. toward the "integrity" culture pictured above if it is a serious problem blocking the needed improvement. If that's the case. it would of course be necessary to start an on-going behavior change program in advance, applying appropriate OD interventions from Chapters 18 and 19, and a crucial factor would be the preparation of "the basic human resources policy" if it hasn't already been done.

The basic human resources policy. To be sound, realistic, cover all bases, and be meaningful to all, it must understandably involve a complex combination of philosophy, values, psychology, organization behavior, management technology, and economics— with climate and culture improvement basic targets.

More and more CEOs are beginning to realize the organizational competitive advantage of managing them well, that given the growing equality of technical competence (marketing, finance, manufacturing, etc.) across all industries, they are truly keys to the performance differences that can provide the desired competitive margin, that they are a main determinants, as shown through these chapters, of goal levels, decision quality, decision acceptance, behavior norms, the quality of organizational life, all the human factors that decide the performance level of their technical abilities; and of course the formal written HR policy is (can be) a crucial influence.

Exhibit 7 in the appendix on page 1224 provides a helpful framework that can be used to tailor the policy to the chief executive's own views.[9] Though an excellent policy statement itself and well ahead of its time when prepared, it is not recommended as is. A number of improvements are possible, and especially important, CEOs should think through each issue and decision to better assure their commitment the policy has to have.

As said in Chapter 18, it is the top HRD executive's obligation to recommend such a policy, but it must be a reiterative process of refinement of an HRD draft between the two, in which the CEO crystallizes his or her own concepts with the aid of the discussions.

Noteworthy about Exhibit 7 is the scope of issues covered, befitting a master policy intended to guide associated subpolicies needed to implement it and all related policy-making down the line; every manager does some, much of it informally. Some points that seem particularly commendable:

- A section for each of the basic human parts of an organization: the larger organization, the units, the superior-subordinate relationships, the individual, and the special situation, the union.

- The first two sections (IA and B) clearly emphasizing climate ("culture" should be added) as the overall goal, plus the leadership characteristics best able to create and maintain the desired culture and climate: Theory Y, ethics along the lines of page 176, intrinsic satisfaction, participation, leadership development, technical-social integration, and leadership that, with Theory Y in mind and intent on closing the I-O gap (p. xxiii), is flexible to the demands of the situation.
- The stress on valuing and managing "the whole person," a matter of interpersonal attitude as well as job enrichment.
- Top management status assigned to the head of HRD (VI), and the personnel function raised to an important responsibility of every manager.

It can be seen from a reading of it that it does express broadly the principles that can guide the subpolicies for the operating and HR systems past chapters have described:

Values (humanistic)	Promotion
Communication	Participation
Motivation	Career planning
Appraisal	Leadership development
Selection	Succession
Compensation	

But it still behooves CEOs to make sure their leadership development programs fill in the details as desired. For example, items IIIA2 and IIIB1 briefly express the organization's goals and stand on employee *rights* and *justice*, but they will plainly remain no more than wishful thinking if they aren't spelled out and backed up with an effective administrative system.

Unfortunately, those brief expressions themselves still disturb most upper executives as opening the door to a stream of threats to their ability to manage, that they are actually a threat to the entire free enterprise system. But the following will demonstrate they are neither, that in truth, taking action on them is of major importance to the viability of the entire economic system in the years ahead as our society's standards continually rise.

Their absence in all but a few progressive firms has been fittingly labeled the "black hole" of organizations,[d] correctly connoting not only the devastating effect it has on abused employees but the organization-wide negative motivation the absence creates. It also suggests the ultimate consequence to the image of organizational life in general as well as in specific if the hole is not eradicated. The requisites for doing it, carrying forward the best thinking of philosophy and science (Chapter 5), can most easily be explained by dividing it into three parts: rights, constitutionalism, and justice:

Rights[e]

Recall that the first five criteria for moral decisions on page 176 concern the rights of others. The traditional fears of managements regarding them are certainly partly due to the centuries of the master-servant relationship described in Chapter 11, a condition and attitude solidly embedded in common law, reinforcing the believed need for it. To this day "the law has adhered to the age-old rule that all employers may dismiss their employees at will... for no cause, or even for cause *morally wrong*, without being thereby guilty of legal wrong,[f] a license that has of course been extended to a wide variety of injustices and abuses short of as well as including dismissal.[g]

It's no wonder that management through command, obedience and fear with all its subtleties is still the dominant mode, and that top managements still thoughtlessly persist in promoting the foolish idea that it as the top authority is always right. Those executives quick to deny it need but reflect what happens to a manager who openly disagrees with a top policy, the blackballing actions that are set in motion to force resignation, the non-person wipeout that follows (which even happened to this author).

The conditioning to this mode has in fact been so thorough that the average older manager, most of whom have been numbed by the amount of humiliation they've taken from it, has already lost sight of what's wrong, that from 9 to 5 all of one's constitutional rights as a citizen are suspended: (a) freedom of speech, (b) freedom of conscience, (c) the right to privacy, (d) freedom from defamation,

(e) freedom from sexual harrassment, and(f) the right to due process.

The infringement is commonly further extended to losses of freedom off-the-job by restrictions on activities that have no bearing on the organization or performance. For the others—

Freedom of speech. In organizations it refers to the right to criticize (vocally or in print) any actions or policies of management or superiors that are believed illegal, immoral, unsafe or irresponsible and to do so without being penalized in any way.

Some call it "whistleblowing," others "ratting " About 14 million in public service in the U.S are protected by law, but about 80 million non-union employees (all levels) are not, and the importance to society of this omission is insufficiently appreciated.

For example, a person is taught in school that testifying in court against a crime is a duty of citizenship, but is prevented from doing it in an organization when they see the violations of the law and morality that take place—defalcations, theft, bribery, unsafeness of products, lying and all the injustices. Besides the costs of non-disclosure, how can a society allow the silencing of the truth on-the-job without getting a carryover of reluctance to speak up off-the-job? The chronic non-involvement.

Importantly, the United States Sentencing Commission, the agency of the judiciary cited above, has now established strong guidelines also for the uniform sentencing by federal judges of corporations, executives and all organizations on violations covering banking, securities dealings, fraud, antitrust, work safety, etc., moreover, changing them from felonies to criminal acts that can send executives to jail and have mandated fines exceeding $500 million—all of which violations must still rely in most cases on whistleblowing for exposure.

Nevertheless, few employees need to be told that whistleblowing can still be risky in spite of the laws and/or a good well-run program; but it doesn't have to be if you know how to go about it. Some advice presented in Forbes magazine:[11]

First, be aware of your own liability. If as a manager, say of sales, you know of a subordinate bribing a PA and do nothing, you too are breaking the law, as is any employee who knows of a co-worker's wrongdoing and remains silent (an employee at CBS found later to have lied about it was fired and had no recourse).

Second, even where the policy is to protect those who do "you never know who else might be involved (besides the one you're exposing) or how internal politics might twist events," Forbes warned, and only a few states will back you up if you're correct, are fired and sue; we're reminded again that in a number of states the employer's right to fire "at will" is still the law.

The wise approach is almost always one of anonymity, but still, if the firm has an ombudsperson who, or system that, promises it, find out who the person you speak to reports to and gauge the possibility of the superior's involvement. You might also be promised anonymity by the company's internal lawyer, but in either case, one can be sure of safety only for culprits up to middle management. When the person is important to the firm you're apt to get no more than lip service and later feel some heat. On all higher-ups go to an outside lawyer for guidance. The SEC will be glad to listen, but be absolutely sure of your facts should you be requested to testify.

Third, ask yourself could it do any good to talk to the person, calmly stressing the damage to the company; it may work if you point out that the misdemeanor is being noticed by others (adding that as a consequence, retaliation against you alone would not be a defense) But don't unless you consider the person a basically friendly type.

Under any circumstance, you must build a case and support with evidence of the wrongdoing. Whether or not proof is available, keep a journal with dates, details, your actions in alerting management or the board and their refusal to investigate and act. A list of caveats (from *Business Week*, 6/3/91, p. 138): Do not use the media; they're always looking for a juicy story of malfeasance, can sorely distort your tale, can get you into serious trouble with your whole industry. Keep in mind that the company can sue you for theft of confidential documents you use in your evidence (but not if it's proof of illegal activity). Know the state laws on false claims, libel, and limits on damages if you're wrongfully fired (e.g., no punitive damages). Know whether or not the action done is in fact permissible via a legal technicality. Know if the state requires special procedures to sue for wrongful dismissal. List the worst-case scenario of possible damages to yourself in the event that you are dismissed, and talk it over with your family. The best initial move when you're thinking of doing it: find a lawyer with white-collar crime experience. He/she can contact your firm for you, preserve your anonymity, negotiate a deal with authorities if it should be necessary. For more information, contact Trial Lawyers for Public Justice, 2000 P Street, N. W., Suite 611, Washington, DC 20036; 1-202-463-8600.

Naturally, organizations themselves should facilitate whistleblowing for their own good and do all they can to remove the fears, starting by mandating free speech across-the-board as spelled out by David Ewing below, the only restrictions being those implied in any employment agreement to refrain from mischievous, malicious, or inane interference, obstructions, or disclosures that are inimical to the welfare of the organization's legitimate business. No employee:[12]

1. should have a right to divulge information about legal and ethical plans, practices, operations, inventions and other matters that the organization must keep confidential in order to do its job in an efficient manner;

2. should have a right to make personal accusations or slurs which are irrelevant to questions about policies and actions that seem illegal or irresponsible;

3. should be entitled to disrupt an organization or hurt its morale by making speeches and accusations that do not reflect a conviction that wrong is being done;

4. should be entitled to rail against the competence of a supervisor or senior manager to make everyday work decisions that have nothing to do with the legality, morality or responsibility of management actions;

5. should be entitled to object to discharge, transfer, or demotion, no matter what he has said about the organization or how he has said it, if management can demonstrate that unsatisfactory performance or violation of a code of conduct was the reason for its action.

These negatives however should not cloud the basic issue, the importance of an organization-wide norm of telling the truth, blowing the whistle only being with regard to blatant immoral situations. Indeed the norm has to be encouraged in every way to avoid the condition Argyris described on page 222 (that intelligent managers know, if you can't tell the truth in an organization it's worthless to put up with the organization), and, if effective leadership is at all an organizational objective. A little thought on it makes the reason quite obvious: the unyielding linkage of truthfulness, executive integrity (consistent honesty), trust, and followership.[h]

Freedom of conscience—another dimension of it. As David Ewing said in his superb book on rights and justice quoted above, thousands of organizations maintain high ethical standards and thousands more try, but in even the best (and often in the worst) there are times when temptation wins, judgments go awry, evil prevails (an accountant is asked to falsify the records, a secretary to submit to sex), and the absolute power of the boss makes refusal to do his or her bidding tantamount to asking for a pink slip.

Subordinates furthermore commonly view the conduct of their superiors as either sanctioned or winked at by the management above, so for those above who don't condone such behavior, especially the CEO, there are few issues more important than to establish and make well known a strong policy and system that protects the troubled and unwilling.

Of course, many situations can occur in which both parties have a valid argument or there are significant differences of conscience-sensitivity. The rules can be fair to both by allowing the employee to refuse (assuming a sincere, reasonable objection), the superior to ask another to do it (time may be of the essence), and the superior to challenge the disobedience later in a hearing. The integrity of the boss should be able to keep most of such incidents separated from the simple non-compliance examined in Chapter 11; the hearings can handle the latter also.

The right to privacy. The IBM policies on privacy described in Chapter 17 provide as fine a model as can be found covering all the important issues:

> data collection
> internal access (who to what)
> external access (who to what)
> data removal and when
> desk, files and locker search
> tapping of phones[i]
> polygraphing (none allowed)
> personality tests[j]

Also, three points as to their management were particularly impressive: the top management commitment to them, their inclusion in the management training of everyone entering management, and the check on adherence through the periodic employee opinion surveys.

Most superior-subordinate problems are in fact resolved in their performance review meetings, and for those that are not or any other complaints, everyone has the right of appeal through the "open door" grievance system described ahead.

Freedom from defamation.[k] After subordinates resign, are discharged or are transferred, superiors are often tempted to "knock" or defame them when prospective employers ask for references; whether it is guilt, vindictiveness, callousness or otherwise, ego needs seem to dominate fairness, honesty and judgment. And it's well known that whole organizations, even industries connive in blacklisting a person who's offended them or denigrated their policies, actions or powerful personalities.

The laws of many states now protect employees from such treatment, and most large organizations prohibit reference responses over the phone, require that requests be made and answered by mail to ensure careful wording. Nevertheless, a policy is still needed to make clear the organization's stand and to encourage ethical behavior. (Also see footnote i on page 384).

Freedom from sexual harassment. There's still considerable confusion on how to define the act. Essentially it's pressure for sexual favors, deliberate touching, letters, phone calls or excessive asking for dates, lewd jokes, sexual remarks; and a 1986 Supreme Court decision has added verbal or physical conduct that creates an intimidating, hostile or offensive work environment or unreasonably interferes with an employee's job performance... the antithesis nicely phrased in the title of DuPont's training seminar to eliminate it: "A Matter of Respect." The Civil Rights Act of 1991 moreover ensured the victim's right to trial by jury and compensation with punitive damages up to $300,000.

The ugly and demoralizing Anita Hill/Clarence Thomas senate hearing certainly highlighted strongly the issue and prompted many large firms to take at least some preventive actions. In general there's a growing realization that the problem not only exists but is pervasive, but the present states of affairs is still shameful:

- *Time* reports that 90 percent of the Fortune 500 have had to deal with complaints in the last year (1992);
- A National Association of Female Executive's survey found that 60 percent of its 607 respondents had experienced sexual harassment since the hearings; more than half said their firms hadn't addressed the problem;
- The NOW Legal Defense Fund has stated that there has been no change in corporate behavior;
- And it can even be a problem with customers and clients: a *National Law Journal* survey of 900 female attorneys found that 10 percent of them had received pressure for dates, 9 percent complained of offensive touching, cornering, pinching, 4 percent directly for sex.

The common attitude has been to issue a policy statement and institute a pitiful token one-hour program on gender awareness as a defense in suits... which clearly doesn't face up to the total cost, not only of litigation but absenteeism, sickness, downtime, the costs of replacing the departed. And of course in letting complaints go public to a court everyone loses.

There are two steps to dealing with it effectively as DuPont has done: curb it by:

- drafting and circulating a strong policy defining it and warning about punishment;
- remind employees periodically that top management is committed to fighting it;

- hold sensitizing seminars for all with men and women together, using videos, lectures and role playing;
- set up dispute-resolution procedures that permit private, confidential complaint, bypassing immediate supervisors (often the alleged offenders).

And second, resolve the disputes by:

- investigating claims immediately and thoroughly regardless of level involved;
- retain confidentiality;
- when a complaint is found valid, apply the appropriate discipline quickly, starting with a warning letter leading to demotion, suspension, transfer or firing.
- ensure no retaliation against the complainant regardless of the outcome.

Other actions by a number of firms:

- a 24-hour hotline to call in for advice and support (e.g , at DuPont, AT&T, Honeywell);
- a complaint counselor or ombudsperson who first contacts the accused immediately, then may ask the employer to set up an independent investigator or mediator, the conclusion non-binding on the employer, or a panel of peers;
- a requirement that complaints go first to one's superior unless the person is involved, or if uncomfortable about it then to the complaint counselor;
- posters in conspicuous places and "handbooks" distributed to all employees

It seems wise to try to somehow educate the women (by in-house memo?) about the three simplest ways to nip an offense in the bud:

- tell the person bluntly to stop—it has been found to work 61 percent of the time;
- say you'll tell other colleagues—effective 55 percent of the time;

- pretend to ignore it—usually doesn't work.

Indeed, when a victim has called on the complaint counselor at AT&T, one of the first questions asked is "did you tell the person you didn't like it, and how many times?"

Companies would be wise to publish on their bulletin boards or in their newsletters the November 1993 quick decision of the Supreme Court that stated "an employer has broken the law if a "reasonable person" would find the workplace so filled with sexual improprieties that it had become a hostile and abusive environment."

Interestingly, when employees have been caught in the act after going through seemingly good programs, it's almost always been found to be in firms with indifferent management attitude and/ or poor handling of complaints or weak censure, and all too often there's been increasing leniency up the ladder to but a frown around the top.

The right to due process. The larger the organization the greater of course will be, for that organization, the number of managers who don't agree with entitlement to some of these rights, but also there are many occasions, we know, when those who do agree will violate them due to differences of values, opinion or interpretation. And there are too the violations out of ignorance, frustration, pressures, fatigue, stupidity, indifference and power abuse. To rely on faith or hope that rights will be honored by managers after only telling them the policy would obviously be foolhardy.

Furthermore, if these issues are truly rights, employees must be entitled to enforcement, which means a right to a hearing and to redress not only for the violations themselves but also for a superior's retribution against one for having asserted a right. Constitutionalism is the solution.

Constitutionalism

The word means no more than adherence to the principle of constitutional government, for example those established in Philadelphia in 1776. Overcoming our forefathers' tradition of totalitarianism within business and government organizations, however, is only now getting under way.

The trade unions started organizational constitutionalism after World War II when they began to succeed in forcing many firms to adjudicate the economic grievances of members. Today virtually every collective bargaining contract requires compulsory arbitration for such disputes during the period of the contract— over 18 million blue collar workers and 3 million professionals.

But not until the 1960s did the unions and the arbitrators take an interest in *civil rights.* The rising level of education and expectations of union members, along with the rest of society, began to make them more acutely aware of the rights issues, and we have seen not only the addition of rights rulings in arbitration but new legislation covering a variety of areas on the perimeter, on related subjects such as equal opportunity, health and pension protection, then close behind, laws on managerial responsibility for workplace safety, product safety, and pollution of the environment.

And in case any executives might think the "worst" is over, they might note that a trend was identified back in the 1970s, though temporarily slowed by conservative administrations in the 1980s, promises much more, to parallel the spreading public consciousness of values and the quality of life for everyone. In addition to the increasing spread of the auto industry's QWL programs described in Chapter 13, we have the evidence as long ago as a 1977 *Harvard Business Review* survey that, in comparing its 1958 responses of managers with a similar one in 1971, found the following encouraging developments:[13,1]

—96 percent would reinstate a fired conscientious objector;
—most privacy issues were overwhelmingly supported;
—a majority would protect whistle blowers and dissidents;
—some 75 percent felt an employee is entitled to know why he or she is fired;
—the majority no longer believed the corporation serves only stockholder interests; they agreed with the statement that it should "serve as fairly and equitably as it can the interests of four sometimes competing groups—owners, employees, customers, and the public."

One need only look at the labor law record to be reminded of the pattern law-making follows: the growing public awareness of managerial abuse building a constituency for controls the law makers soon have to acknowledge and produce, the pattern of all labor law since the Wagner Act, and it's now a growing one on management behavior issues also. Additionally, the resort to the courts by employees is clearly exploding, each case costing companies in the tens of thousands and each ruling helping to compile a "common law" in support of the individual.

The handwriting would seem to be on the wall. The efforts of some individual CEOs may indeed be noble, but they must also lead their industry associations into a massive upgrading of attitude, values and behavior to affect the pattern; there's plenty to gain by doing so and an awful lot to lose by not; managements will:

- forestall ill-conceived legislation that hostile forces may produce,
- avoid the loss of needed ethical decision discretion,
- eliminate the high legal defense costs,
- avoid the unionization of lower and middle management that often follows abusive treatment and lack of response to needs,
- improve superior-subordinate relations, employee performance, intrinsic satisfactions, and pride in the organization.

The two instruments needed to succeed: a bill of rights and a due process enforcement system.

A bill of rights. The constitution of the U.S.S.R. up to 1991 that promised many of the human rights our own does is a convincing example of how important the philosophy of the leadership is to such a document's integrity. Their authoritarianism made it no more than fraudulent propaganda. A management that tries similarly to use one as window-dressing will gain the same disrespect free people around the world accorded the Kremlin. It would be better not to publish one until ready to back it up.

Even among those executives who have genuinely democratic views however, there commonly are objections to a bill of rights due to fears of the consequences, for example, that one would:[m]

- be a threat to free enterprise's hierarchy of authority, already limited by collective bargaining and other laws;
- reduce a superior's authority to get the job done;
- reduce a superior's authority to induce compliance on the unpleasant work that has to be done;
- cause a mountain of paperwork, lower efficiency, higher costs, lost time;
- result in higher product prices and lower profits.

But they need only analyze the true nature and intent of a bill, and all of them will evaporate. At the same time, a few justified fears are not undesirable: fears of the revelation of poor management, malfeasance or misbehavior. The only time there's added work or costs is when rights have been violated; otherwise:

—no managerial authority is transferred to employees,
—a bill does not deal with economic matters,
—there is no involvement in or voting on managerial decisions (it has no relationship to the Swedish or German worker democracy),
—no management work is added—a bill should only be "don'ts,"
—there are no limitations placed on the ability to manage the legitimate affairs of the organization; it only rules against abusive treatment of employees.

And a bill does set standards of behavior that the honorable will know ought to be adhered to and the less than honorable will be less ready to disregard.

To those few organizations in which the top management already does model and encourage the recommended regard for these issues, it may seem superfluous to publish a bill, but their boards only need ask, will subsequent CEO's have the same philosophy or give it the sustained support it has to have?

Moreover, a bill not only clarifies and spreads the policy news but makes it very difficult to regress or engage in exceptions without a great deal of objection.

David Ewing has supplied an excellent set of minimum precepts, reproduced in Figure 21.3, that, like the human resources policy in Exhibit 7, can be used as a base to build on. He called it a "working paper," reminding that different industries, even companies, may have to have differences of wording.[14]

His suggestions for drafting one's own, which suggestions the Figure illustrates, merit consideration:

- make each statement an imperative (imperatives are unequivocal, normatives are weak),
- make them negative "don'ts" (they are not delegations of power),
- make the total bill of rights succinct (start simple and build over time),
- make the English easy to understand (not legalese),
- be sure each imperative is enforceable.

Due process. Ewing's "comments" on each of the nine rights in Figure 21.3 should be read by anyone planning a bill,[n] but others too will find that those he made on #9, due process, can clear up doubts about its seeming vagueness.[15]

This very important right is the organizational equivalent of due process of law as we know it in political and community life. Without due process in a company or agency, the rights in this bill would all have to be enforced by outside courts and tribunals, which is expensive for society as well as time-consuming for the employees who are required to appear as complainants and witnesses. The nature of a "fair hearing" is purposely left undefined here so that different approaches can be tried, expanded and adapted to changing needs and conditions.

Note that the findings of the investigating official or group are not binding on top management. This would put an unfair burden on an ombudsperson or arbitrator, if one of them is the investigator. Yet the employee is protected. If management rejects a finding of unfair treatment and then the employee goes to court, the investigator's statement will weigh against management in the trial. As a practical matter, therefore, employers will not want to buck the investigator-referee unless they fervently disagree with the findings.

EMPLOYEE BILL OF RIGHTS
(a preliminary working paper)

1.   No organization or manager shall discharge, demote, or in other ways discriminate against any employee who criticizes, in speech or press, the ethics, legality, or social responsibility of management actions.

2.   No employee shall be penalized for engaging in outside activities of his or her choice after working hours, whether political, economic, civic, or cultural, nor for buying products and services of his or her choice for personal use, nor for expressing or encouraging views contrary to top management's on political, economic, and social issues.

3.   No organization or manager shall penalize an employee for refusing to carry out a directive that violates common norms of morality.

4.   No organization shall allow audio or visual recordings of an employee's conversations or actions to be made without his or her prior knowledge and consent. Nor may an organization require an employee or applicant to take personality tests, polygraph examinations, or other tests that constitute, in his opinion, an invasion of privacy.[p]

5.   No employee's desk, files, or locker may be examined in his or her absence by anyone but a senior manager who has sound reason to believe that the files contain information needed for a management decision that must be made in the employee's absence.

6.   No employer organization may collect and keep on file information about an employee that is not relevant and necessary for efficient management. Every employee shall have the right to inspect his or her personnel file and challenge the accuracy, relevance, or necessity of data in it, except for personal evaluations and comments by other employees which could not reasonably be obtained if confidentiality were not promised. Access to an employee's file by outside individuals and organizations shall be limited to inquiries about the essential facts of employment.

7.   No manager may communicate to prospective employers of an employee who is about to be or has been discharged gratuitous opinions that might hamper the individual in obtaining a new position.

8.   An employee who is discharged, demoted, or transferred to a less desirable job is entitled to a written statement from management of its reasons for the penalty.

9.   Every employee who feels that he or she has been penalized for asserting any right described in this bill shall be entitled to a fair hearing before an impartial official, board or arbitrator. The findings and conclusions of the hearing shall be delivered in writing to the employee and management.

Figure 21.3

Nevertheless, a due process system can become the Russian dressing warned against if it is not given the distinct characteristics needed to make it work. Ewing listed seven:[16]

1. It must be a procedure with rules to minimize subjectiveness and arbitrariness;
2. It must be visible so that potential violators know of it;
3. It must be predictably effective;
4. It must be "institutionalized," that is, part of the management system;
5. It must be perceived as equitable;
6. It must be easy to use;
7. It must apply to all employees.

And an eighth necessary to make and keep it that way is assumed: it must have the unqualified and active support of all top executives, which includes the willingness to accept rulings they do not agree with.

The 1977 HBR survey quoted earlier listed the six most popular processes in use and calibrated the percent usage of each in 1971 and 1977 as shown in Figure 21.4. The preponderance of authoritarianism among organizations is once again seen in the fact that even among these select leaders (HBR subscribers) and where there is some conscience about rights, the preponderance of them concede only the weakest procedures, the bottom two. It's common knowledge that because of the arbitrators' bias and the possibility of feedback to one's superior, employees have to be truly desperate to use them. But of course the same feelings will arise about poorly supported or poorly run "strong" methods.

The growing popularity, however, of the three strong processes at the top of the Figure and decline of the bottom three is more evidence of the trend, and it is interesting that the choice among the strong ones is fairly evenly balanced, suggesting that each is believed effective and that organizations tend to select the one that best fits their management philosophy and organizational culture. Some points on the top three may help in making a choice among them for one's own.

"Due Process," 1971-1977

Figure 21.4

Mechanism

Percent of companies
0%   25   50   75

Management grievance committee. — 14%, 9%

Corporate "ombudsman" or "ombudswoman." — 11%, 8%

Hearing procedure that allows employee to be represented by attorney or other person, and with a neutral company executive deciding on the evidence. — 11%, 6%

Assistant to the president or vice president who investigates grievances and reports to top management. — 11%, 14%

Personnel executive who investigates grievances and reports to top management. — 42%, 43%

Senior executive whose "door is always open" to employees who think they have been wronged. — 63%, 68%

White = 1971, Black = 1977

1158

Management grievance committee. The two main forms of this method are for the committee to be composed of uninvolved members of management selected by top management or to be a group elected by the employees; both would be a revolving permanent committee.

In either case, a feature that is important to its success is for the plaintiff to be allowed counsel, since the average employee lacks the articulateness and objectivity needed for a convincing argument and may be cowed by a panel of seniors.

Polaroid Corporation applies a provocative combination. The non-union employees (about 12,000) elect from the ranks a committee that is made responsible for representing each employee before a management committee, and any employee who loses may submit the case to an outside arbitrator.

Ombudsperson. The ombudsperson method is largely based on the fact that, if the superior's action was not immoral, both sides can usually be brought to a mutually agreeable settlement by guiding them with understanding to seeing the facts; and if the superior knows that his/her action was immoral, a fear of its getting to his or her superior may do the job. It has a surprisingly high record of achievement when managed well, so warrants a fairly full description of its two forms, *the individual* type and *the system* type... in each case the pages 1144-1146 cautions to employees on whistleblowing holding true for the present.

The ombudsperson in *the individual* type reports directly to the CEO of the organization or large sub-division but has no authority, has no position in the hierarchy, and brings problems to the CEO only as a last resort (but occasionally enough to remind managers of the relationship).

It is a job of fact gathering, listening, objective reasoning, and tactful persuasion of both sides. If the superior is unwilling to accept a fair settlement, his or her superior is approached, on up to the CEO when necessary. Grievances do not get bogged down in paperwork because the ombudsperson has little or no staff, therefore little paperwork is possible; problems have to be resolved rapidly.

Typical cases handled: employees who've been fired, demoted, undesirably transferred, passed over on a promotion, harassed to resign, given excessive overtime, denied medical payments, wronged in some way. Or it may be a non-grievance problem of "where do I stand with my superior?" or "How can I get ahead," but always of personal impact as compared to complaints about organization policies.

Confidentiality is of course vital. The ombudsperson never goes to a superior without the plaintiff's permission, and the location of the ombudsperson's office is best placed in an inconspicuous spot where entry can be made covertly if desired. Yet a widespread, clear awareness of the function is most important. As one GE ombudsperson stated:[17]

> The mere existence of the ombudsman encourages managers to be sure they can justify their actions. This preventive aspect is due largely to the high visibility the position is given, as well as to its high level organizationally— reporting directly to the top man. It would seem that trying to establish the role at a lower level or with less exposure could only result in failure.

There are also two other stipulations, and they would appear to go without saying: (1) it is not a position for an over-the-hill executive; the person has to be selected with the greatest care for a competence, independence, honesty and evenhandedness that will build a respected reputation. The record of one at Xerox seems to be a good illustration of the desired evenhandedness; he said in an interview that about 40 percent of his decisions favored the employee, 30 percent were compromises, and 30 percent went against the employee.[18]

(2) The CEO should keep in touch with the person's workload to avoid overloading that taxes quality as some have permitted. One person can usually handle about 150 cases a year, but it varies with the number of employees, the type of work, the management systems, and the authoritarianism among managers. MIT, for example, has two because of its large number of employees, as does the Aircraft Engine Group at GE.

Those who have installed the method have concluded unequivocally that it pays off in both user satisfaction and performance. The benefits listed earlier should be motivating enough for every organization to investigate it and there are at times unexpected dividends. For instance, an analysis at the above GE Group of a most common complaint, promotion selections, led to a study of the selection procedure used and the institution of their "open selection" systems, now a corporate policy.

Of course, the interpersonal benefits one can expect are limited; it will not:[19]

- Please people whose idea of justice is having their own way,
- Change managerial styles, even when they could objectively be considered wrong,
- Instill the vital need for an employee and his/her manager to be honest and open with each other.

An example of *the system* type of ombudsperson procedure is the "Private Lines" program at New England Telephone Co. described on pages 548-549. It differs from "the individual" type in that it is a staff department service, and at the telephone company it is but one in an extensive upward communication system operated by the staff; in fact, the service evolved there as a dividend of the upward system as employees sought solutions to their personal grievances through the staff.

Recall that the employees' information needs serviced were divided into the two categories of those directed to general management on the organization and its policies, concerns that had to be handled anonymously, and those that were personal grievances, most of which required disclosure (disclosure was still only with a plaintiff's permission).

IBM has separated the two into a distinct system for each. The "Speak Up" procedure described on page 550 is for the first, one in which all interrogations are kept anonymous, and the second is a pure ombudsperson system for the grievances that they call "Open Door," all of which require disclosure, confrontation being the only way such problems can be truly settled.

In the "Open Door" (no relation to the bottom mechanism in Figure 21.4) any employee with a superior-subordinate grievance who has tried unsuccessfully to settle it with the superior (the rules require this first effort) can write any senior executive of his or her own choice to set the "Open Door" procedure in motion. The response is quick and personal, followed by selection from among the management of an objective ombudsperson not involved in the dispute. The selected person goes through the same procedure as in "the individual" type, moving unresolved problems up the ladder for satisfaction, finally to the corporate CEO as last resort, and apparently many get that far.

IBM's basic rule for all investigators is particularly important to justice: start out on the side of the plaintiff, and we are told there are no aversions to making bosses uncomfortable if necessary. As a result, those who plan to fire, demote, or otherwise penalize a subordinate "learn to anticipate an immediate Open Door unless they have taken exceptional precautions to avoid it,"[20] and management training includes instruction on how to keep adequate support records which help them evaluate the wisdom of any contemplated action.

Especially admirable about the procedure is the participative character of it. Every manager is subject to involvement along with the aggrieved, that is, subject to part-time call for ombudsperson duty (a plus on one's record), subject to its rigor's if subordinates have grievances, and a potential client of the system for his or her own grievances. The motivation to be fair is strong, and apparently the cases are handled thoroughly and rapidly, always within a couple of weeks.

Both the telephone company's "Private Lines" and this one, incidentally, can be used before or after the damage. An employee may call or write (writing is required at IBM) immediately when threatened by a perceived injustice and avoid much unnecessary misery that can arise from being too late.

The hearing procedure. This is also called the "informal court." An impartial executive, usually the head of HRD, is the judge, another executive is the "attorney" for the company, a third argues in behalf of the plaintiff, and other employees who may contribute are asked to be present. The case is formally recorded with copies to the parties, one to the CEO and one to the files.

Company managers at times object to the system and try to denigrate it, feeling it's an infringement on their prerogatives, but probably no more so than the same persons would about any other due process procedure. What is important is that aggrieved employees get a quick hearing (less than 2 weeks) and generally a fair judgement as compared to letting it fester, taking it to a formal court which can take years for a settlement, or going through a formal arbitrator that averages 3-6 months.

Lastly for this section on due process, top managements of organizations operated by humanist principles—therefore having participative and integrative management, open personnel systems and OD—might conclude that there is no need for such a process, that the internal openness, trust and collaborative management of the culture obviate it. However, in addition to the risk of regression by the next administration, as mentioned for the bill of rights, two realities make it indispensable regardless of the management system in force:

- In spite of the best intentions of individuals, human relations are too complex for there to be no grievances or differences of opinion between superiors and subordinates, and there will always be some superiors who are poor at interpersonal skills, and those with the best unable to handle some situations.
- There will always be a *basic* difference of goals between the individual and the organization (the matrix on page 231) that has to be reconciled, and, the "control" role responsibility of leadership will always include some behavior control, discipline, rules, and penalties for infraction; conflicts of perceived injustice requiring a third party are over time inescapable.

Justice°

The astronomy analogy, the "black hole" of organizational life, is certainly an apt description. Sages have long said that human rights are essential to a free people and to individual dignity, but even a discussion of them is taboo in most organizations.

An employee's existence is truly a dichotomy—freedom in the community and tyranny at work—and no matter how benevolent the management team, the *power to* tyrannize for lack of a balancing system of justice will itself always be demeaning and a mark against the organization (and CEO) as not a genuinely humane one.

A widespread institution of systems of justice is going to be necessary to retain the hierarchical management system's acceptability as society's standards of behavior continue to rise. The dismal decline in public regard for authority and leadership in business and government but manifests the growing awareness of the immorality of a lot of managerial behavior, and it's only a short step to blaming the whole system and to the calamity that would follow.

The trend must and can be reversed, and internal constitutionalism is fundamental to getting it started. The reasons to get moving on it are clear enough, and it is patently no threat to a manager's or organization's ability to manage; they both can only gain. We need but note that the firms that do try to ensure justice for their people (like IBM, GE and Xerox) are usually also very profitable and among the toughest competitors on their product lines.

A person with a true sense of justice, though, realizes that there's more to organizational justice than constitutionalism. It's quite possible for a management—for instance, one with an asocial attitude—to install a bill of rights and due process and yet be aversive. Organizational justice is a product of the total management system for which constitutionalism provides but a subsystem, one covering only standards and enforcement for employee rights, and, one that management may not be committed to.

There are five basic requisites, along with the commitment, of *a total system of justice*:

- Participative management (i.e., the System 4 goals)
- Open personnel systems (the four listed on page 379)
- Organization development (Chapters 18 and 19)
- Constitutionalism (the principles of justice and employee rights)
- A humanistic basic human resources policy.

Any knowledgeable traditionalist can, however, present a pretty good argument that the organization doesn't really have to go to all that trouble (and would probably add "risk") to get satisfactory performance and profit. The open personnel systems alone highlight conditions (and inequities) that take a lot of energy and time to handle and moreover reduce one's control over controversial decisions or issues that can be sustainted with closed ones.

Virtually all of the Fortune 500 can be used to illustrate the point. Those that are managed by System 3 can be counted on two hands; the balance are System 1 and 2; furthermore, generally only a few units within the most advanced can claim to be practicing even two of the above four. And yet all but a few earn acceptable-to-good profits.

However, they are all capitalizing successfully on outstanding advantages with regard to size, resources, technology, markets, developed image, or unique assets that are not necessarily long-lasting.

An especially interesting example is IBM, because it had succeeded quantitatively up through the 80s beyond any early stockholder's fondest dream, had done so with essentially a System 2 and only half of one of the four factors, constitutionalism without the bill of rights.

Looking at its history to see how it all happened, one finds it a consequence of a fortunate coincidence: a unique personality, philosophy and competence in the person of Thomas Watson, Sr., and a circumstance, one of a company in an industry ready to take off—a combination that led to a steady multiplication of the competence over time and to the organization's astounding growth.[p]

It's a lucid illustration of the importance of philosophy even if it has flaws. Hired in 1914 at age 40 (after 21 years under John Patterson at NCR) to turn around a small group of faltering firms called The Computing Tabulating Recording Company, Watson had already developed a singular commitment to six tenets that he demanded of all his managers and employees:

1. treat every individual with dignity and respect,
2. do well every job assigned,

3. appear neatly dressed,
4. be clean, "forthright" (honest) and optimistic,
5. be obedient,
6. be loyal

And to this day, the norms, managerial behavior and virtually all personnel policies can still be traced to one or more of them. Its systems of justice and communication were clear attempts to reflect the first; its training (twice that of any other computer company) was dedicated to the second; the stories, jokes and edicts about the third and fourth are legend; and for the importance of the last two, young managers needed only observe those who got ahead.

What evolved was a sophisticated paternalism that satisfied the most ambitious material hopes of every recruit who would work hard and conform, providing personal growth, advancement, munificent reward.

The competitive advantages gained by this combination of benevolence, traditional management and industry opportunity are of course well known to every follower of business news; the more obvious ones:

- such a dominant leadership in many of the industry's technologies that its products and services often set their worldwide standards;
- a size and growth rate that provided a continuous enormous number of openings and opportunities to move up;
- the resources and profitability to maintain the highest pay rates in most functions;
- the preponderant share of the market in the U.S. such that with its technological leadership, every door was open to IBM salespeople if just to find out what's going on in the industry;
- an image because of these that appeals strongly to the pick of competent upward-mobile prospects on the outside looking in.

But less obvious was the management system that evolved and was so badly misread until recently by analysts blinded by the above picture. Worse, it seemed to have had the same effect on the management itself, both undoubtedly influenced by the old saw that "you can't argue with success," its prolonged success producing a self-satisfaction and arrogance that precluded the necessary flexibility to adapt to the rapidly changing environment. The IBM story is a prime illustration of the closeness or inseparability of the culture, climate, technical, and social components of an organization. Mismanagement of any one of them will affect the others and performance negatively.

Indeed any firm need but a cursory look at what on the social (HR) alone was missing and compare it with their own for a good guess, if similar, at their own future down the road (the following from research by the author and a comprehensive interview in 1987 of an IBM human resources executive):

- No "open selection;" each superior had total "candidate" and "career" authority over subordinates (p. 868).
- Complete pay secrecy (pages 318-320 for the consequences).
- No formal career planning, further reinforcing superiors' control.
- No participation on individual management development planning; one headquarters planned program fits all: orientation on entry, functional courses on reaching middle management, executive courses at universities for a select few on entering the top group (there seemed to be nothing on values, philosophy or climate, and for interpersonal skills only the "modeling" technique on page 1095).
- No OD department or OD personnel, though opinion-climate surveys were conducted every 18-24 months for managers to review with subordinates, a measure of collaborative management to the extent that the managers were open to feedback and decision influence.
- The leadership behavior norm: "be firm, directive and fair" with a laissez-faire policy on leadership style. Different styles discussed in training, none promoted; authoritarianism okay it the superior thinks it works.
- The basic human resources policy (not formalized) was composed of three parts instead of the five on pages 1224-1227:

Authority—the emphasis on a combination of position power and management technology competence.

Communication—"Speak Up" (page 550), the periodic employee surveys, many internal publications.

Constitutionalism—the policy of respect for private rights and the "Open Door" ombudsperson due process system (page 1160), but no bill or rights.

Undoubtedly, the communication and constitutionalism were important to making the authority approach tolerable, but consider too the extent to which the competitive advantages had contributed to the tolerance; for example:

- The corporate image for growth opportunity plus fast advancement and top pay attracted and retained hard-driving, single-minded upwardmobiles, a type well known for willingness to take orders for such rewards.
- The top pay and fast movement minimized problems and complaints about pay secrecy.
- The fast movement itself minimized complaints about the selection system (the superiors' "career authority") and the absence of career planning.

What it added up to was high attention to material needs, little to the psychological, and getting away with the neglect. True, those on the move were being substantially satisfied on their aspirations for attention, recognition and self-actualization, but it can hardly be claimed for the other 90 percent of the white collar personnel (not to mention the blue), and no one had the benefits of the missing factors.

There is no question that for superiors with traditional values and their misconceptions the three italicized components above are in the short run a lot easier to manage than the five. No time needs to be "wasted," as traditionalists see it, on integration, the open systems, and OD, and it may have been that the company felt its communication and degree of constitutionalism with its Open Door sufficiently filled any need for participation.

The Open Door, though, only dealt with grievances, the communication that occurred was predominantly one-way with minimal power-sharing, and the directive attitude restricted the nature, degree, and reception of the feedback that might occur. In *The Change Managers* by Kanter a Hewlett-Packard executive was quoted in 1982, describing the "progressiveness in the treatment of people" of his firm, comparing it with "Chipco" and IBM on a scale of 10: "Chipco," he said, "would be rated 10, H-P 4 and IBM 1." "Chipco" was used in the book to disguise the real name of another well-known large computer firm.[22]

So here you had the technologically most advanced firm in the country, "one of the great technical treasures of the world" (from Nobel winner Lederberg), in an abysmal decline largely due to a dated authoritarian attitude, unable any longer to adapt to and cope with the greatly increased pace of technological development, resulting in a horrendous bureaucracy and unworkable type of centralized decision-making (e g., all major product and pricing decisions made by the top Corporate Management Committee).

By the time Louis V. Gerstner was brought in (August 1992) the weaknesses had apparently become apparent to everyone in industry but itself. As listed by the press: a company choking on its culture, arrogance and misguided strategies, preoccupied with internal processes, a dysfunctional company with huge disproportionate costs. $28 billion had been written off since 1986, over 120,000 of its 250,000 employees laid off, and its stock price had declined 75 percent by 1992.

Gerstner's own added findings on the internal in his first 6 months (well qualified to judge: a prominent McKinsey consultant, former president of American Express and CEO of RJR Nabisco): compensation, data processing and administration systems a mess, company hamstrung by internal wrangling, oversight by headquarters strangling action (some deals requiring 18 signatures), "bureaucracy run amok."[q]

Fortunately, his actions and programs to date have been prodigious and highly commendable with good promise of turning the behemoth around. A sampling:[24]

- The top 24 executives told to count on working closely with him on planning and firming up down-sizing, strategic direction, and employee morale improvement.
- An 11 member top executive panel set up to find out how to get the units to work together better.
- A World Management Council of 34 IBM top leaders around the world to meet 4 to 5 times a year for review, evaluation and planning of global performance (similar to GE).
- Plans to "ignite a cultural revolution" by overhauling the IBM training and development programs (probably similar to GE after a long meet with CEO Jack Welch, hopefully instituting the "total system of justice").
- 9 task forces set up to study how to improve the information system, inventory management, purchasing, transportation, other administrative functions.
- 11 strategy task forces charged to find ways to get IBM growing again, the strategies being studied ample evidence that he and his team are finally on top of the industry's technology and direction:

Client/server computing	Other software
Multimedia and mobile computers	Semiconductors
	Distribution channels
Networking services	Competitive evaluation
Hardware architecture	Systems design, data
Software architecture	processing and
Application software	maintenance services

And in the May 1, 1995 issue of *BW* the chart below was published as an example of the progress to that date.

Perhaps a caveat should be added for CEOs who still can "buy" only one or two of the five elements of the total system of justice or think a partial effort on all five is adequate. Unfortunately, any effort so limited would seriously tax the ever-present interdependence mentioned of the culture, climate, technical and social components of an organization. There is, further, the interdependence among the five requisites of justice that supply each other mutual support.

The Score So Far
**A look at Big Blue today—
and when Louis Gerstner took over**

	1993	1995
SHARE PRICE	50	88
RETURN ON EQUITY	None (loss)	18.1%*
EMPLOYMENT	301,542	219,839**
MAINFRAMES AND MINIS	Sales and profit slump	Sales and profits up
PERSONAL COMPUTERS	No. 1 worldwide	No. 2 worldwide, No. 4 U.S.
SOFTWARE	Betting on OS/2	Betting on OS/2

*Dean Witter Reynolds, Inc., estimates   **As of the preceding December

For instance, as explained about *genuine* participation, the personal systems (pay, selection, appraisal. personal information) have to be open for it to be achieved; but then even if they are opened, how can participation gain the desired commitment to organizational goals without technical-social integration, which to be continuously applied requires OD as proposed? Moreover, how can integration occur where authoritarian attitudes and injustice are permitted?

The mutual support among the five elements is self-evident, manifesting itself particularly through the necessary mutual trust between superiors and their subordinates, such that superiors readily solicit opinions, listen, communicate, are supportive, and share power; the subordinates offer their creativity, collaboration, commitment, and the benefit of their doubts.

NOTES

a.   One industry education service firm offers a guide for preparing 106 different personnel policies alone. Note that a number of these are in fact strategies, perhaps not recognized as such 30 years ago.

b.   "Nearly every major company has put together some form of written code of ethics ranging from Exxon Corporation's one page "Policy Statement on Business Ethics" to Citicorp's 62-page booklet; a comment recently of one major corporation CEO however: "The only thing all these new ethics codes proves for sure is that every company believes that appearing to be ethical is good public relations."

c. About 30 percent of all business failures are due to dishonesty, the cost of white collar crime is about 10 times that of street crime, and see Chapter 1 for the prevalence and variety of other types of immorality.

d. First encountered by this writer in David Ewing's book, *Freedom Inside the Organization* (New York: E.P. Dutton, 1977).

e. For an excellent essay on why humans have inalienable rights and what they are: "Justice and Equality" by Gregory Vlastos in *Social Justice*, (ed.) R.B. Brandt (Englewood Cliffs, N.J.: Prentice-Hall, 1962), pp. 31-72. Reprinted in *Ethical Issues in Business*, (eds.) T. Donaldson and P.H. Werhane (Englewood Cliffs, N.J.: Prentice-Hall, 1979).

f. Quote of C.D. Stone in his excellent book on what to do about managerial immorality .

g. It has been estimated that each year over a million full-time employees, including managers, are fired without a fair hearing. However, a change seems to be slowly getting under way. A number of states now prohibit firing except for just cause, and the courts in 46 are helping workers challenge believed wrongful dismissal (called "employment-at-will" cases) Some 25,000 cases have been reported as currently pending, and of course not included are the many thousands of low level workers each year who do not sue because of the litigation costs. For the upper levels in general, "employment-at-will" is no longer a reliable corporate defense anywhere, New York even enforcing oral contracts. Advice to corporations: (a) keep good records on dismissals, give several warnings; (b) push for specific legislation because of the unpredictability of juries.

h. For useful specifics see Steven Kerr, "Integrity in Effective Leadership," in *Executive Integrity* (eds.) S. Srivastva et al (San Francisco: Jossey-Bass, 1988).

i. No tapping or taping of a person's phone conversation without permission, and no taping of a meeting without prior announcement

j. Note that behavioral authorities on the subject of personality tests agree on the impropriety of violating privacy rights, that is, asking questions not directly relevant to job performance, but they do not reject the tests in themselves. For example, standard tests of intelligence, interests, dominant-motivation (TAT), cognitive style and behavioral-fit provide important information for appraising and planning without such violations.

k. Defamation: a false statement maliciously uttered (slander) or written (libel) that tends to injure the reputation of another.

i Once more one has to keep in mind that these subscribers form a comparatively small select group of progressive managers.

m. Apologies again for repeated listings, but when dealing with a raft of facts, points are less apt to be lost than in lengthy prose.

n. Another comment of his that's particularly relevant to the *Individual-Organization gap*: "Due process is a way of fighting institutional indifference to the individual."

o. Two contributors to the book "Moral Education" wrote, "Commitment to justice is the only way for an adult to maintain his moral authority over the young, and without this *kind* of superiority, there is no basis for authority."[21]

The authors make it clear that the "justice" referred to is the moral justice of Kohlberg's principle stage #6, not the legalistic orientation of #5 (page 000). Such a requirement for managing the young is obviously essential for maintaining moral *equality* in the leadership of adults.

    p.   The current name adopted in 1924; the sales history:

1914 — $4.2MM	1982 — $34.4 billion
1922 — $10.7MM	1988 — $59.7 billion
1932 — $18.4MM	1990 — $69.0 billion
1942 — $119.4MM	1992 — $65.1 billion
1952 — $333.7MM	(a $4.9 billion loss)
1962 — $1.9 billion	1994 — $64.1 billion
1972 — $9.5 billion	(a $3 billion profit)

    q.   In fairness to IBM units that have risen above the bureaucracy of headquarters, it should be mentioned that some of them have made admirable progress, one example being its relatively independent Electronic Card Assembly and Testing plant in Austin, Texas. Starting in 1986, it "reengineered" its environment, now has among other changes some 200 self-directed work teams, each involved in all of product design, planning, production and selling with customer contact at both ends. The unit goals: people empowerment, customer satisfaction, supplier partnerships, cycle-time reduction, process improvements, with periodic benchmarking.[23]

REFERENCES

1. Booz, Allen & Hamilton, Inc., 1956.

2. Skinner, W., "Manufacturing—missing link in corporate strategy," *Harvard Business Review*, May-June 1969.

3. Stone, C. D., *Where the Law Ends* (New York: Harper & Row,1975).

4. Fortune, Apr. 20, 1992.

5. Paine, L. S., "Managing for Organizational Integrity," *Harvard Business Review*, Mar.-Apr. 1994.

6. Bowman, J. S., "Altering the Fabric of Work: Beyond the Behavioral Sciences," *Business Horizons*, Sept.-Oct. 1984, pp. 42-48.

7. *Business Week*, Oct. 14, 1985, p. 66.

8. Paine, L. S., op. cit.

9. Milton, C. R., *Ethics and Expedience in Personnel Management* (Columbia, South Carolina: University of South Carolina Press, 1970), pp 226-231.

10. Blades, L. E., "Employment at Will vs. Individual Freedom: on Limiting the Abusive Exercise of Employer Power," *Columbia Law Review*, Vol. 67, pp. 1404-1435.

11. *Forbes* magazine, Oct 21, 1985, pp. 166-169.

12. Ewing, D. W., *Freedom Inside the Corporation* (New York: E.P. Dutton, 1977), pp. 109-110.

13. Ewing, D. W., "What business thinks about employee rights," *Harvard Business Review*, Sept.-Oct. 1977B. His survey sample: 36% top mgmt., 36% middle mgmt., 20% lower mgmt., 7% professional and retired; 55% in firms of over 1000 employees, 45% under; 40% in gen. mgmt., 47% functional, 12% other.

14. Ewing, D. W., op. cit. (1977A), pp. 146-9.

15. Ibid, pp. 149-150.

16. Ibid, p. 156.

17. Dunn, F. E., "The View From the Ombudsman's Chair," *New York Times*, May 2, 1976.

18. "Where ombudsmen work out," *Business Week*, May 3, 1976.

19. Dunn, F. E., op. cit.

20. Foy, N., *The Sun Never Sets on IBM* (New York: William Morrow & Co, 1974), p. 126.

21. Sizer, T. R. and N. F. Sizer, "Introduction," *Moral Education*, op. cit, p. 8 (T. R. Sizer was then Dean of the Harvard Graduate School of Education).

22. Kanter, R. M., *The Change Masters* (New York: Simon and Schuster, 1983), p 132.

23. *Commitment Plus* (Schaumburg, Ill.: The Quality and Productivity Management Assn., April 1993).

24. *Business Week*, 10/4/93.

Chapter 22

Solutions to the Problems

The art-science of *Leadership of Organizations* is obviously much more than the traditional concept of management technology plus-telling-people-what-to-do, and the surveys in Chapter 1 made evident at least the social consequences of that approach: the individual-organization gap, organization behavior problems, and poor performance, all apparently increasing across industry.

Experienced managers who are satisfied they've become successful with the traditional (and in spite of it), however, only naturally are not about to change their way of managing subordinates, even if they accept the news about the gap, unless positive proof is given on what's wrong about what they're personally doing and how to correct it. So the 6-step problem-solving procedure on page xxiii was set up and followed throughout Part I in the hope that a logical systematic explanation of the right and wrong of leadership behavior might be persuasive. And of course the procedure was followed also for the *Technical* and *Integration* of Parts II and III, the text to this point completing Steps 1, 2 and 3.

Recall now that the hypothesis on page 34 postulated as a crucial need in any attempt to close the I-O gap and solve adequately both the social and technical problems, postulated that not only social and technical competencies are required but so is a major effort on the part of society. Dividing what has to be done into "the internal" of leadership and "the external" of society...

The internal

As stated on the 6-step procedure page, since analysis is a continuous mental process that goes on throughout the Step #3 formal investigation, the analytic reasoning aroused by the detail

1175

in each chapter was described along the way, a brief summary of that on The Social given at the start of Part II (pages 433-434), that on The Technical at the start of Part III (pages 433-434), and the summary of Part III's Chapter 18-21 will be as follows, thus summarizing for Step 4 the key points of all three Parts.

The analysis, Step #4. For a quick orientation review of the project's highlights, one can outline that the causes of the gap and problems could be any one or combination of five factors:

1. the management of the technical;
2. the management of the social;
3. the management of the integration of the two;
4. the degree of incompatibility of the individual and the organization due to their respective natures (asking too, is it a variable?);
5. human values that cause conflict in the superior-subordinate relationship and among peers.

It soon became apparent that each except #4 were, or could be, important causes of poor performance. On the #1, dysfunctional behavior as well as poor performance can occur when needed controls, structures, processes or appropriate strategies are either missing or poorly designed or managed, many examples provided throughout Part II. Two factors were clearly the causes of problems on #2 and #3: the inadequacy of social and integration skills and the human values "paradox" of #5, the conflict of the values held by managers as superiors summarized by Douglas McGregor in Theory X (page 16) and those that dominated them as subordinates, the needs on page 143. Depressing lists of the conflicts' destructive consequences were presented on pages 6-8, 449-450 (under "bureaucracy"). And the #4 was disposed of fairly early, the disposal subsequently validated convincingly.

It was quite evident therefore that the solutions to the gap and problems would require a change of the #5 values first, followed by more education on #2 and basic education on #1 and #3. The finding on #3 in Part II on the Integration verified this and showed the specifics of what has to done. The Part III Integration and analysis highlights:

1. *Individual change.* The value misconceptions and wrong assumptions held by managers in both positions, as superiors and subordinates, have to be corrected, but those in the former have to be changed first before success can be achieved on the latter. Many can be corrected quickly by the simple acquisition of relevant information, and many others can be, taking a little longer, by social change processes (Chapters 18 and 19 described them), both feasible within or sponsorable by the organization. But there are a number of deep-seated values that are crucial for adequate change success, changes that can be brought about only by society itself over an extended period of time.

2. *Organization change* (OD). The mechanisms of change best for different growth stages were described by Edgar Schein and presented in Chapter 17 (pages 904-907), the interventions of OD being major components; the key concept: collaborative management of the management technology and HR policies with participative processes.

The OD discipline has so far had in general a poor record of achieving its goals, but it has the framework needed for the total internal solution for the problems and it can be made wholly successful by adding the missing imperative functions that must precede all its interventions: the values upgrading as described in #1 above, the creation and maintenance of a freed-up climate, and the teaching of the technical-social integration skills - with a recognition that it all takes time, the missing management patience.

3. *Leadership.* Until recently knowledge about how to best program training and development either in-house or out has been poor as to both design and coverage, but the profound and vast changes that have taken place in the last decade has resulted in a significantly different paradigm for the "out" as well as the "in." The combination of competitive pressures and information technology advances alone have required a plethora of new requirements (covered in the text) to survive and prevail, particularly analysis-planning-decision-making skills, interpersonal and motivational skills (including social-technical integration), strategy planning, team philosophy, reengineering, and process/team structures, using MIS and EDI for competitive

advantage, computer networking and groupware, the use of the Internet, leadership principles and roles, and the total programming of leadership development to be carried on through participants' years in employment, all built intó the restructuring to optimum flatness of the new post-hierarchical organization.

4. *Technical-social integration.* Successful direct integration is the ultimate demonstration of one-to-one leadership because it engages all the principles and role responsibilities of leadership. And successful indirect integration—the direct has to precede it— can be said to be the hallmark of superior organizational (or group) leadership because it demonstrates both the social and management technology competencies as well as the integration competence of the person.

Optimum technical-social integration, however, awaits, as said, the change by society of numerous deep-seated value misconceptions and erroneous opinions, but substantial behavioral progress is possible before then.

5. *Policies.* An essential part of top management leadership competence would be the common sense to formalize basic guidelines on how it wants decisions made down the line on both the technical and social for situations that it is known will occur or are probably.

For an organization to be truly just, its top management must be committed to at least the basic requisites of a *total system of justice*: participative management, open personnel systems, OD, a humanistic basic HR policy and constitutionalism that includes justice and employee rights.

The validation of the three parts of the hypothesis on page 34 can be seen in these five Part III summaries. Logic alone makes evident the primary position of section (i), that effective management of the organization toward its technical purpose must obviously come first, but close behind must be the principal means by which the technical is achieved, the management of the social, management that entails developing a congruence between the goals and methods of the organization and the needs and aspirations of the doers, as stated in (ii). The text's "formal investigation" (Chapters 3-21) validated it through its comparison of all types of successful organizations with unsuccessful ones.

Those that succeeded had intrinsically-satisfied managers and high output, those that didn't had less satisfied, indifferent or dysfunctional ones and lower output.

The formal investigation also repeatedly illustrated what the wrong values and missing skills causing the failures were and additionally made evident what only society and education can and must do on the values. The need for section (iii) was made clear.

Finally, problem-solving Step #4 on page xxiii required the "verification or correction of the system model as consistent with the research findings," the model being Figure 7.1 on page 228. It could now be said that nothing had surfaced to weaken the reasoning underlying the model or to diminish the soundness of the whole system depicted or any of its parts.

Design and choice, #5 and #6. Although the development of a hypothesis at the beginning of a research project always involves a choice from among the initially perceived alternatives as done on pages 29 to 33, the formal investigation usually uncovers or develops others. Carrying forward the letter designations applied on page 29 of "m" to "q" for the initially perceived ones ("q" given there to "the current OD solution" described in Chapter 19), "r" will be assigned here to the "Leadership development with upgraded OD," the upgrading being the addition of T-grouping and the teaching of direct integration, and "s" adds the external requirements theorized to be necessary for the total solution.

This completes the Design Step #5, and the process of making the Choice Step #6 that follows will be based on the best management system each has the potential to achieve, determinations that were made by analyses of the many organizations examined in the formal investigation. The results are in the right hand column below.

		Mgmt. system potential
m.	The Theory X solution	1
n.	The "leadership theorists" solution, the label given to the second	2
o.	The human relations school solution	2.1
p.	The benevolent authoritarian solution	2.1
q.	The current OD solution	3
r.	Leadership development with upgraded OD (internal only)	3.5
s.	The adopted hypothesis (that adds the external)	4

We do know this much from the studies: Theory X will clearly produce a System 1 (an example in Figure 13.7 (a), page 577), and n, o, and p, are in fact variations of Theory X with degrees of "softness" that might make a small improvement in climate: n recommends the organization first try to get its way with persuasion, training and rewards before resorting to unilateral orders and punishment; o says the easy method to get your authoritarian manipulative way is with kindness; and p is the n approach that adds consideration for material human needs (disregarding the psychological), retaining the executive's "right" to be unilaterally arbitrary, like IBM in the 80s.

So the principal comparison on what's in the marketplace today turns out to be between the Theory X group (m to p) and the q, the current OD solution. The text has, however, pointed out the fact that the number of organizations that have tried to apply OD comprehensively can be counted on two hands, those used for illustration being the Harwood-Weldon project, TRW Systems, the limited applications at the GM assembly plants, and the company in Exhibit 6 (Appendix).

Figure 13.2 (p. 565) and 13.7 (pp. 577-579) together supplied the basic information needed to verify the "management system potential" in the table above used as the basis for choosing. In January, 1962 before the acquisition the Weldon managers rated Harwood as a system 1, Likert's designation of the exploitive-authoritative one in the 13.7a Figure. In April 1964 after the application of current OD, they rated it at a 3—no T-grouping or direct integration taught as in "r"; but with societal values upgrading still missing, the "r" has to be rated between the 3 and 4, at about 3.5.

A contrived analysis for choice and presumptuous to generalize from one example? Of course. But because of the crudity of even the best analytical tools, there is no other recourse, short of a prohibitively expensive longitudinal study of a large sample, than to use what's available like the carefully executed Weldon project and what else is available in literature, add logical assumptions for the unknown, and reason through to a conclusion somewhat like this.

What has been done seems to confirm that the hypothesis provides the best model for both solving the problems and optimizing performance, which suggests an additional principle of management following the XIII on page 000 that packages the essentials. A draft open to improvement:

IX, *the principle of Technical-Social Integration*: the procedural skill of management that will best optimize employee performance, achievable when the managers possess/apply:

- technical competence, including the needed technical integration,
- enlightened social knowledge, humanist attitude, participation, and team philosophy,
- advanced leadership development that builds OD with values upgrading into the management system for continuous self-renewal and teaches the skills of technical-social integration,
- a total system of justice (ahead).

But still to be done for organizations to reach their full potential-for iii of the hypothesis:

The external

Because organizational leaders are as members of society commonly either community leaders also or important influences, communities and the nation will naturally gain as well as organizations to the degree that leaders (and all potential or would-be leaders) are aware of the impact on both their internal efforts and the whole social system of all the crucial external forces, and aware of what they as citizens can do about them. Indeed, a moment's reflection on all that's involved in developing superior organizational leaders makes clearly evident the scope, the *totality*, of what is involved.

Consider first, for example, the profound and pervasive *international* importance of values. One need but note their comparative influence on the management of societies and nations themselves that have different sets of values, be they in form of philosophies, ideologies, or different cultural patterns of behavior.

The dominant problem in the management of any organization including nations is after all gaining the collaborative effort of members toward its goals, and in each it is the leadership philosophy and values that decide the modus operandi, the two basic choices being:

Democratic   —concern for others that enlists their decision involvement, or
Authoritarian —non-concern, Theory X, and do it my way or else.

Unquestionably, the dire conditions of some of the less developed nations require an authoritarian approach just as emergencies often do in corporate organizations. But in advanced societies where the political process is democratic, the incompatibility with it of authoritarianism in the work place should be clear. It is impossible for an individual to hold honestly the two conflicting sets of values at one and the same time—an authoritarian one for organizational subordinates and a democratic one for society—without compromising basic principles. Fcr example, a person with integrity must either hold for both sectors the principle of participation—to have a say in decisions that affect one's work and life—or hold it for neither.

Organizational managers additionally have to face the fact that this fundamental idea of democracy is already turning into *a right* of organizational membership as well as citizenship (the survey data on page 10).

A recent study of "Alternative Futures" for the United States and the world lucidly illustrated both what's at stake and what the options are, showing not only the importance and commonality of the values foundation across the two sectors but the awesome opportunity, the immense challenge, and the foreboding urgency of societal action. The Stanford Research Institute (SRI) did it for the U.S. Office of Education, using newly developed techniques that take into consideration all relevant forces and variables, their strengths, possibilities, probabilities, co-existence, sequencing, and timing, producing the five alternative societal conditions

"Tree" of Alternative Future Histories (Open-Closed Dimension)

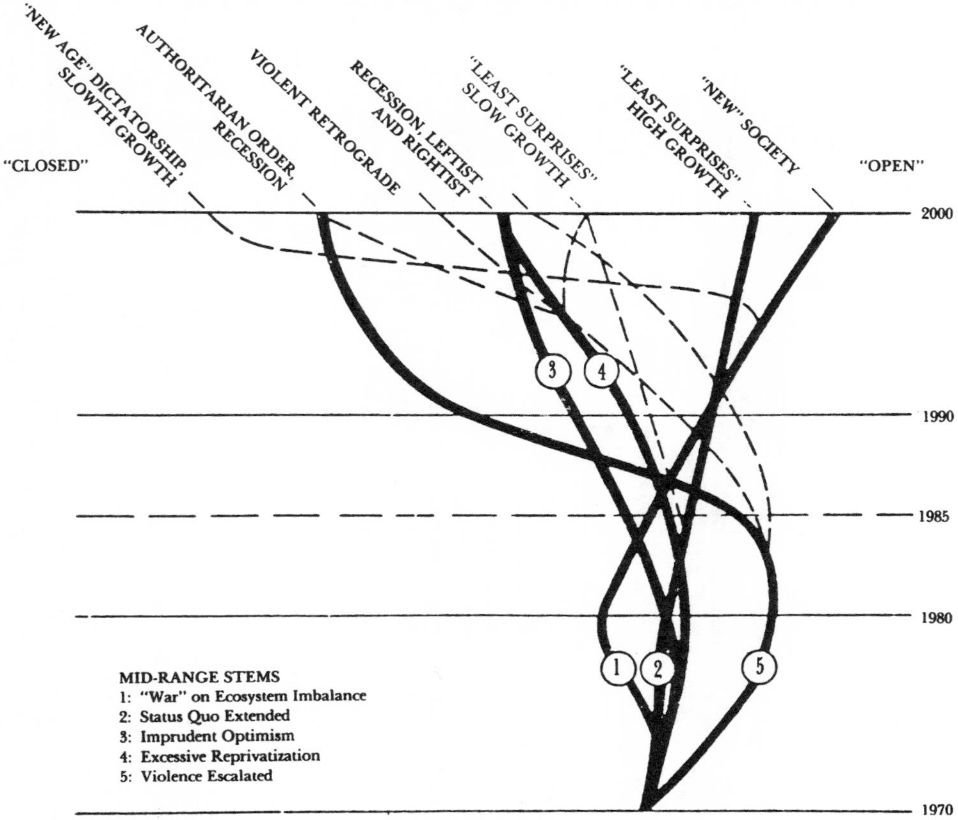

"CLOSED"
"OPEN"
"NEW AGE" DICTATORSHIP, SLOWTH GROWTH
AUTHORITARIAN ORDER, RECESSION
VIOLENT RETROGRADE
RECESSION, LEFTIST AND RIGHTIST
"LEAST SURPRISES" SLOW GROWTH
"LEAST SURPRISES" HIGH GROWTH
"NEW" SOCIETY
2000
1990
1985
1980
1970
3
4
1
2
5
MID-RANGE STEMS
1: "War" on Ecosystem Imbalance
2: Status Quo Extended
3: Imprudent Optimism
4: Excessive Reprivatization
5: Violence Escalated

Figure 22.1

shown in Figure 22.1.[1] The solid lines trace the mid-rang stems of the five dominant histories, taking the forces into account. The dashed lines are distillations of some 40 highly plausible alternatives to the five options. The calendar dates could of course be off by several decades without lessening the validity of the research.

During the early stage of the study it became apparent that the impact of one central set of societal problems, an interrelated network of social forces, had to be considered in all possibilities:

a. proliferating knowledge,
b. industrial development unmoderated by social responsibility,
c. increasing population,
d. an expanding have/have-not gap.

This set was named the "world macroproblem," and as the study advanced it was found that (1) the set manifested a fundamental cultural condition of our Western society; and (2) society "awaits only increased levels of population and technological application (for the condition) to become intolerable."

The findings, the report stated, raised the question of the future appropriateness of the operative values of our society that brought us to our present point of development, and they impugned the values as **out of phase and wrong for solving the problems created by that development,** which is itself responsible for the rising level of expectations that is hastening the intolerability. It is obvious that values are important causes of all four factors of the macroproblem, a dominant one being the inadequate concern of the "haves" for the gap (d).

The researchers concluded that, to achieve *any* desirable future, "significant changes in operative values and cultural Morality" would be necessary.

The following thumbnail sketches of the five, condensations from the report, will themselves help one appreciate the tenuousness of the present stability, how easily the best of conditions can go to the worst, and how risky it would be to let ourselves drift with present trends. Plainly, none are forecasts; they are the five most probable alternatives, one of which describes the essential features of what is most likely to happen or that we can try to make happen:

1. *War* (the moral equivalent of) *on the ecosystem imbalance.* A national effort to (a) reestablish a balanced physical ecosystem, (b) control population growth to a satisfactory level, (c) redistribute material wealth enough to eliminate extreme domestic poverty, economic growth and prosperity assumed. Required: a national consensus plus the necessary leadership and education to make the needed substantial changes in cultural values and premises.

2. *Status quo extended.* An optimist's view of scenario #4 below (the excessive reprivatization), one the researchers call the "good" "luck" version of it. It assumes (a) the world macro-problem has been grossly overstated, (b) economic and political patterns of the last 15 years can be extrapolated, (c) trends of social, cultural and technological change will slow down.

3. *Imprudent optimism, leading to a left-centrist recession and bureaucratic stultification.* Efforts by government to correct perceived social and environmental ills are too many, too hurried and too fragmented. Top down controls of remedial programs are inept and commitments exceed national productivity. A persistent pursuit of welfare policies under bureaucratic controls locks in a slow drift toward recession as industry's concern for stability and growth causes a decreasing level of capitalization. It was dubbed the "bad luck" version of scenario #1.

4. *Excessive reprivatization, leading to right-centrist recession and garrison state.* A possible reaction, that might find its roots in present conditions, to the inadequacy of bureaucratic interventions to deal with the social problems and the economic problems (especially inflation). Emphasis on private enterprise, market forces and the profit motive to solve the problems, ignoring the fact that (a) they accentuate macroproblems b and d; (b) they all stress short-term results, and (c) market forces cannot anticipate side-effects and long-term consequences of actions and policies, so do not provide the information needed for good long-range decisions.

There is initial optimism as a percent of the population (the "haves") "get theirs," but hands-off government fails to keep economic forces in balance or abuses of property, power, and greed in check; national policy and decisions favor short-term results and the most powerful special interests.

The inequities lead to severe forms of repression against those who protest; the repression and short-term and ultra-conservative asocial thinking lead to recession, then economic isolation, then chaos and violence in and from the third world, posing a serious threat to the entire North Atlantic community.

5. *Violence escalated.* This scenario evolves from (a) an escalation of present tendencies to use confrontation and one-issue politics to accomplish societal reforms and/or (b) institutional encouragement of "stakeholder" differences by inept attempts at participatory planning.

Trust and confidence throughout society breaks down, authorities have to increasingly rely on force as a means of maintaining control; power replaces consensual authority. The paralyzing effect of terrorism and the repressive inflexibility inherent in an authoritarian response makes recessive trends most plausible. A Caesarist take-over is one possible consequence.

The final paragraph of the report concisely summed up the key issues in the determination of which future (or mix) will occur:

> Note that virtually all aspects of the world macroproblem are manmade, and that the future is dependent on the choices man makes to an extent never dreamed possible in times past. Thus the future is predominantly management limited, rather than resource limited.
>
> Since the various critical societal problems must somehow be solved, the long-term choice is between democratic forms of management of the nation and the planet and authoritarian/oligarchic/bureaucratic forms.

It is possible now to appreciate that "management limited" in fact means "judgment" limited—limited especially by the values and premises that guide the decision-making of the managers— for almost all the critical decision alternatives and their consequences for each scenario are known.

The planning the nation must do and the sequencing would seem to be clear:

First, decide what scenario should be the long-range goal.

Second, do the necessary values research: what values and philosophies will induce the solution of the macroproblem and lead to the desired future?

Third, participatively assemble a national plan to make the changes, and then implement it.

On the *first,* scenario #1 undoubtedly appeals most to educated people, who also realize that as a goal it is essentially a long-range ideal that will take decades to reach—and must be pursued within a framework of the principles of democracy, free enterprise and social responsibility.

Chapters 5 and 6 have presented some of the best research done and books written so far for the *second.* Pages 117-121 listed the most glaring value problems for organizations, and page 176 gave guidelines for everyone and every walk of life. And a brief outline for the implementation of the *third* was given on page 194 listing some of the urgent tasks that should be considered by the three basic institutions society will have to depend on. To repeat it for reader convenience:

A. Education
  1. Research on what values the nation wants to hold and should hold and how to teach them to
     a. children and adolescents
     b. college students and adults
  2. Educational programs
     a. Type #I values (page 191) and the relevant ethics
     b. Type #2 values and associated ethics by behavioral techniques
     c. A long-range plan for type #3 values and associated ethics
     d. Value systems education (within a, b and c): orientations, philosophies, ideologies
     e. The education necessary for B and C below.
B. Industry and professional associations
  1. Education on and promotion of leadership development with its values upgrading and ethics as described in Chapters 17, 20 and 21.

2. The definition of and promotion of leader, corporate and professional social responsibility.
3. Leading the reform of corporate governance.
4. Codes of ethics for both internal and external relations.
5. Professionalizing organizational leadership.

C. **Government**
   1. Industry regulation, to the extent that industry makes it necessary, through agencies such as SEC, FDA, others.

   2. Federal Laws, to the extent that self-management by industry is inadequate, on governance, employee rights, behavior.

However, the *totality* of what has to be done should again be stressed because of its desperately urgent importance, the totality of the requirements to develop and motivate effective organizational leadership in a free society, meaning every aspect of the binternal—the organizational behavior and ethics (throughout and especially in Part I), technical competence and the technical-social integration (**Parts II** and **III**)—and every aspect of the external by the three institutions (A, B and C above), industry and government paying particular attention to the structures and processes that in some instances motivate even mismanagement and actions seriously damaging to the future of the nation. Indeed, as far back as 1980 the futurists of SRI's think tank touched on it when they stated that this country's democratic form of government itself "may have difficulty surviving as it is faced with increasing special-interest lobbying, ballot initiatives, and litigation."[2]

Some thoughts and proposals for each of three external categories, beginning with the most basic one:

Education. Plainly, we have to go back to the fundamental circular process: schooling that will carry from students to parents and teachers to employees and back to preschool children. And education has not been wholly remiss. A surprising amount of progress has been made by its research for the young, evidenced by a growing number of scattered successful experiments. But then there's the catch-22 of the larger picture it's faced with described on pages 126-128: the inability around the country of getting started on values education at the most elementary level of public schools where most children begin, e.g., the refusal still of the New York State Board of Regents to approve the first step, *policy*, in the public schools.

The refusal is typical across the nation, an outstanding exception being California which has already moved past the basics to the next steps, the what and the *how*, and which started teaching the fundamentals to children in 1973. However, there are encouraging reports of communities across the country waking up to the need for schools to teach at least agreed-on behavioral values, that experience shows society too often can't count on parents.

Certainly the process could be greatly speeded up everywhere if managers themselves (hopefully enlightened) would get involved for the sake of their children and grandchildren, at least through PTAs. Chapter 5 gave a general idea of what is involved—the learning process from Kohlberg's stage #1 through Stage #6 (page 123), the values education scheduled to educability.

As he pointed out (in the Harvard book *Moral Education*), we must at least go to work immediately on teaching the most fundamental value to any society, respect for individuals' rights, just as we teach the laws of the land. Indeed, given that the Constitution itself makes clear that a principal rationale of government is the preservation of the rights of individuals—*justice*—our public schools must be committed to justice just as our courts must be.

Then, because justice plays a crucial part in each of the other fundamental values as shown on pages 161-163, it can supply a base for studying them and for putting morality to the test in judging others, preparing the way to move up the stages to full maturity, moral autonomy, and principled decision-making.[3,a]

Moral autonomy is the capacity to make moral decisions regardless of peer pressure or the dictates of higher authority, thus, a capacity for pro-social non-compliance on unacceptable social rules,[4] Martin Luther King's leadership on page 124 a superb example. Its importance to the advance of society is manifested in its impact on "socialization," socialization being the degree to which its people have internalized the values and rules of the society and are therefore committed to the status quo. Clearly, moral autonomy would be essential to the progressive modification of the status quo. It is, further, a major force in personal social change and is probably necessary to move from Stage #5 to the principled decisions of #6.

A lot of progress has also been made for higher education. The five lectures of the *Moral Education* book are themselves good primers on teaching values in universities as well as lower levels, and the "Hastings Center" has supplied an excellent phrasing for the goal that business schools should pursue with an outline of what has to be imbued in our present and future leaders to achieve it:[5]

> *The educational goal*: develop the capacity for moral judgment in business contexts and how to integrate a concern for the welfare of people with one's managerial role and to implement that concern competently
>
> And *the six capacities* on which moral judgments of all types depend are (abridged):
>
> 1. Moral imagination—a sensitivity to the hidden dimensions where people are likely to get hurt with the ability to anticipate them and imagine how to keep them from happening.
>
> 2. Moral identification and ordering—the ability to see which moral claims are relevant, locate the risks and benefits, and link them to available resources, that is, to address them rationally, in the course of regular activity.
>
> 3. Moral evaluation—to relate the protection of human welfare to the ongoing processes of institutional purposes, weighing and reasoning through the alternatives that can do this.
>
> 4. Tolerating moral disagreement and ambiguity—a corollary to understanding the diverse commitments and needs of the many whom managers affect.
>
> 5. Integrating managerial competence and moral competence—which includes the "ethics of anticipation," anticipating the consequences in the future of decisions affecting people.
>
> 6. A sense of moral obligation—the absence of which may be uncorrectable but for those who have it the teaching process can help demonstrate the relevance of morality in the managerial context.

The authors who summarized the Hastings Center research in the quoted booklet also cited the major obstacles within business schools that have to be overcome just to get moving beyond the current "business and society" courses used to teach ethics in a limited way. Noble efforts have been made as far back as 1962 by men like George Steiner to promote a business ethics course (his try at UCLA after some 20 years of work on designing one), but it is still not required by the American Assembly of Collegiate Schools of Business (AACSB), which only recommends it be considered within existing courses and it's generally agreed that the ethics referred to has been preponderantly with respect to only an organization's external relations.

The authors pointed out additionally that probably the most formidable threat to success for the present is the absence of qualified and interested faculty. Though leading schools are beginning to address the need seriously, we still have in them many educators who were trained in the same asocial system as the current one that's delinquent on ethics. They not only don't have the commitment to teach ethics per se or in their courses, but they're very uncomfortable with the language and terms of ethics.

However, writers and opinion leaders on the subject have too often made an assumption about students and adults themselves that seriously handicap any effort: that little if anything can be done about their values and behavior anyhow because they've by and large already been firmly formed as if—the old cliche—set in concrete. Therefore the most that can be done, they go on, is sensitize those few who know enough about ethics to be receptive to it.

A reading to this point must have made evident how too sweeping that is, that much can be done with information alone on the type #1 values when ignorance is the problem (page 191), behavior change techniques have had important success on the type #2, and the deep-seated of #3 are at different depths in different personalities, such that some can be budged by the authority of educators, by impressive models, and/or by operated programs like the four-part first step on pages 962-963, which itself can have impressive authority.

As for imbuing ethics in the functional courses,[b] an objective of Part II has been to provide the basics, and the professors don't have to be professional philosophers, can become adequately qualified for their own classes with a study of Parts I and II or the like and seminars that advance as felt needed the information on values, organization behavior, the philosophies, ethics sensetizing, and the ethics analysis described on page 178 (the application to ethics situations of the various philosophy principles that appear most appropriate, ranking them, choosing the best per one's own values, priorities, and conscience). Then as part of the analysis education after values and philosophies, a recent book giving more on how to understand, change, and cope with the social behavior of others and whole organizations is well worth study by professors, students, and managers alike: *The Hard Problems of Management* by Mark Pastin (San Francisco: Jossey-Bass, 1986) that shows particularly how a participative utilitarianism (Bentham, Mill, Dewey), deontology (rules, Kant), and/or the social contract model (Plato, Hobbes, Adam Smith) might be applied.

Nonetheless, it does seem to behoove graduate schools to offer all four parts of the pages 962-963 program if they hope to achieve anything like the Hastings goal, to develop ethical leaders. There are plenty of behaviorists available for numbers 1, 3, and 4 of the program but as yet not the needed business ethics philosophers for number 2. However, efforts to develop them are increasing. Seven major business schools now offer doctorates in business ethics, and a rapidly growing volume of literature on the subject is building a substantial base for the essential "case method,"[c] the Hastings Center booklet supplying a wealth of subjects to cover— to which the internal interpersonal relations concerns should be added.[d,e]

These comments of course do not lessen the importance of what society and lower education levels must still do on the #3 type in general, especially toward the critera on page 176. Indeed, the present values condition at the college level is such that a substantial proportion of the students are at or below the Kohlberg Stag #4 on page 118, students who, as he expressed it, "kick conventional morality, search for their thing, for self-chosen values, but can't tell an autonomous morality of justice from one of egoistic relativism, exchange, or revenge."

Industry and professional associations. Most educated members of an open free enterprise society accept the promise that organizations should upgrade their own behavior and government step in only where and when they're unable on their own to stop damaging society in the ways they do. And the greatest power for a general upgrading is their associations, and individual members can—usually have to—lead the way.

The five areas listed under B on pages 1187-1188 are where they can produce the most beneficial results, the two key ones that comment will be limited to being corporate (or social) responsibility and corporate governance.

Corporate responsibility.[f] The recent profusion of articles on this is truly encouraging, but one has to wonder why in virtually all instances the discourses have been limited to external relations to the exclusion of the internal human resources policies and behavior other than working conditions.

It's possibly a result principally of the combined denunciations by society about corporate misbehavior and the palpable ethics neglect on the external along with little pressure from within due to authoritarian dominance. But managerial conduct on the external and internal have as a base the same set of values, so the two are inseparable.

Granted, the initial and paramount questions are external: (1) what social values and priorities does the nation as a whole want to hold, (2) what of them should be considered institutional responsibilities, and (3) how should those responsibilities be divided between government and non-government organizations, the non-government (ex Education) being principally corporations and their associations (other associations subject to the same reasoning that follows[f])?

Chapters 5 and 6 can, as said earlier, supply enough of a foundation to assemble the answers to the first, but for the second and third one has to start with specifically individual social responsibilities because they are the source of the answers.

A definition of an individual's social responsibility would be the same definition given by Erich Fromm to duty (that is, social duty, or morality) on page 222: *duty* is love and advancing the full potential of the self, others and the institutions of society, in which love is knowledge + care + respect + responsibility, the knowledge referring mainly to values, priorities, others' needs, psychology.

How then can we ascribe any of such responsibilities to organizations and, additionally, divide those ascribed between corporations and government? In this way. Naturally every citizen is responsible wherever his or her own social values are involved as defined on page 119 wherever voluntary ideas, judgments, intentions, decisions or actions concern or have a bearing on:

a.　other individuals
b.　the institutions of society, or
c.　the formation of one's own character;

and since all organizations, non-government and government, are but collections of citizens, those in them, especially the managers, are obligated to do likewise also when acting in the name of the organization.

Thus the primary social responsibility of any organization derives from the morality of its managers, and the organization should be designed to insure that all structures, processes and leadership foster moral behavior on (a), (b) and (c), particularly on decisions and actions concerning:

- Hiring policies,
- Human resources (internal policy and practices),
- Interpersonal relations,
- Internal rights and justice,
- Health and safety in the workplace;

and corporations would add:

- Customer, supplier, stockholder and other external relations,
- Product, service and promotion integrity,
- Community environment (especially pollution),
- Obeying the laws,
- Paying the taxes,
- Plant movings and closings.

As for the institutional separation, government responsibility is obviously set by the legislative and executive branches, but it is necessarily minimal and more social effort is always needed, which is what leads people to turn to corporations for responsibility and contribution; and to decide just how much should be forthcoming one needs but consider three realities: (1) the economic purpose of corporations, (2) the fundamentally social purpose of government, and (3) present public expectations.

The first and second together seem to spell out a clear-cut dividing line, but not adequately if one considers that the public would only naturally have some expectations, the third, due to and in proportion to the *power* of corporations, which are after all instruments of society, social as well as technical.

Those who have given a lot of thought to the subject have by and large concluded that, in light of #1 and #2, corporate responsibility for community involvement is to help their communities where their special expertise or resources are needed as supplements to the efforts of government or voluntary organizations, the degree kept in balance with responsibilities owed stockholders, employees and customers. Deep-seated local or national problems however, are wholly the territory of government, corporations brought in on a contract basis when needed and paid for their help befitting their need for ROI to survive.

This is of course all very general, much having of necessity to be left to executive judgment, and we know that almost any decision made may be subjected to criticisms ranging from social irresponsibility to unwarranted distribution of assets and exceeding delegated authority.

Two organization behaviorists recently condensed the key points into three principles for decision guidance, and executive maturity (especially criterion #6 on page 176) has to take it from there:[8]

- *Primum non nocere*—above all, do no harm.
- Organizational accountability for consequences, intended or not.
- The power-responsibility equation—the larger the organization the more actual and potential its social influence therefore the greater the responsibility.

Certainly the first goes without saying; more on the second under "governance" ahead; and as the authors said for the third, executives have to face the fact that the public sees corporate responsibility as a cost of success and accordingly proportional to it. Managements therefore have to make a real effort to be sensitive to, indeed anticipate, what the expectations are if they wish to avoid a damaging image...and/or conversely want to generate public admiration and goodwill the way TRW Corporation's social program did as far back as the 70's; A thumbnail sketch of it published in 1976:[9,g]

...The economic contribution of TRW during 1972 was positive. Sales, profits, dividends, wages, fringe benefits and taxes all increased. Employment increased by 12 percent, providing about 8,500 jobs. Capital and work-planning improvements to increase productivity have been significant. As in prior years, many divisions were cited by their customers for the outstanding quality of their products and services.

...TRW emphasized its equal employment opportunity programs and increased its minority population significantly The company also promoted educational opportunities and job enrichment programs designed to upgrade the skills and abilities of all employees with special emphasis on providing training courses for the disadvantaged. Occupational health and safety received major attention. Facilities and equipment which meet or exceed all regulations for the operator's safety were installed. TRW was proud of its environmental record with respect to air and water quality problems. During the past five years virtually all major sources of industrial pollution were eliminated.

...In Boston the company's AB&W Division was formed several years ago to provide meaningful employment for inner-city blacks and whites. Managed by black employees, this operating unit performs quality manufacturing and assembly functions at competitive prices for other TRW divisions while also actively building additional business outside the TRW organization. In Cleveland there was a need for a neighborhood health facility near one of TRW's plants. Working with concerned community leaders and area medical professionals, TRW provided a convenient location and financial assistance to establish the Polyclinic Family Health Care Center.

...Los Angeles teenage Mexican-Americans are getting a better break when they enter the work force in Southern California in part due to the efforts of TRW employees who formed an organization called Career Opportunities for Youth. COY volunteers work with Chicano youngsters, motivating them to remain in school through tutoring and rap sessions,

helping them to select a trade or field, and instilling the confidence needed
to obtain and hold meaningful jobs.

It's undoubtedly evident that economically feasible community
involvement is but a high level of basic corporate morality, which
fortuitously creates goodwill that often plays a big part in product
acceptance and preference. All social responsibility is discernibly
no more or less than *social exchange*, therefore "enlightened self-
interest," the give and take balancing out in the long-run,
including what happens when a corporation tries to take more
than it gives either externally or internally.

In sum, the integral nature of individual manager responsibility
and organizational responsibility for the morality of organizations
goes without saying; but equally clear must be the fact that, in
order to develop the morality of both present managers and future
ones—*therefore develop moral organizations*—the burden falls on
all of Education, individuals, organizations, and the associations
together.

Such an educational joint effort should include in the least the
variety of recommendations presented in the three parts of the text;
those that should particularly be highlighted and promoted
(expanding on the B1 and B2 on pages 1187-1188):

- The recognition that organizations are social instruments of
  society as well as technical and legal entities, and that more
  than half the leadership function is human relations and
  therefore a matter of morality in one regard or another.
- The basic information about values and morality (Chapter
  5 & 6), immorality and the six capacities for mortal
  judgements (page 183).
- The behavior change program on pages 962-963, that
  includes the "information" above and the ethics training on
  pages 177-178.
- The organizational requisites:
  a. formal codes of ethical conduct for both internal and
     external relations:
  b. an ethically sound and well respected human resources
     policy statement;
  c. a total system of justice (page 1164).

- And leadership at all levels teaching and promoting the policies and moral decision making by example, continuous personal attention, and systematic periodic review.

Corporate governance. The term, we know, refers to the authority, actions, and responsibilities of the board that can be detailed as-

- The *selection* of the CEO and involvement in officer selection;
- Taking part in the *planning* of basic objectives, strategies, policies, major resource allocations, and succession planning, and *evaluating* and *approving* each;
- *monitoring* the CEO's performance, corporate performance, plan compliance, strategy progress, organizational technical and social (culture and climate) health, and the legal and ethical conduct of officers and employees.

Patently, the board's own degree of felt responsibility and integrity, therefore its values and philosophy, will operate as the leading influence on every aspect of its corporation's behavior - if it does its job.

Governance has certainly been greatly improved over the last 20 years, but surveys, research and court records have shown that it is in general still grievously below acceptable standards. For examples of what still prevails in most of them:

- The character of the board: self-perpetuating, clubby rubber stamps of management that aim to please management more than benefit the stockholder;
- Control of the board by management through its election of at least the majority of the members and having the CEO be the chairperson; the conflicts of interest are ignored;
- The questionable reliability of the judgements of board members from the standpoint of the adequacy of the decision-making information and knowledge they possess or are given and the legal advice they get.

- The dubious credibility of the company books because of their flexibility to convey the messages the management decide to convey.
- The misuses of corporate resources, for example, approved excessive top management compensation, stock options, perks, secret funds, bribes, illegal contributions, golden parachutes, greenmail, and managements buyouts with company cash and credit, the compensation for CEO's being particularly egregious: those of the major corporations get 160 times what the average bottom level workers earn vs. 20 times in Japan and 21 times in Germany, each company in the top 200 averaging in 1991 $2.8 million/year.[11]
- Indifference to stockholders interests and opinions, for example, making substantial changes in the structure, business, or share value of the firm without stockholder consent; abuse of the proxy system.[h]
- Neglect of the culture and climate of the corporation and failure to question and act on either the evidence of corporate internal injustice or the factors that allow it.
- Indifference about the morality of managers as long as they generate profits.[i]

Given that the fundamental foundation of organizational leadership is the leadership of the board, if these problems aren't corrected corporate prospect for the future looks grim. A 1989 comment from an ex-CBS president now teaching at Fordham's graduate business school: "The system doesn't work the way it's supposed to... there's a sense of rot here."

The Business Roundtable, the CEOs of some 200 top corporations, did publish as long ago as 1978 a set of recommendations on the composition and role of corporate directors and one on ethics in 1987, but as Kenneth Andrews editor of HBR at the time, said, the SEC must have asked, "Is that all?"[12] Unfortunately, they reflected the common contention at the top that the laws on the books and market forces are sufficient to induce adequate responsibility and integrity and weed out the bad apples—conveniently closing their eyes to the limitations of the law (that it covers only gross offenses and their after-the-damages-are-done nature).[j]

Moreover, to say further that market forces will also encourage responsibility and eventually weed out the bad apples ignores the fact that the market forces can only allocate capital, labor and production; they're incapable of responding to basic human needs (page 143), and untouched by them are the harmful side-effects and undesirable long-range consequences of business decisions, actions, and products; for example, pollution, certain herbicides, carcinogenic drugs, asbestos, the Columbia Pictures case (in j.)—and all the asocial and authoritarian indifference to people still extant.

The "laws" argument brings to mind again Lawrence Kohlberg's Stages #5 and #6 of mental development to toward maturity (on page 123):

> Stage #5: contractual legalistic orientation
> Stage #6: conscience or principled orientation.

Many lawyers, trained in and saturated with the fine points of the law, illustrate stoppages at #5 in their willingness to defend immoralities if loopholes in the law allow them, which fits nicely their financial self interest, the way the legal argument does for top executives. And the main evidence of a person reaching Stage #6 is a developed trait of evaluating and being morally influenced by the consequences of his/her decision and their alternatives, which includes both obedience of "good" laws and a readiness like King to challenge the "bad" ones (page 124).[k] Of course most corporate leaders today are guided by a fair amount of moral principles under Stage #6 as well as the laws of #5, so it's a question of what social responsibilities they're inclined to carry out and what ones they're not. If this can be determined, the separation of self-regulation by corporations and government regulation is easier to discern.

The impracticality of using individuals principles as criteria must be apparent, but a very simple distinction supplied by Christopher Stone will do the job eminently—two classifications of executive behavior:[14]

Class A behavior—there is a considerable range of social problems on which top managers agree with the public, and their social decisions on them will fulfill public expectations if they are fully informed of the facts.

Class B behavior—there are a number of areas where there are conflicting views, and most top managers and directors will act differently even if fully informed unless required by the law (e.g., on many issues of pollution, consumerism, labor, human resources management, authority, the governance conduct on pages 1098-1099, and much of social responsibility in general).

The way to ensure at least the best of Class A compliance by CEOs is obviously a combination of electing high caliber ones educated about behavior as well as on technical leadership and CEOs who believe in continuing their education in the years ahead.

The staff of every industry association should further study Stone's proposals for Class B behavior to give their members the knowledge and options needed for an open informed debate toward a stand that will best serve society as well as themselves. The associations should then promote behavior policies on the conclusions for their members or propose legislation (e.g., footnote d), without which Congress may act on its own; indeed the next subsection is specifically on what government needs to do about Class B behavior in both corporations and on Wall Street that is beyond the capability of self-regulation. Comment here would best serve the reader by only saying that Stone's book is a classic that will influence thinking on the subject for some years to come. It is engrossing, timely, shocking, and well written.

Finally for industry associations, they are in the best position to fill a current glaring vacuum, the widespread ignorance of directors of the specifics of the role and responsibilities of the position, a principal reason for the deplorable performance of most boards in living up to them. They've all observed the traditional behavior pattern of passive attendance for the perks and the characteristics on pages 1098-1099, see that that's the way it's done and readily fall in knowing no better (aside from "loyalty" to the

CEO).

Seminars should be made available for all current and to-be directors (several top graduate schools now offer them) and seminar attendance made the norm at least for new directors, in which three subjects in particular should be taught while and within covering the three basics (*selection, planning and monitoring*):

(1) *strategy*—what it means, its importance to corporate performance, the options (e.g., page 742) and examples of them, demanding good shareholder value and return (pages 761-763). Few are adequately informed, and the many inane diversifications, conglomerations, selloffs, buybacks, etc. are ample evidence. Moreover, CEOs, who are usually selected for financial or operating performance, commonly also know too little about strategy, compounding the problem.

(2) A clear awareness of constructive vs. destructive *types of conflict* as self-evident as it seems, with heavy stress on the importance to the corporation of the constructive; many board members are or have been top executives who abhor conflict of any sort from subordinates.

(3) *The responsibilities and performance expectations* of boards of publicly held corporations—one can begin with the list at the start of this governance section, add the 8 rules below proposed by the General Motors board chairman, John Smale[15] (the directors subsequently issued a more detailed "magna carta for themselves, 6 pages of 28 guidelines), and what follows.

Clearly the outside directors must dominate; indeed it is generally agreed that the compensation, audit and nominating committees should be composed of only outsiders, that in each case the chairperson should not be the CEO, and the proposed "lead director" of the outside members—who would probably be the chairperson of one of the committees—would convene regular outside director meetings without the CEO for an evaluation of CEO and corporate performance (say, at a 2-3 day retreat) and a periodic meeting with distinguished outside analysts for objective critiques. Then add to these the following:

1 There clearly should be a majority of outside directors.

2 The independent members of the board should select a lead director.

3 The independent directors should meet alone in executive session on a regularly scheduled basis.

4 The independent directors should take responsibility for all board procedures.

5 The broad should have the basic responsibility for selection of its own members.

6 The board should conduct regularly scheduled performance reviews of the CEO and key executives.

7 The board must understand and fully endorse the company's long-term strategies.

8 The board must give an adequate amount of attention to its most important responsibility: the selection of the CEO.

a. Boards should be involved in developing and setting corporate goals for quarterly performance evaluations.

b. In medium-size to large public firms a small staff independent of management should evaluate and report directly to the audit committee and board quarterly on needed objective knowledge: significant *external* events about products, markets, competition, changing market and technological conditions, customer requirements; the *internal* as to progress in developing new technologies and products, and on organizational structure, processes and social health (culture, values, ethics and climate).

c. Directors should establish qualifications and performance expectations of board directors and evaluate the performance of each member annually (making dissatisfactions apparent); set the maximum number of other directorships acceptable (preferably three); set standard term limits (e.g., 12 years); set moderate competitive director compensation (eschewing the temptation to give themselves retirement benefits as some have done—violating their fiduciary duty to shareholders), informing investors what has been decided—it's after all their money.

d. The CEO should not remain on the board after retirement unless the outside directors unanimously want it, but then for no more than two years.

e. Directors should create an "investor relations committee" of the chairpersons of the board, the audit, compensation and nominating committees, the CEO, and the lead director if one, for periodic briefings of shareholders (particularly large ones) in addition to the annual stockholders' meeting for questions and answers on performance, plans and processes; the improved relations would pay off in many ways including the avoidance of costly proxy fights (a move proposed by L.M. Thompson, Jr., president of the National Investor Relations Institute).[16]

Probably needless to say, there is widespread doubt among the CEOs of large corporations that the board chairman should not be the CEO; essentially they simply fear interference. Moreover, when the CEO is also chairman, the person can easily avoid discussions of "unpleasant" issues, whereas an outside chairman can result in the directors demanding and getting what they want to see on performance: financial, production, marketing, market share of products, quality, safety, health, investment return, diversity, and so forth.

The only exception: an organization in a long-term decline and in deep trouble at IBM (Gerstner made holding the two positions a condition of employment). GM is a rare exception for a troubled organization due to the personalities involved. The smooth functioning of the GM board under Smale and CEO Jack Smith is a prime example of what a well-run separation can do for even the country's largest corporation. The board, revitalized by their joint leadership, now gets a constant flow of all of this, develops long-term strategy, and the (a) to (e) above are largely followed.

Finally, a Harvard Business School professor, W.J. Salmon, who has served on many boards recently proposed an excellent set of questions, Figure 22.2, for CEOs, boards and major investors to judge the adequacy of their boards' structures, processes and performance, the set listing or elaborating on much of the below.[17]

An overaching objective of all this worth putting in writing though obvious: CEOs and boards must be made accountable to stockholders.

Government. The underlying reason for the present failure of our laws to prevent corporate irresponsibility was the understandable inability in 1776 to foresee 200 years down the road how large and omnipotent the private sector and its units would be.

The Constitution, in guaranteeing the rights of private individuals against powerful government, provided the balance of power needed through most of the 19th century, but it was inconceivable at that time that the little businesses in existence when it was formulated would some day become so large that they would themselves have virtually the power of government over more people than individual states. As David Ewing pointed out back in 1977, AT&T at the time had more employees than the three largest colonies combined in 1776; GM and the Postal Service had more than the largest of them, and ten companies had more than New York State.[18,1]

22 Questions for Diagnosing Your Board

If you answer yes to all 22 questions, you have an exemplary board.

1. Are there three or more outside directors for every insiders?
2. Are the insiders limited to the CEO, The COO, and the CFO?
3. Do your directors routinely speak to senior managers who are not represented on the board?
4. Is your board the right size(8 to 15 members)?
5. Does your audit committee, not management, have the authority to approve the partner in charge of auditing the company?
6. Does your audit committee routinely review "high-exposure" areas?
7. Do compensation consultants report to your compensation committee rather than to the company's human resources officers?
8. Has your compensation committee shown the courage to establish formulas for CEO compensation based on long-term results - even if the formulas differ from industry norms?
9. Are the activities of your executive committee sufficiently contained to prevent the emergence of a "two-tier" board?
10. Do outside directors annually review succession plans for senior management?
11. Do outside directors formally evaluate your CEO's strengths, weakness, objectives, personal plans, and performance every year?
12. Does your nominating committee rather than the CEO direct the search for new board members and invite candidates to stand for election?
13. Is there a way for outside directors to alter the meeting agenda set by your CEO?
14. Does the company help directors prepare for meetings by sending relevant routine information, as well as analyses of key agenda items, ahead of time?
15. Is there sufficient meeting time for thoughtful discussion in addition to management monologue?
16. Do the outside directors meet without management on a regular basis?
17. Is your board actively involved in formulating long-range business strategy form the start of the planning cycle?
18. Does your board, rather than the incumbent CEO, select the new chief executive - in fact as well as in theory?
19. Is at least some of director's pay linked to corporate performance?
20. Is the performance of each of your directors periodically reviewed?
21. Are directors who are no longer pulling their weight discouraged from standing for reelection?
22. Do you take the right measures to build trust among directors?

Figure 22.2

A serious consequence of the growth has been a deleterious imbalance of power between the parties involved—management, board, stockholders, employees, and the public (the welfare of communities and the nation)—with management holding dictatorial power on top and not at all reluctant to promote only its self-interests. The original power equalization imposed on government was not carried over to these new quasi-governments.

Plainly, what is needed now is a definition of the balanced legal relationships that ought to exist among them, something that's never been spelled out, and a determination of ways in which the balance can be feasibly instituted and sustained.

We know that individual federal agencies now attempt important controls—the SEC, FDA, OSHA, EPA and so on—and they're now recognized as indispensable, but what they do is like fighting the drug traffic by arresting street peddlers; the core problems remain untouched.

Until education and the long-range values-change programs of society shift the bulk of Class B behavior over to Class A—which is many decades down the road—government rules, incentives and penalties on responsibility and accountability through operating rules will have to fill the void just to stop the trend toward "the intolerable" (due mainly to (b) and (d) on page 1184).

One particularly potent tool that deserves more attention than business lobbies will allow—because it is potent in these regards—is the packaging of much of what is needed under *federal corporate chartering*, a solution that was considered by Teddy Roosevelt, Taft and Wilson, and again after the 1929 crash more seriously by Franklin Roosevelt. But FDR felt that unregulated speculation in securities was the primary problem and set up The SEC; federal chartering got lost in the effort.

The smallness of businesses in 1776, their largely intrastate nature, and the states' rights attitudes only naturally resulted back then in state regulation of commerce, and a minimal amount of it, in the form of state chartering that's changed little since then: a taxing technique and practically no controls. Few states have even one employee on enforcement of charter requirements. Moreover, it has now degenerated into a competition for the endowment of freedom from accountability for a fee. Way-out-in-front Delaware now has about half of the largest 100 and half of the largest 1000 corporations, providing the state with over 20 percent of its total revenue.

There's little disagreement among progressive thinkers on the subject that our free enterprise system has a dire need for three key benefits federal chartering can significantly contribute to, all of:

- a balance of power between the parties involved that will result in optimal benefit to the nation and its free enterprise system;

- corporate behavioral standards and a uniformity of the standards across the nation;
- management and board accountability;
- social responsibility to employees, suppliers, community and nation.

It is obvious that the states have no interest in attending to any of them and no interest in the problems beyond their borders resulting from their disinterest. Moreover, any reasons given that little Delaware should charter General Motors and other giant national and international firms can only be based on groundless nonsense.

The four benefits must of course be the sole goals, the overriding purpose to legislate only on the social, the moral obligations of the corporation that have been ignored, with studied avoidance of interference in the technical, the legitimate business decisions of managing the organization.

The principle is once again a social exchange. the state (the nation state) symbolically gives a corporation life and legitimacy with a franchise and backs it up with a multitude of laws that facilitate its functioning because it expects to benefit from the commerce. But it is entitled when it does so to protect its society from damaging behavior of the corporation not covered by the current laws on the books, to do so by attaching conditions to the charter.

Managements have of course vehemently objected from the first mention of the federal chartering idea, saying that it would impose that much more red tape tying their hands, and that it would deprive them of the flexibility they need to cope with the diverse and dynamic market conditions, when in fact it would affect only business integrity and moral obligations.

Anti-business? Plainly not any more than traffic ordinances or laws against theft.

However...federal chartering would not alone have the potential to be an adequate solution after the 1970s, when two major events occurred: (A) a new power surged in and soon not only corrupted governance, but overpowered the whole U.S. corporate financial system; and (b) "The Ownership Revolution" foreseen by Peter Drucker back in the 1950s came into full bloom.[19]

Up to the 1970s anti-trust enforcement, disclosure, and the SEC had held *the stock market trading to the stock market's intended purposes* fairly well: to provide capital to commerce and industry, to supply a measure of individual corporate performance and prospects, to allocate resources according to performance and prospects (therefore most effective use), and to provide liquidity for ownership transfer. But the almost total laissez-faire policies of the Reagan administration in the 1980s resulted in a complete undermining and overpowering of these purposes by unbridled greed, "commoditizing" the market and changing it substantially to a speculation and manipulation machine to get-rich-quick... the new power of (A) above.

Instability and hypervolatility became its dominant characteristics, sorely aggravated by the speculators' creative financial "derivative" securities at the time for greater winnings, and the substitution of market timing for sound investing based on corporate fundamentals. The New York Stock Exchange and Chicago pits resembled and largely still do resemble gambling casinos, and their use of the term "free market forces" became wholly misleading.

The dilemma was and still is that if the stockholders would or could exercise their rights of ownership—select the board members and demand the execution of its responsibilities—governance and management performance would much less often be major problems, but because of corporate size (of thousands of firms) and the great number of stockholders in each, the individual investor knows his or her attempted input would be ignored, and the directors and managements count on it. So "The Wall Street Rule" as Lowenstein phrased it in his book, "What's Wrong With Wall Street," has become the universal attitude: if you don't like what's going on in a firm, don't get involved, sell it.[20]

However, the second event mentioned, "The Ownership Revolution" (B), had taken place. As most market observers know, the public (individual stockholders) share of the equities dropped precipitously after the 1987 crash (to under 5%) because of not only the volatility but the blatant trading dishonesty, greed and thievery.

By 1994 they'd returned but principally via mutual funds to play it safe, and, particularly significant, institutions as a group (pensions funds, insurance companies, investment bankers, S&Ls and the mutual funds) held over 50 percent, the pensions owning over 40 percent of the top 200 Fortune-500 firms.

But these institutions had their own dilemma; selling large holdings of poorly performing corporations could be expensive not only because of the excessive turnover of an institution's portfolio but also due to the negative message to the market in each instance of a huge scale, depressing its price. An alterative: get the laggards to improve by pressuring their boards and CEOs, which a number of large ones did, notably the California Public Employee's Retirement System (CalPERS), the biggest boardroom activist.

(In the Spring of 1994 CalPERS sent 200 of the large firms in its portfolio a letter-survey suggesting they examine the GM precepts, asking them to think about how their boards operate and give CalPERS their thoughts on it. The responses were graded from A (IBM, Merck, Eastman Kodak, Squibb, Exxon, 31 others) to F (CBS, Bankers Trust, MCI, DuPont, Johnson & Johnson, American Airlines, Gannett, others.)

Indeed, four events have been changing the picture: the continuous institutional pressure, a growing recognition and acceptance by many boards and CEOs that their recommendations often had value, the need to avoid bad publicity in the press on not only poor performance but high-handed obstinacy (which the F's got in a 10/17/94 *BW* write-up), and the change of proxy rules by the SEC allowing stockholders to confer (virtually prohibited previously), to have access to stockholder lists and to place their own nominees on a slate for new directors.

Additionally, the institutions have now concocted a new structure known as "Relationship Investing" that results in what might be viewed as nontakeover takeovers. Groups are formed either by activists or institutions themselves for the sole purpose of friendly buy-ins of big poor performers, buy enough to be taken seriously be boards and CEOs, provide advice on how to improve, sometimes take a seat on the board, monitor them, and in essence ensure patient capital for longer-term decisions, better governance, and accountability. In actuality, it aligns management with at least major owners.

However, it only attends to large firms and only poor performers, and even if the groups collaborate with each other to spread the load over a fair number of firms, still untouched will be the thousands of others whether poor performing or not. Needed: an upgrading of the whole governance system. Back to the federal chartering proposal that should correct many of the behaviors listed on pages 1198-1199, to which the government should add law changes to bring our 1930s free enterprise system up to the competitive world of the 1990s.

Lester Thurow of MIT's Sloan School of Management summarized the key needs succinctly (with the Keiretsus in mind):[21]

a. Let groups of companies own substantial shares in one another and put executives on one another's boards; let financial institutions own shares in public companies (20% is common in Japan's Keiretsus).
b. Require anyone or company owning 20 percent or more of a publicly traded company's equity to give a day's public notice before buying or selling that company's stock.
c. Make voting rights increase with the length of time that shares are held, with full rights attained only after, say, five years.

The first (a) is indeed a main advantage the Japanese and Germans have. The holdings by the banks in members of their Keiretsus and by the German hausbanks ensure the pursuit of long-range goals; as a result of their capital interest they gain when their holdings gain and vice versa; like the big institutions they're not interested in applying the Wall Street Rule to the ups and downs of short-term quarterly earnings. Thus the Glass-Steagall Act that prohibits such investments has to be repealed. The intercompany stock ownership simply strengthens the many alliances already in force described in Chapter 15's strategies (page 742).

Item (b) would substantially reduce the drop in share price of large sell-offs and also reduce profiteering from inside knowledge, and the (c) would block the speculators and piratical raiders while making more probable long-range objectives for decisions. One arrangement: no voting rights given to those owning shares less than two years, one-third given in the third year, another third in the fourth year, and full voting in the fifth; the gains would be many, especially:

- stock traders would not be treated as owners;
- the use of speculative financial derivatives for trading profit would be greatly curtailed;
- market hypervolatility as in October 1987 would be unlikely;
- portfolio managers would eschew short-term gains from market timing and intuitive betting, begin taking more interest in the fundamentals and value of equity selections;
- corporate boards and CEOs would have another good reason to think and plan long-range.

Other desirable actions on the part of Congress:

- the denial of interest tax deductions on bonds or loans used for takeovers when they are sold or put back on the market within the first two years;
- raise the cost of going Chapter 11.

Wishful thinking for any of these law proposals? Probably so. In fact one does have to be quite pessimistic about any constructive legislation from a Congress largely controlled on these subjects by special interest PACs, the core factor preventing the solution of virtually all the nation's major financial problems. In this case, for example, The Security Industries Association, Inc. has been one of the largest contributors via both its huge PAC and "honoraria," the fees handouts to legislators for speeches or just being present at breakfasts, lunches, etc., fees that go directly into their pockets to influence voting on specific bills before them at that time.

A postscript. Of course, our executives, managers and society can muddle along for a long time in indifference about the leadership issues in this book—values, the principles, role responsibilities, OD, organization design and operations, justice, governance, and the rest—and doubtless many ask the question on page 166, "why give a damn about my culture which will probably hold up as long as I live." After all, as an Englishman (Keynes) once said, in the end we're all dead.

Many young people in fact believe the answer to at least the organization problem is self-employment as implied in the statement of William Blake: "I must make my own system or be a slave to another's." But one can see from the text that our knowledge of organizations and how to build them into desirable places to work can make the idea—which is too often true now—as obsolete as the old-style egotistic individualism that prompted it (the type that Rollo May said "makes one intolerable to all men").[22]

Indeed, to make our organizations both technically effective and humane ought to be perceived as the most inspiring challenge and opportunity of all, and it will be the organization leaders who will play a major part in achieving it and achieving the most desired alternative future.

NOTES

a. Kohlberg gives in this monologue (his p. 82) an excellent illustration of how the educational process can succeed, an application of Lewin's "Unfreeze-change-refreeze" principle to "the Platonic view" of virtue, moving students progressively up the moral development stages that were presented on p. 123.

b. In many business graduate schools ethics was during the 1980s and still is discussed only in "business and society" or "corporate policy" courses, and then "largely treated as another problem with which management must learn to cope, "oriented toward helping managers defend themselves in a hostile environment with little thought of the normative."[6]

c. For example, the ten books cited on page 182; and note that the University of Virginia's "Center for the Study of Applied Ethics" creates and is a source of teaching material—also, that its business school requires an ethics course for all first-year students.

d. An executive vice-president of General Motors suggested the following "Alternative Ethical Guidelines" for managements and managers who must weigh competing claims and interests, a very common dilemma (abridged): 1. First, management itself should provide a broad statement of corporate purpose, eliciting employee input from all levels, and periodically evaluate it, and (2) make organizational health and fitness a high priority, so that it can attend to the purpose on a stable long-term basis; then (3) when there are important social interests that the market fails to protect, management's overriding obligation is initially to protect the firm's financial health, then to solicit appropriate government intervention to protect those social interests, using its judgment to remove and overcome competitive impediments to the corporation's social responsibility, and (4) consider too whether the moral issue involved would be better addressed through legislation; if so, there may well be a duty to propose and pursue regulatory reform. (5) Individual managers should reject alternatives that violate basic human dignity, betray trust, or are unlawful, and (6) before presuming an obdurate conflict of interest among constituencies, consider the extent to which they share goals and use your communication skills to instill mutual understanding of what they have in common.[7]

    e.   A procedure outline that may be helpful for decision dilemmas:
  1. Write down your own perception of what alternatives there are that are ethical. This is the place for Ethics Analysis.
  2. Determine who the stakeholders are (those affected).
  3. Find out the opinions each individual (or group) has of your preferred conclusions in #1 (demonstrating your interest in their views). Next, don't rely on what they say (their "espoused theories"—Argyris), determine their "theories-in-use" in this way (a-d from Pastin):
     a. Examine their past actions on such subjects.
     b. Identify the decisions that produced them.
     c. Determine the premises, assumptions underlying them.
     d. Evolve the resulting "ground rules" they concluded and used.
     e. Weigh the probabilities of success of each alternative.
     f. Preferably via participative "utilitarian" discussion with each (group), conclude a ranking of the final alternatives with (d) and (e) in mind. Then make a choice (with their concurrence if possible) per your values and felt responsibilities to each stakeholder (or group).

    f.   Social responsibility to professional and non-corporate entities.

    g.   A promising sign: the Conference Board found in a 1986 survey of 140 large firms that a major community concern of theirs for the next five years would be the quality of primary and secondary education, motivated by their sense of "corporate responsibility." Other leading concerns were aging, health care, and unemployment.[10]

    h.   "Imagine a country where the election results aren't known for weeks after the vote. Where incumbents can keep the polls open longer than scheduled to rustle up more favorable votes. Where they can lobby voters to change their ballots long after they are cast and cut confidential deals to sway votes. Where they can ignore the results of a referendum. This is no banana republic. It's corporate democracy." (*Business Week*, July 4, 1988, p.37).

    i.   A 1978 case at Columbia Pictures: a top executive who was particularly good at picking movie winners was caught stealing from employees by forging "pay to" himself on bonus checks, so the president fired him. But the board forced his reinstatement even though other serious offenses came to light. However, a public outcry forced his removal again, at which time the board gave him a contract to continue as a consultant and fired the president to get even with him for firing the man in the first place. The message to employees: we don't care if you're a crook as long as you make money for us. In 1981 United Artists made him its chairman and chief executive officer. This is the industry with probably the greatest impact on the formation of public values.

j.   For another example of their ambivalence. when the American Law Institute decided recently to study governance toward designing stronger laws, the Roundtable chairman and other members called it a major threat lo capitalism, tried to derail the project (in a Mar. '84 paper), and did succeed in forcing them to scale it back. Then as recently as 1991 they tried to prevent the new SEC ruling allowing communication among stockholders.

k.   Rollo May recommends the development (by Education) of an ethic of intent: "We are responsible for the effects of our actions, and we are also responsible for becoming as aware as we can of these effects."[13]

l.
1776 Population		*1976 Employment*	
Virginia	493,000	AT&T	939,000
Pennsylvania	284,000	General Motors	681,000
Massachusetts	252.000	Postal Service	696,000

REFERENCES

1.   Markley, O.W., *Alternative Futures: Contexts in Which Social Indicators Must Work* (Menlo Park, CA: Stanford Research Institute, 1970). U.S. Office of Education contract #OEC 1-7-071013-2474.

2.   "What they see in the future," *New York Times*, Jan 11, 1981.

3.   Kohlberg, L., "Stage and Sequence: The Cognitive-Development Approach to Socialization," *Handbook of Socialization Theory and Research*, (ed.) D.A. Goslin (Chicago: Rand McNally, 1969).

4.   Hogan, R., "Moral Development and the Structure of Personality." *Moral Development*, (eds.) D.J. DePalma and J.M. Foley (Hillsdale, NJ: Lawrence Eribaum Associates, 1974), p. 162.

5.   Powers, C.W., and D. Vogel, *Ethics in the Education of Business Managers* (Briarcliff Manor, NY: Hastings Center, 1980), Section III.

6.   Ibid, pp. 35-36.

7.   Johnson, E.W., "Alternative Ethical Guidelines," *Harvard Business Review*, Jan.-Feb. 1988, p.146.

8.   Dalton, D.R. and R.A. Cosier, "The Four Faces of Social Responsibility," *Business Horizons*, May-June 1982.

9.   Mertes, J.E., "Case Study—TRW Inc., A Social Policy Statement," *Business and Society* (eds.) R.D. Hay, E.R. Gray and J.E. Gates (Cincinnati, OH: South-Western Publishing Co., 1976).

10.   *Forbes*, March 10, 1986, p.9.

11.   Crystal, G.S., *In Search of Excess* (NY: W.W. Norton, 1991).

12.   Andrews, K.R., "The Roundtable statement on the board of directors," *Harvard Business Reviews* Sept.-Oct., 1978.

13.   May, R., *Power and Innocence* (NY: W.W. Norton, 1972).

14.   Stone, C.D., *Where the Law Ends* (NY: Harper & Row, 1975), pp. 138-9.

15. *Fortune,* November 29, 1993, p.10.

16. *Harvard Business Review,* Jan.-Feb. 1993, p.81.-17. Salmon, W.J., "Crisis Prevention: How to Gear Up Your Board," *Harvard Business Review,* Jan.-Feb. 1993.

18. Ewing, D., op.cit. (1977), pp. 12-13.

19. Drucker, P., "Reconning with the Pension Fund Revolution," *Harvard Business Review,* Mar.-Apr. 1991.

20. Lowenstein, L., *What's Wrong With Wall Street* (Reading, MA: Addison-Wesley, 1988).

21. Thurow, L., "Let's Learn From the Japanese," *Fortune,* Nov. 18, 1991.

22. May, R., op.cit., p.259.

EXHIBIT 6*

A CASE OF CHANGING AN ORGANIZATION'S CULTURE

This case describes a strategy for changing the "culture" of an organization, in this instance, from a family-owned, family-managed organization to a family-owned, professionally managed organization.

BACKGROUND

A large food and catering company (annual sales volume $600,000,000; 30,000 employees) had, over the years, enjoyed a commanding position in its markets. In recent years this position had deteriorated seriously. Major causes for this included increased competition and increased costs, both of which had contributed to a squeeze on profits. Other causes were a rather "traditional" marketing strategy not geared to the times, and a relatively rigid management style.

The company culture was modeled on a "royalist" pattern with the family members holding all the top management jobs. (Your father had to be a member of the owning family for you to hold any job above department head). Most of the management and work force were long-term employees and were generally satisfied with this state of affairs. There had been relatively little pressure for productivity and efficiency. Historically the organization had existed in a relatively stable, predictable world. There was a heavy production orientation in the organization so that production people had highest influence on the top management.

---

*Referred to page 1033.

THE NEED

One of the more progressive and more influential members of the family (we'll call him Mr. A) headed several sections of the enterprise including the largest single business. He was acutely aware of the problems in the organization; the need for increased marketing capability; the need for new organization forms, and the need for promotion by merit rather than heredity. He and some of his brothers undertook to persuade their family colleagues to consider moving toward a change in the culture and the introduction of more professional management After some years of negotiation, they were able to get approval for an experimental change program in the largest business segment.

At this point Mr. A called in consultants to help diagnose the situation and develop a change strategy.

INITIAL DIAGNOSIS AND STRATEGY

As the initial consultant, I worked with the family member and a member of the personnel staff. We addressed ourselves first to the following questions:

What is the specific change problem?
What systems and subsystems are specifically affected?
What is the "state" of each of these subsystems?
How *ready* for change? How *capable* to make the change?

The change problem was defined as changing the management of this division from a relatively low-autonomy group, with centralized decision-making by the family leadership, to a *relatively* autonomous profit center with professional management. A secondary change target was to continue to move the culture of the business from a heavily production-technical orientation to a more heavily marketing-oriented stance.

The systems most affected were

1. The family member who had been manager and would now be a group executive.
2. The new division manager.
3. The top division staff who now reported to a family member and would report to the new man (presently one of their colleagues).
4. Several of the corporate staff groups which interfaced with the division management and in which control was divided.

We looked at each "system's" readiness and capability for change.

	Readiness	Capability
Family member	High	High
New division manager	High	High
Top division staff	Medium to low	Low to high
Corporate functional groups	Medium to low	Medium to high

The above analysis was arrived at through discussions with key people in each of the systems. Additional facts about the state of things were:

1. There was some high management potential in the existing management team of the division.
2. The change in management would be very dramatic and probably traumatic for a number of management people.
3. The first professional manager should have a strong marketing capability.
4. There was such a man heading the marketing function in the division (Mr. B).

5. He had some relationship problems with some of his colleagues, partly due to his personal style but largely due to his role and the increased stature of marketing in the company.
6. If Mr. B were to be the "nominee," it would be necessary to give him and opportunity to further develop a *general* management orientation and to work on his own management style before the organization change.
7. It would be necessary to prepare the division-management group for the change, to get out some of their feelings and attitudes about the new leadership, and to find ways of getting their commitment to making the new mode work.
8. The family member, Mr. A, who would move out of direct management operations and function as a group executive to whom the division manager would report, was well loved and respected by the team. His personal conviction and desire to really carry out the change would have to be well communicated to the members of the team.
9. Mr. A would have to be prepared to fully support Mr. B's decisions. Based on this diagnosis, the following initial strategy was developed:
1. Mr. B would go to an advanced management program at a major business school.
2. An off-site meeting would be held with the top management team immediately following his return from the course and before any public announcement was made.
3. Just prior to this meeting all members of the group would be interviewed by the consultant to get their feelings and thoughts about the barriers to optimum effectiveness in the division management; the kinds of changes they would like to see occur; their concerns about a "non-family" manager; their career problems and interests.

4. The actual changeover of management would not take place for several months after the first off-site meeting.

5. Following the actual announcement, additional kinds of activities would be scheduled, including team building with the new management team, some work on intergroup relationships between the new team and the relevant central-staff service, and some goal-setting activities for the management team and later for the subunits of the division.

ACTIONS

1. Mr. B went to the business school course.

2. During the period of the course, he met several times with me. We talked about his role in the planned off-site meeting, including some of the problems that would exist with his colleagues. I made it clear that an essential condition for an effective team meeting was his personal conviction of the worth of such an activity, his commitment to doing it, and his willingness to openly discuss whatever information came out on business or organization problems or on attitudes and feelings of his colleagues.

Without such commitment, I proposed we should not hold the team meeting. Mr. B originally was quite skeptical about the worth of this activity. As he thought more about it, he decided that it *would* be useful to bring the group together to clear the air and begin to build toward a new team. He saw this as practical since it was similar to the way he had operated in his marketing leadership role with the marketing team.

3. During this same period (the 12-week course) Mr. B returned to his company for a meeting with Mr. A. The purpose was to think trough the new role relationships between the two men and to decide how things would be handled and decisions made in this new mode.

4. After the course ended, as previously planned, I interviewed the nine members of the management group about their feelings concerning the change; about the kind of organization and the kind of management that would be required to improve the division's position in the field and to build a stronger organization. Several interesting findings emerged from these interviews.

a) Several who were interviewed felt threatened by the change. They had spent their entire working lives reporting to a "member of royalty," the *family*, and now were about to find themselves reporting to a "commoner," one of *them*. This was perceived as a loss of status, both in the firm and in the community. It was also seen as a loss of contact and upward influence with the power center, since the family would still own the business.

b) Another significant finding was the deep concern expressed by the production and technical people about the increasing influence of the marketing people. The change was perceived as a real takeover by the marketing "hot shots."

c) Some others interviewed feared they would be faced with more restrictions, and would have less autonomy and less influence.

d) There was a considerable lack of trust in the real motivations of the family in making the change. Was this a gimmick? Was it for real? What were the intentions of the family? Was this a device to upgrade marketing? What would happen to the young and sometimes incompetent family members; would they *really* be asked to report to a non-family manager?

e) A number of other historical problems surfaced in the interviews. A real conflict had existed between the technology and production departments as to who should control quality in the production process.

f) The financial manager had his primary loyalties in the central finance office, which he saw as his "home." He felt that he was a representative of the family ownership in the division. He was not a "regular" member of the management team and he did not see himself as really accountable to the general manager. He feared that Mr. B's appointment would be a threat to his role. He felt there would have to be a confrontation between the headquarters financial people and the new division manager to get things straight.

5. The day after the data were collected, Mr. A, Mr. B, the department heads, and the consultants (myself and an in-company personnel man) went away for a three-day meeting. The first evening was spent in an informal get-together by the group while the consultants were summarizing the data that had been collected. The next morning I fed back the interview results to the group. We had put the information into several categories. There was a group of items about Mr. A's intentions, motivations, reasons, and plans; a second group; related to attitudes toward Mr. B; and another group of items about the fears of a marketing takeover. A fourth group related to the financial management situation; a fifth, to intergroup or interdepartmental difficulties, including the technical/production quality-control problem. A final category dealt with division policies and practices.

After the feedback of the total information, the group selected one set of items on which they wanted to work. It quickly became apparent to all that it would be necessary to hear from Mr. A about his plans and intentions before anything else could be profitably discussed. He was quite prepared to do this. He made an open disclosure about his thinking, his feelings about the firm, about the question of promotion through competence versus heredity; about the difficulties he'd had in getting support from some of the family colleagues for his ideas; and about his strong conviction as to

the necessity to continue down this course. He responded to a number of questions, including some about other younger family members, two of whom were present, and who would now move into roles subordinate to a non-family man. He announced his planned timetable for making the general announcement of the change several months after this meeting. To his surprise, the group suggested strongly that, after hearing him and seeing the situation, it made much more sense to them for him to make the change immediately. They suggested, "Let's start the new ball game and get to work on increasing the productivity and effectiveness of the organization." He agreed to this new timetable.

The next major agenda item was the feelings and anxieties about Mr. B, who was to be their boss. Using the interview information as a starting point, there was a very frank discussion of their concerns. Mr. B was queried about his past managerial style and proposed practices. People expressed their concerns about his past over-controlling style. Some voiced the worry that he would favor marketing to the detriment of other departments. He responded to these questions and shared his plans and concerns. He asked for continuing feedback on his behavior in the months ahead. He and the group worked out mechanisms for keeping this subject on the agenda for the next few months at all staff meetings.

At the end of the three days, a number of positive action steps emerged. These included:

a. Scheduling a similar off-site meeting for the technical and production managements to work through their problems of relationship and control.

b. A reorganization of the administrative staff.

c. A rethinking of the kinds of agenda to be dealt with at staff meetings.

d. An agreement to have at least one meeting a month that would look at how the management group was functioning so that continuous temperature-taking was part of the process.

e. An agreement to leave this whole group function as members of the management staff for three months, but with the knowledge that it was the intention of Mr. B to cut down this very large team.

f. Recognition that it might be too difficult for some management people to accommodate to the change in management style from Mr. A's to Mr. B's style—that this would be a matter for continued discussion and negotiation.

g. An agreement to examine the financial-management role question.

h. Clarification on how Mr. A, in his new role as group executive would participate in division matters, for example, he would no longer attend management meetings except as specifically requested.

i. An agreement on the condition under which matters were to be brought to Mr. B or to Mr. A.

6. The next step was for an extensive team-building and goal- setting program by the top team. This went on for several months. Their continued work together did build a cohesive and quite enthusiastic team with one exception—the financial manager. He became more and more uncomfortable and his performance more frustrating to his colleagues. A series of meetings was set up between the central financial-management staff and Mr B, who strongly believed in decentralized control. A new arrangement was worked out which was different from the traditional patterns of highly centralized control that had existed in the company.

The financial manager was transferred back to the central office. A new man was brought in from outside who had an operating orientation. He was able to provide the management with accounting and management services that Mr. B felt were essential and, at the same time, to meet the needs of the central office for financial information.

7. Moving down the organization, the members of the top team began spending so much of their time and energy with each other that they began to lose contact with the people immediately below them. the middle managers began griping to the personnel staff and to Mr. B. They felt they had less communication to and from the top than before. They felt helpless to influence the division. They felt their bosses were less accessible than in the past.

As he became aware of this, Mr. B talked with his top team, which did not see the problem as clearly as he did. Mr. B felt that immediate action was required. He asked for some consulting help. After examining the situation, we decided on a meeting of the entire management group to get the feelings aired, the priority problems identified, and action plans started for dealing with these priorities.

From this situation we invented the confrontation meeting (described in *Chapter 19*). A one-day meeting was held in a hotel. After an opening session, the total management group met in small *ad hoc* groups. They identified problems and behaviors that were getting in the way of communications and performance. They then met as functional teams: sales, marketing, production, engineering, and finance. They took information from the *ad hoc* groups and made plans for doing something about it. Each group also produced a list of items to which Mr. B and the top team should give priority attention. In a general session, Mr. B responded to each of these. He made a commitment to action of some sort on each item.

This meeting tended to bring the whole organization together and to mobilize a considerable amount of energy toward systematic organization improvement. In effect, it was an organization-wide, *goal-setting* exercise.

8. Changes in an organization of this kind do not stay stable, and a few months later another off-site meeting seemed indicated. Let me quote from a talk made by Mr. B at a national management meeting some years later.

His talk describes the whole effort but what follows looks specifically at this phase:

And then the top team began to get frustrated with itself, feel cynical of its own achievements—I now find I didn't believe at the time that they would be, but the top team then went through the same process of confrontation. We sat down again over two or three days with the aid of Dick Beckhard and worked through the problems, in a very candid and open way, that were bugging us. What were the barriers to team effectiveness? Now these exercises involve talking about things which might, in another culture, sound like weakness. Sometimes we lacked competence. Well, we all knew we lacked competence in a certain area. We all talked about our lack of competence in certain areas in the back staircase, but were we willing to confront it? What were the risks in so doing—would there be a blowup? Would somebody resign? Would somebody get fired? We took the risk and in fact this turned out to be a fear which was unsubstantiated. Also the question of trust—did we really trust other people? One looked at the actual behavior of members of the group and saw the way in which that behavior, predicated as it was on certain assumptions about how to be effective, did nothing but arouse anger, mistrust, and anxiety in other members of the team. We then made a conscious attempt to look at the top team to see how we could reduce these barriers. I want to emphasize my grave concern about this exercise. Was this weakness? Was I letting the lunatics run the asylum? Was I abdicating this thing called leadership? Or was this leadership? Well, it seemed to work out okay, so we then passed on to the next logical phase: It's all right for the top management—what about the operating management? So we went through the process as a division, then, of trying to get the entire management, I suppose between 150 and 250 people, to have this same kind of experience, to go through the same processes which in a more intensive way we had gone through.

9. They set up a series of programs using the managerial Grid. Their entire management organization went to these programs. Senior division-management attended laboratory-training programs; team-development meetings were held with marketing, sales, and production groups, and systematic annual team goal-setting meetings were started.

Let me go back to another quote from Mr. B's remarks to the management association:

What have we got from this exercise? We believe we have obtained, as a product, a freed-up society—candor is practiced—confrontation is valued, goal orientation, new patterns of behavior, sounder concepts, sounder values—task-group possibilities—maximization of resources.

He then goes on to describe a number of specific things that are different—hourly people showing considerably more concern about quality control and efficiency and effectiveness; foremen being concerned about absenteeism much more than they used to be and being concerned about job satisfaction.

SUMMARY AND ANALYSIS

This case describes the first steps in an organization-wide effort to change the culture of an enterprise from family-owned, family-managed to family-owned, professionally managed.

The strategy was to start the change with a pilot effort in a significant (largest business) sector of the enterprise. The basis for this strategy choice was developed by the management with consultant help. Significant factors were:

1. The change would be dramatic and probably traumatic.
2. Many new relationships would have to be established.
3. Many would fear the change so it would need to be not too threatening.
4. The first efforts had to be successful if further efforts were to be effective.
5. The top management (family) needed to learn how to handle the change, so a pilot effort was best.

Having decided the pilot population, a diagnosis of that environment was made. Using a "model of planned change from behavioral-science research" the management and consultant developed:

1. A refinement of the statement of the change problem.
2. An analysis of the relevant units of the organization.
3. An analysis of each unit's attitudes and capacity to handle the change.

From this diagnosis, an action strategy was developed. It included:

1. Attitude assessment and development for top management (Mr. A).
2. Attitude change, behavior change, and wider orientation for the new division manager (Mr. B—business school, consulting conferences).
3. Attitude analysis, behavior change for division team (interviews, first off-site, follow-up meeting).
4. Change in influence of middle management (confrontation meeting).

In order to assure up to date information on the effects of the change effort, a number of information-collecting mechanisms were developed. These induced:

1. Follow-up minutes on action plans from first off-site.
2. Periodic discussion on the "state of things" between both outside and inside consultants with Mr. A, Mr. B, and top-team members.
3. Total organization confrontation meetings.
4. Periodic temperature-taking within teams (management team, functional teams, and task groups).
5. Building in critique or analysis as an organic part of staff and other meetings.

The consultant roles in this case were:

1. To help in a total-organization diagnosis and strategy plan (pilot project).
2. To provide a model for analyzing the change problem and strategy (system analysis).
3. To counsel with key individuals and pairs (Mr. A, Mr. B, production managers) on roles and relationships.
4. To get information on the state of the system and to feed it back (division team, total group, departments).
5. To function as procedural guide and consultant at team-development meetings (division team, division and group managers).
6. To convene and consult with groups having interface difficulties (production, technical).
7. To counsel with key management on continuing strategies (Mr. A, Mr. B).
8. To periodically "take a reading" with the organization on its own health and effectiveness as a basis for planning.

EXHIBIT 7*

GUIDE FOR A CORPORATE PERSONNEL POLICY

Source: *Ethics and Expediency in Personnel Management* by C. R. Milton (Columbia So. C: Univ. of So. Carolina Press, 1970), pp. 226-230. Author's title: "The Total Personality Model of Personnel Philosophy."

I. Company and Employee Relationships.

    A. Leadership Climate.

Although the philosophical foundation for management rests upon the rights of private property and a freedom contract, leadership is eclectic; that is, authoritarian when necessary but democratic when conditions permit. Based upon the decentralization of authority and decision-making, executive leadership formally encourages employees to function as a social unit by participation in decisions appropriate to the level at which employees work.

Positive leadership prevails that is directed toward earning cooperation, interest, and goodwill through the possession of human understanding, fairness, and consideration for the dignity, self-respect, personal interest, and security of employees.

Sound personnel relations are not incompatible with profits, but encourage rising productivity and business efficiency.

Relationships with each employee are governed by the highest standards of conduct and ethics; the personal satisfactions of employees is one of the measures of company success.

    B. Motivational Climate.

Management is committed to the promotion of a work environment that gives balanced consideration to economic, psychological, and social needs; gratification of one set of needs is not emphasized at the expense of minimizing others.

Management creates conditions which will keep the objectives of the company and employees as harmonious as possible by dealing with employees to their greatest advantage and by developing motivations which spontaneously generate employee efforts.

Having a basic faith in the employee's capacity and willingness to direct his behavior toward organization goals or sub-goals, as well as his capacity to assume responsibility, management strive to arrange work conditions and methods of operation so each employee can achieve his personal goals by the direction of his efforts toward organization objectives or sub-goals.

Relying upon the employee's self-control and self-direction, management seeks to provide guidance and opportunities for growth and development.

    C. Social Responsibility. The employee's standard of living, security, and welfare are intimately linked with the company's welfare.

        1. Work environment.

            a. To provide good working conditions that appeal to the self-respect and dignity of employees.

            b. To provide adequate protection for the health and safety of all employees.

        2. Economic security.

            To maintain personnel policies that provide adequate compensation, hospital and medical services, sickness and accident insurance, life insurance, and other feasible employment benefits.

---

* Referred to on page 1141.

3. Job security.
   To provide steady employment for employees insofar as possible by careful planning and good management.

D. Labor Concepts.

1. Consumer—Public.
   Satisfactory employee-management relations are the basis for public relations, and long-term profitable operations must be based on public, customer, and employee goodwill and loyalty since these groups are essentially the same.
2. Partnership (Optional).
   Make each employee a full partner in the enterprise through profit sharing or stock ownership so that the employee shares in the profits and growth of the enterprise.

II. Supervisor and the Work Group.

A. Social Concept of Labor.

Since social needs find expression through formal and informal associations, both top management and supervisors are involved in effectuating an adequate social work environment. Those measures requiring the support of top management, since staff and engineering assistance are required, and therefore only indirectly under supervisory influence, are as follows:

1. Supervisory training directed toward the promotion ·of leadership to understand and cope with the social phenomenon of work.
2. The restructuring of small work groups, built around common experiences and interests, and the concomitant physical arrangement of production.
3. Establishment of congenial groups of employees by sociometric grouping.

B. Immediate Supervisor

Activities that are necessarily implemented by the work group's immediate supervisor are as follows:

1. Encourage employees to function as a social unit, both formally and informally by strengthening team work and group solidarity.
2. Promote group activities on the job and recognize group members for work performed collectively.
3. Apply group incentives when appropriate.
4. Assist the development of a common positive purpose while working under a minimum of supervisory pressure.
5. Encourage the group to develop his own means for internal self-control.
6. When practical, respect the standards, norms of behavior, and values that the work group believes are proper.
7. Identify and cooperate with informal group leaders to minimize conflict and to assure that the informal leadership in promoting company objectives.
8. Use consultation and participation in the making of decisions to minimize conflict of managerial objectives and group values before technological innovations are made and to solve problems that involve the group as a whole.

III.   Supervisor and the Employee.

    A.   Humanistic Labor Concept.

        1.   The practice of employee centered leadership.

            a.   To provide a gratifying personal relationship through considerate and understanding treatment.

            b.   To provide direction based upon persuasion and suggestion.

            c.   To provide a gratifying work relationship through general directions and the evaluation of performance.

        2.   Respect for the right of each employee.

            a.   To be treated as an individual and respected as a person.

            b.   To fairness and justice in all his relations with fellow employees and superiors.

            c.   To prompt, fair adjustment of complaints of every kind.

        3.   Communications.

            a.   To provide each employee with the knowledge of where he stands in terms of job performance and promotion potential.

            b.   To inform the employee on matters that may affect his economic psychological, and social well-being.

    B.   Citizenship Labor Concept.

        1.   Free expression.

        To assure each employee the right of free expression on matters that concern his own and company welfare.

        2.   Consultation.

        To give each employee an opportunity to contribute to the best of his ability in the solution of common problems.

        3.   Participation.

        To encourage each individual as a group member to participate in discussing and solving problems that involve the group as a whole.

IV.   Individual and Job.

    A.   Uniqueness Labor Concept.

        1.   To select differentially and fill all jobs with the best applicants available so as to provide the individual with purpose and satisfaction in his daily activity.

        2.   To encourage and foster individual development and advancement by training each employee to his maximum capacity.

        3.   To base promotion on merit and seniority; all other things being equal, the employee with longest service should be given preference.

    B.   Humanistic Labor Concept.

        Provide a psychologically gratifying job function insofar as possible and give adequate attention to job enrichment and job rotation when necessary.

V.   Company and the Union—Labor Relations.

Management works with the union on a fair and businesslike basis when employees choose to bargain collectively. Labor relations are conducted willingly and frankly with the employees' authorized representatives and with regard for the rights and responsibilities of the union.

Since positive advantages are seen as accruing from bargaining with a strong and well-disciplined union, management encourages workers to support their union.

Labor-management relations are based upon consultation and cooperation, rather than unilateral imposition or working around the union. Management separates areas of conflict and mutual interest as a means of increasing cooperation.

Management accept the viewpoint that it is possible for employees to be loyal to both the company and their union—dual loyalty.

Management recognizes the compatibility between sound personnel relations and collective bargaining with the elected representatives of their employees. Labor relations do not preclude the need for personnel relations, and consequently, management strives to maintain a balance between its relations with employees as a group and as individuals.

VI. Personnel Management for the Total Personality Personnel Philosophy.

To implement the philosophy previously outlined requires that the personnel management function be characterized by the following conditions:

Top management function be characterized by the following conditions.

Top management accept the ultimate responsibility for personnel relations, and personnel management is accepted as a basic function of management.

Personnel executives or managers have assimilated the ethical and philosophical foundation of personnel administration as a scientific discipline. Consequently, both behavioral principles and techniques provided by the social sciences are employed to promote harmonious personnel relations.

The personnel manager is an active participant in top management planning when policies are formulated that have an impact upon human relations and advises management of the personnel implications of proposed policies or courses of action. Consequently, human values, motivation, and attitudes are considered prior to the adoption of managerial plans and programs.

Personnel management is a major function of every person having supervisory responsibilities. Consequently, each person in a managerial capacity is in effect a "personnel manager" who fully understands the personnel philosophy, policies, and procedures formulated by top management.

Labor relations are integrated with personnel relations in order to achieve a consistent and balanced program of employee relations.

The personnel program contains the essential elements of personnel management, supplemented by relevant, appropriate techniques; such techniques and tools, however, are only a means to the promotion of personal satisfaction and job adjustment.

Bibliography

Adams, W. & J.W. Brock, "The hidden costs of failed mergers," *New York Times*, June 21, 1987, 3F

Achoff, R.L., *A Concept of Corporate Planning* (New York: John Wiley, 1970)

Adler. A., *Practice and Theory of Individual Psychology* (London: Lund Humphries, 1923)

Adler, M., *Aristotle for Everybody* (New York: Macmillan, 1978)

————, *Six Great Ideas* (New York: Macmillan, 1981)

Adorno, T.W. et al, *The Authoritarian Personality* (New York: Harper & Row, 1950)

Alfred, T.M., "Checkers or choice in manpower management," *Harvard Business Review*, January-February 1967

Allport, G.W., *Personality: A Psychological Interpretation* (New York: Holt, 1973)

————, "Historical Background of Modern Social Psychology, Handbook of Social Psychology," (ed) G. Lindzey, (Reading, Mass: Addison-Wesley, 1954)

Allport, G.W., Vernon, P.E., & Lindzey, G., *The Study of Values* (Boston: Houghton Mifflin, 3rd Revision, 1970)

Ancona, D. - See Nadler, D.A.

Andrews, K.R., "The Roundtable statement on boards of directors," *Harvard Business Review*, September-October 1978

Ansbacher, H.L., "Individual Psychology," *American Handbook of Psychiatry* (ed) Silvano Atieti (New York: Basic Books, 1974)

Ansoff, H.L. *Corporate Strategy* (New York: McGraw-Hill, 1975)

Argyris, C., *Personality and Organization* (New York: Harper & Row, 1957)

————, *Interpersonal Competence and Organizational Effectiveness* (Homewood, Ill.: Irwin-Dorsey, 1962)

————, "T-Group for organizational effectiveness," *Harvard Business Review*, March-April, 1964

————, "Interpersonal barriers to decision making," *Harvard Business Review*, March-April, 1966

————, *Management and Organizational Development* (New York: McGraw- Hill, 1971A)

————, "Beyond freedom and dignity by B.F. Skinner, A Review Essay," *Harvard Educational Review* Vol. 41, No. 4, 1971B)

————, *Increasing Leadership Effectiveness* (New York: John Wiley, 1976A)

————, *Argyris on Organization* (New York: Amacom, 1976B) four audio cassettes.

Argyris, C. & Schon, D.A. *Theory in Practice: Increasing Professional Effectiveness* (San Francisco: Jossey-Bass, 1964)

Aristotle, *The Nichomachean Ethics*, trans, by W.D. Ross (London: Clarendon Press, 1925)

Arnstein, W.E., "The Fundamentals of Profit Planning," *The New York Certified Accountant*, May 1962

Axelrod, R., *The Evolution of Cooperation* (New York: Basic Books, 1984)

Austin, N.K. - See Peters, T.J.

Azrin, N.H. & Holtz, W.C., "Punishment," *Operant Behavior* (ed) Honig, W.K. (New York: Appleton-Croft-Century, 1966)

Baird, L.S., - See Schneier, C.E.

Bamforth, K.W. - See Triste, E.L.

Barnard, C.I. *The Functions of the Executive* (Cambridge, Harvard Press, 1938)

Bartunek, J.M., "Why did you do that? Attribution Theory in Organizations," *Business Horizons*, September-October 1981

Bass, B.M., *Stogdill's Handbook of Leadership* (New York: Free Press, 1981)

Baumhard, R., *Ethics in Business* (New York: Holt, Rinehart & Winston, 1968)

Bayles, M.D., & K. Henley (eds), *Right Conduct*, (New York: Random House, 1983)

Beatty, R.W. - See Schneier, C.E.

Beckhard, R., "The confrontational meeting," *Harvard Business Review*, March-April, 1967

————, *Organizational Development* (Reading, Mass: Addison-Wesley, 1969)

Beer, M. & Ruh, R.A., "Employee growth through performance management," *Harvard Business Review*, July-August, 1976

Bell, C.H., Jr - See French, W.L.

Bennis, W.G., "Revisionist theory of leadership," *Harvard Business Review*, January-February, 1961

————, *Changing Organizations* (New York: McGraw-Hill, 1966)

————, *Organization Development: Its Nature origin and Prospects*, (Reading, Mass.: Addison-Wesley, 1969)

————, *The Unconscious Conspiracy* (New York: Amacom, 1976)

Bennis W.G., and Shepard, H.A., "A Theory of Group Development," *Human Relations* Vol. 9, November 4, 1965

Bensen, S., - See Johansen, R.

Bertalanffy, L. Von, "The Theory of Open Systems in Physics and Biology," *Science*, January 13, 1950

————, "The World of Science and the World of Values," *Teachers College Record*, Vol. 65, 1964

Bettelheim, B., "Moral Education," *Moral Education, Five Lectures* (Cambridge, Mass.: Harvard University Press, 1970)

Blades, L.E., "Employment at Will vs. Individual Freedom: On Limiting the Abusive Exercise of Employer Power," *Columbia Law Review*, Vol. 67, 1967

Blake, R.R. & Mouton, J.S., *Building a Dynamic Corporation Through Grid Organizational Development* (Reading, Mass.: Addison-Wesley, 1969)

————, *The New Managerial Grid* (Houston, Texas: Gulf Publishing Co., 1978)

Blanchard, K.H. - See P. Hersey

Blanchard, K.H., P. Zigarmi and D. Zigarmi, *Leadership and The One Minute Manager* (New York: William Morrow, 1985)

Bolt, J.F., *Executive Development* (New York: HarperBusiness, 1989)

Bonjean, C.M. & Vance, G.G., "A short-form measure of self-actualization" *Journal of Applied Behavioral Science*, 4, 1968

Boss, R.W., "Trust and Managerial Problem Solving Revisited," *Group Organizational Studies* September 1978, p 331.

Bowers, D.G. - See Marrow, A.J.

Bowers, D.G., & S.E. Seashore, "Predicting Organizational Effectiveness with a Four-factor Theory of Leadership," *Administrative Science Quarterly*, September, 1966

Bowman, J.S., "Altering the Fabric of Work: beyond the Behavioral Sciences," *Business Horizons*, Sept.-Oct. 1984.

Boyatzis, R.E., *The Competent Manager* (New York: John Wiley, 1982)

Brenner, S.N. & Molander, E.A., "Is the ethics of business changing?" *Harvard Business Review*, January-February 1977

Bright, W.E., "How one company manages its human resources," *Harvard Business Review*, January-February, 1976

Brion, J.M., *Decisions, Organization Planning and the Marketing Concept*, (New York: American Management Assn., 1964)(technical planning)

————, *Corporate Marketing Planning* (New York: John Wiley, 1967)(technical planning)

Brock, J.W. - See Adams, W.

Brooke, M.Z. and Remmers, H.L., *The Strategy of Multinational Enterprise* (New York: American Elsevier Pub. Co., 1970)

Burack, E.H. & Mathys, N.J., *Human Resources Planning: A Pragmatic Approach* (Lake Forest, Ill.: Brace-Park Press, 1980)

————, "Career Ladders, Pathing and Planning: Some Neglected Basics," *Human Resources Management*, Summer 1977

————, *Career Management in Organizations: A Practical Planning Approach* (Lake Forest, Ill.: Brace-Park Press, 1980)

Burgess, R.L., "Communication Networks: An Experimental Reevaluation," *Journal of Experimental Social Psychology*, July 1968

Burnham, D.H. - See MacClelland, D.C.

Burns, T. & Stalker, G.M., *The Management of Innovation* (London: Tavistock Publications, 1961)

Buss, A.H., "Aggression Pays," *The Control of Aggression and Violence*, (ed) Singer, J.L. (New York: Academic Press, 1971)

Buxton, V.M. - See Schneider, B.

Byham, W.C., "Assessment Centers for Spotting Future Managers," *Harvard Business Review*, July-August 1970

Campbell, J.P., Dunnette, M.V., Lawler, E.E., III, & Weick, K.E., Jr., *Managerial Behavior, Performance and Effectiveness* (New York: McGraw-Hill, 1970)

Campbell, D.N., R.L. Fleming & R.C. Grote, "Discipline without punishment - at last," *Harvard Business Review* July-August 1985

Campbell, A. - See Gould, M.

Carroll, S.J. - See Tosi, H.

Cartwright, D. & Lippitt, R., "Group Dynamics and the Individual," *International Journal of Group Psychotherapy*, Vol. 7, January 1957

Cattell, R. B., *Personality: A Systematic and Factual Study*, (New York: McGraw-Hill, 1950)

Chandler, A.D., Jr., *Strategy and Structure* (Cambridge, MIT Press, 1962)

Charan, R., "How Networks Reshape Organization - For Results," *Harvard Business Review*, September-October, 1991

Coch, L., & French, N.R.P., "Overcoming Resistance to Change," *Human Relations*, Vol. 1, No.4, 1948

Cohen, P., *The Gospel According to the Harvard Business School* (New York: Doubleday, 1973)

Cohen, S.R. & Zysman, J., *Manufacturing Matters: The Myth of the Post-Industrial Economy* (N.Y.: Basic Books, 1987)

Coleman, J.C., *Psychological and Effective Behavior* (Glenview, Ill.: Scott- Foresman, 1969)

Collard, B.A. - See Waterman, R.H., Jr.

Conger, J.A., *Learning to Lead* (San Francisco: Jossey-Bass, 1992)

Cornwall, D.J., "Human Resources Programs: Blue Sky or Operating Priority?" *Business Horizons*, April 1980

Coser, L., *The Function of Social Conflict* (New York: Free Press, 1956)

Cosier, R.A. - See Dalton, D.R.

Cottrell, N.B., et al, "Social Facilitation of dominant responses by the presence of an audience and the mere presence of others" *Journal of Personality and Social Psychology*, 1968,9

Cox, R.D., "The Concept of Psychological Maturity," *American Handbook of Psychiatry* (ed) Arieti, S., (New York: Basic Books, 1974)

Crane, D.P., "The Case for Participative Management," *Business Horizons*, April 1976

Cronin, M.J., *Doing Business on the Internet* (New York: Van Nostrand Reinholt, 1993)

Crystal, G.S., "Incentive Pay that Doesn't Work," *Fortune* 8/28/89

Crystal, G.S., *In Search of Excess* (New York: W.W. Norton, 1991)

Cummings, L.L. - See Schull, F.A. Jr.

Cyert, R.M. & March, J.G., *A Behavioral Theory of the Firm* (Engelwood Cliffs: Prentice-Hall, 1963)

Dale, E., "Centralization vs. Decentralization," *Advanced Management*, June 1955

————, & Meloy, C., "Hamilton MacFarland Barksdale and the Dupont Contributions to Systematic Management," *The Business History Review*, Summer 1962

————, & Urwick, L.F., *Staff in Organization* (New York: McGraw-Hill, 1960)

Dalton, D.R. & Cosier, R.A., "The Four Faces of Social Responsibility," *Business Horizons*, May-June 1982

Dalton, M., "Conflict Between Staff and Line Management Officers," *American Sociological Review*, June 1950

————, "Changing Staff-Line Relationships," *Personnel Administration*, March-April 1966

————, Lawrence, P.R. & Greiner, L.E., *Organizational Change and Development* (Homewood, Ill.: Richard D. Irwin, 1970)

Davenport, T.H., "Saving IT's Soul: Human-Centered Information Management," *Harvard Business Review*, March-April 1994

Davis, G.B., *Management Information Systems: Conceptual Foundations, Structure, and Development* (New York: McGraw-Hill, 1974)

Davis, K., *Human Behavior at Work* (New York: McGraw-Hill, 1972)

Davis, S. - See Tannenbaum, R.

Davis, S.A., "Building an Organization for the Future," *The Failure of Success*, (ed) A.J. Marrow (New York: Amacom, 1972)

Davis, S.M., - See Lawrence, P.R.

Deikman, A.J., "Bimodal Consciousness," *Archives of General Psychiatry*, 25 December 1971

DeMott, B., "Threats and Whimpers: The New Business Heroes," *New York Times* 10/26/86

Dent, J. - See Mann, F.C.

DePre, M., *Leadership is an Art* (New York: Doubleday 1989)

Dern, D., *The Internet Guide for New Users* (New York: McGraw-Hill, 1993)

Dollard, J., Doob, L.W., Miller, N.E., Mowrer, O.H., & Sears, R.R., *Frustration and Aggression* (New Haven, Yale Univ. Press, 1939)

————, & Miller, N.E., *Personality & Psychotherapy* (New York: McGraw- Hill 1950)

Doob, L.W. - See Dollard, J.

Dowling, W.F., "System 4 Builds Performance and Profits," *Organizational Dynamics*, Winter 1975

Doyle, M. & Strauss, D., *How to Make Meetings Work* (N.Y.: Jove Publications, 1985)

Drayton, C.I., Jr., C. Emerson & J.D. Griswalk, *Mergers and Acquisitions: Planning and Action* (N.Y.: Financial Executives Research Foundation, Inc. 1963)

Driscoll, J.W., "Trust and Participation in Organizational Decision Making as Predictors of Satisfaction," *Academy of Management Journal*, 1973, Vol. 21, No. 1

Drucker, P.F., *The Practice of Management* (New York: Harper & Row, 1954)

————, "Entrepreneurship in Business Enterprises," *Journal of Business Policy* 1970

————, "Reconning with the Pension Fund Revolution," *Harvard Business Review* 1991

Dunn, F.E., "The View From the Ombudsman's Chair," *The New York Times*, May 2, 1976

Dunnette, M.D. - See Campbell, J.P., et al

Emerson, C. - See Drayton, C.I.

Emerson, R.W., "Politics," *Selections from Ralph Waldo Emerson* (ed) Wicher, S.E. (Boston: Houghton Mifflin, 1957)

Emshoff, J.R. & Mitroff, I.I., "Improving the Effectiveness of Corporate Planning," *Business Horizons*, October 1978

England, G.W., "Personal Value Systems of American Managers," *Academy of Management Journal*, March 1966

English, H.B. & A.C., *A Comprehensive Dictionary of Psychological and Psychiatric Terms* (New York: Longman Greens & Co., 1958)

Engst, *Internet Starter Kit* (N.Y.: Hayden, 1993)

Ericson, R.F., "Organizational Cybernetics and Human Value," *Academy of Management Journal*, March 1970

Ewing, D.W., "Who wants corporate democracy?" *Harvard Business Review*, September-October 1971

————, *Freedom Inside the Organization* (New York: E.P. Dutton, 1977)

————, "What business thinks about employee rights," *Harvard Business Review*, September-October 1977

————, & Lankenner, W.A., "IBM's guidelines to employee privacy," *Harvard Business Review*, September-October 1976

Falk, G., P. Evans, & L.E. Shulman, "Competing on Capabilities: The New Rules of Corporate Strategy," *Harvard Business Review* March-April, 1992

Fayol, H. *General and Industrial Management*, trans. by C. Storrs (London: Sir Isaac Pitman & Sons, LTD., 1949)

Ferguson, L.L., "Better management of managers' career," *Harvard Business Review*, March-April 1966

Festinger, L., *A Theory of Cognitive Dissonance* (Stanford: Stanford Univ. Press, 1957)

Fiedler, F.E., *A Theory of Leadership Effectiveness* (New York: McGraw-Hill, 1957)

————, & Chemers, M.M., *Leadership and Effective Management* (Glenview, Ill.: Scott Foresman, 1974)

Fink, C.F. - See Thomas, E.J.

Fleming, R.L. - See Campbell, D.N.

Flesch, R., *The Art of Clear Thinking* (New York: Harper and Brothers 1951)

Flowers, V.S. & Hughes, C.L., "Why employees stay," *Harvard Business Review*, July-August 1973

Fordyce, J.L. & Weil, R., *Managing with People* (Reading, Mass.: Addison- Wesley, 1971)

Foulkes, F.K., "The expanding role of the personnel function," *Harvard Business Review*, March-April 1975

Foulkes, F.E. & Livernash, E.R., *Human Resources Management: Text and cases* (Englewood Cliffs: Prentice-Hall, 1982)

Foy, N., *The Sun Never Sets on IBM* (New York: E.P. Dutton, 1974)

Frankel, M.S. - See Gellermann, W.

French, J.P.R. - See Coch, L.

French, W.L. & Bell, C.H., Jr., *Organizational Development* (Englewood Cliffs, N.Y.: Prentice-Hall, 1973)

Freud, S., *Beyond the Pleasure Principle* (New York: Liverright, 1970)

Fromm, E., *Man for Himself* (New York: Holt, Rinehart & Winston, 1941)

————, *The Art of Loving* (Harper & Row, 1956)

Galbraith, J., *Designing Complex Organizations* (Reading, Mass.: Addison- Wesley, 1973)

————, *Organization Design* (Reading, Mass.: Addison-Wesley, 1977)

Galbraith, J.K., "Technology, Planning and Organizations," *Values and the Future*, (eds) Baier, K. & Rescher, N. (New York: Macmillan, 1969)

————, *The New Industrial State* (Boston: Houghton Mifflin, 1971)

Gellerman, S., *Motivation and Productivity* (New York: American Management Association, 1963)

Gellermann, W., M.S. Frankel & R.E. Ladenson, *Values and Ethics in Organization and Human Systems Development* (San Francisco: Jossey- Bass 1990)

Ghiselli, E.E., *The Validity of Occupational Aptitude Tests* (New York: John Wiley, 1966)

————, - See M. Haire

Gibb, J.R., "Defensive Communication," *Journal of Communication*, September 1961

Gibbs, M., *Absolute Beginner's Guide to Networking* (Carmel, IN.: SAMS Publishing, 1993)

Gluck, F.W., Kaufman, S.P. & Walleck, A.S., "Strategy management for competitive advantage," *Harvard Business Review*, July-August 1980

Goggins, W.G., "How the multidimensional structure works at Dow Corning," *Harvard Business Review*, January-February 1974

Goldenson, R.M., *The Encyclopedia of Human Behavior* (Garden City: Doubleday, 1970)

Gordon, M.E. - See M. Haire

Gould, M. & A. Campbell, "Many Best Ways to Make Strategy," *Harvard Business Review* November-December 1987

Gouldner, A.W., *Patterns of Industrial Bureaucracy* (Glencoe, Ill.: Free Press, 1954)

Green, C.H. - See R.F. Vancil

Greene, T.M., *Kant Selections* (New York: Scribners Sons 1957)

Greiner, L.E., "What managers think of participative leadership," *Harvard Business Review*, March-April 1973

_____ , - See Dalton, G.W. (1970)

Griswalk, J.D. - See Drayton, C.I.

Grothe, M. & Wylie, P., *Problem Bosses* (N.Y.C.: Facts on File, 1987)

Grote, R.C. - See Campbell, D.N.

Grove, B.A. & Kerr, W.A. "Specific Evidence on origin of Halo Effect in Measurement of Employee Morale," *Journal of Abnormal and Social Psychology*, July 1946

Guest, R.H., "Quality of work life - learning from Tarrytown," *Harvard Business Review*, July-August 1979

Gulick, L. & Urwick, L.F. (eds) *Papers on the Science of Administration* (new York: New York Institute of Public Administration 1937)

Guion, R.M., *Personnel Testing* (New York: McGraw-Hill, 1965a)

Guth, W.D. & Taguiri, R., "Personal values and corporate strategy," *Harvard Business Review*, September-October 1965

Hackman, J.R. - See Porter, L.W. (1975)

Haire, K., Ghiselli, E.E. & Gordon, M.E., "A psychological study of pay," *Journal of Applied Psychology Monograph*, 1965

Hamel, G. - See Prahalad, C.K.

Hanson, K. - See Solomon, R.C.

Harriman, B., "Up and Down the Communication Ladder,"' *Harvard Business Review*, September-October 1974

Hartshorne, H. & May, M.A., *Studies in Deceit* (New York: Macmillan, 1928)

Hayakawa, J.I. (quotation)

Heilpern, J.D. & D.A. Nadler, "Implementing Total Quality Management," *Organizational Architecture* (San Francisco: Jossey-Bass 1992)

Heinisch, R.P. - See Kizilos, T.

Hemphill, J.K., "Job descriptions for executives," *Harvard Business Review*, September-October 1959

Henley, K. - See Bayles, M.D.

Herden, R. - See Sussman, L.

Hersey, P. and Blanchard, K.H., *Management of Organizational Behavior* (Englewood Cliffs, N.J.: Prentice-Hall, 1957, Third Edition)

Hershey, R., The Grapevine...Here to Stay but not Beyond Control," *Personnel*, January-February 1966

Herzberg, F., "One more time: how do you motivate employees?" *Harvard Business Review*, January-February 1968

————, "Motivation-Hygiene profiles," *Organizational Dynamics*, Fall 1974

————, - See Paul, W.J.

Herzberg, F. et al, *The Motivation to Work* (New York: John Wiley, 1959)

Heskett, J.L. - See Kotter, J.P. (1992)

Hickson, D.J., Pugh, D.S. and Pheysey, D., "Operations technology and organization structure: an empirical appraisal," *Administration Science Quarterly*, 1969, 14

Hobbes, T., *Leviathan* (1651)

Hofstede, G., "Motivation, Leadership and Organization: Do American Theories Apply Abroad?" *Organizational Dynamics*, Summer 1980

Hogan, R., "Moral Development and the Structure of Personality," *Moral Development*, (eds) DePalma, D.J. & Foley, J.M. (Hillsdale, N.J.: Lawrence Erlbaum Associates, 1974)

Hokanson, J.E. et al, "Modification of Autonomic Responses During Aggressive Interchange," *Journal of Personality*, 36, 1968

Holtz, W.C. - See Azrin, N.H.

Homans, G.C. *The Human Group* (New York: Harcourt, Brace & World, 1950)

————, "Social Behavior as Exchange," *American Journal of Sociology*, Vol. 62, May 1958

Horney, K., "Culture and Neurosis," *American Sociological Review*, 1" 221- 235, 1936

Hower, R.M. & Lorsch, J.W., "Organizational Input," *Systems Analysis in Organizational Behavior*, (ed) Seiler, J.A. (Homewood, Ill.: Richard D. Irwin, 1967)

Huberman, J. "Discipline Without Punishment," *Harvard Business Review* July-Aug., 1964

Hughes, C.L. - See Flowers, V.A.

Jackall, R., "Moral mazes: bureaucracy and managerial work," *Harvard Business Review*, September-October 1983

Jackson, J., "Structured Characteristics of Norms," *Current Studies of Social Psychology* (eds) Steiner, I.D. & Fishbein, M. (New York: Holt, Rinehart & Winston, 1965)

James, W., *The Principles of Psychology* (New York: Dover, 1950)

Jamison, B.D., "Behavioral Problems with Management by Objectives," *Academy of Management Journal*, September 1973

Jacques, E., "In Praise of Hierarchy," *Harvard Business Review* January-February 1990

Jennings, E.E., *The Executive* (New York: Harper & Row, 1962)

Johansen, R., D. Sibbet, S. Benson, A. Martin, R. Mittman & P. Soffo *Leading Business Teams* (Reading, Mass.: Addison-Wesley, 1991)

Johnson, E.W., "Alternative Ethical Guidelines," *Harvard Business Review* January-February, 1988

Judson, A.S., "The awkward truth about productivity," *Harvard Business Review*, September-October, 1982

Jung, C.C., *Psychological Types* (New York: Harcourt Brace, 1933 reprint)

Kahn, R.L. - See Katz, D. (1978)

Kantner, R.M., *Change Masters: Innovation for Productivity in the American Corporation* (New York: Simon and Schuster, Inc. 1983)

Katz, D. "Motivational Basis of Organizational Behavior," *Behavior Science*, 1964

Katz, D. & Kahn, R.L., *The Social Psychology of Organizations* (New York: John Wiley, 1978, 2nd Edition)

Katzenback, J.R. & D.K. Smith, "The Disciplined Teams, " *Harvard Business Review* March-April, 1993

Kaufman, S.P. - See Gluck, F.M.

Keele, R.L. et al, "The Down Side of Monitoring," *Trainer's Workshop*, May 1987, p. 61

Keen, P.G.W. - See McKenney, J.L.

Kellogg, M.S., *What to Do About Performance Appraisal* (New York: Amacom, 1975 revised)

Kerr, S., "Integrity in Effective Leadership," *Executive Integrity* (eds) S. Srivastra et al (San Francisco: Jossey-Bass, 1988)

Kerr, W.A. - See grove, B.A.

Kirchner, W.K. & Reisberg, D.J., "Differences between better and less effective supervisors in appraisal of subordinates," *Personnel Psychology*, 1962, 15

Kirkpatrick, D., "Groupware Goes Boom, " *Fortune* 12/27/93

Kizilos, T. & R.P. Heinisch,"How a Management Team Selects Managers, " *Harvard Business Review*, September-October 1986

Klineberg, O., *Social Psychology* (New York: Holt, 1940)

Kluckholm, C., "Values and value orientations in the theory of action," *Toward a General Theory of Action* (eds) T. Parsons and E.A. Shils (Harvard Univ. Press, 1954)

Kohlberg, L., "Stage and sequence: the cognitive-developmental approach to socialization," *Handbook of Socialization Theory and Research* (ed) D.A. Goslin (Chicago: Rand McNally, 1969)

————, "Education for Justice, A modern Statement of the Platonic Viewpoint," *Moral Education, Five Lectures*, (eds) Gustafson et al (Cambridge: Harvard University Press, 1970)

Kolodny, H.D. - See Lawrence, P.R.

Kotter, J.P., *Power and Influence* (N.Y.: The Free Press, 1985)

————, *The Leadership Factor*, (N.Y.: The Free Press, 1988)

Kotter, J.P. & J.L. Heskett, *Corporate Cultures and Performance* (N.Y.: The Free Press, 1992)

Kouzes, J.M. - See Posner, B.Z.

Kouzes, J.M. & B.Z. Posner, *The Leadership Challenge*, (San Francisco, Jossey-Bass, 1987)

Kraut, A.I. & Scott, J.G., "Validity of an Operational Management Assessment Program," *Journal of Applied Psychology*, Vol. 56, 1972

Kraynak, J., *The Complete Idiots Guide to PCs* (Carmel, IN: Alpha Books, 1993)

Ladenson, R.F., - See Gellermann, W.

Lankenner, W.A. - See Ewing, D.W.

LaQuey, T., *The Internet Companion: A Beginner's Guide to Global Networking*, (Reading Mass.: Addison-Wesley, 1993)

Lawler, E.E., III, "Management's New Gurus," *Business Week*, May-June, 1986

————, *Pay and Organizational Effectiveness, A Psychological View*, (New York: McGraw-Hill, 1971)

Lawler, E.E., III & Porter, L.W., "Predicting manager's pay and their satisfaction with their pay," *Personal Psychology*, 1966, 19

————, - See Porter, L.W. (HBR 1968B)

————, - See Porter, L.W. (Irwin-Dorsey 1968A)

————, - See Porter, L.W. (1975)

————, - See Campbell et al.

Lawrence, P.R. - See Dalton, G.W. (1970)

Lawrence, P.R., Kolodny, H.F. & Davis, S.M., "The Human Side of the Matrix," *Organizational Dynamics*, Summer 1977

Lawrence, P.R. & Lorsch, J.W., *Organization and Environment* (Cambridge: Div. of Research, Grad. School of Bus. Adm. Harvard, 1967)

Learned, E.P., "Problems of a new executive," *Harvard Business Review*, May- June, 1986

Leavitt, H., *Managerial Psychology* (Chicago: Univ. of Chicago Press, 1964)

Levin, R.I. - See Behrman, J.N.

Levinson, H., "Management by who's objectives?" *Harvard Business Review* July-August 1970

Levitt, T., "The managerial merry-go-round," *Harvard Business Review*, July- August 1974

Lewin, K., *Principles of Topological Psychology* (New York: McGraw-Hill, 1936)

_____, *Resolving Social Issues*, (New York: Harper Bros., 1951)

_____, *Field Theory in Social Science* (New York: Harper Bros., 1951)

Likert, R., *New Patterns of Management* (New York: McGraw-Hill, 1964)

_____, *The Human Organization* (New York: McGraw-Hill, 1967)

Likert, R. & Likert, J.G., *New Ways of Managing Conflict* (New York: McGraw-Hill, 1976)

Limpert, T.M. - See Nadler, D.A.

Lindzey, G. - See Allport, G.W.

Lippitt, G., *Organizational Renewal*, (New York: Appleton-Croft-Century, 1969)

Lippitt, R. - See Cartwright, D.

Litwin, G.H. and Stringer, R.A., Jr., *Motivation and Organizational Climate* (Boston: Harvard University, 1968)

Livernash, E.R. - See Foulkes, F.E. (1982)

Lock, E.A., "Toward a theory of task motivation and incentives," *Organizational Behavior and Human Performance*, 1968, 3

Locke, D. - See Weinreich-Haste

Lodahl, T.M., *Man on the assembly-line: Job attitude at two and fourteen years* (Cornell University School of Bus. & Pub. Adm., 1964)

Lodge, G.C. - See Martin, W.F.

Loew, C.A., "Acquisition of a hostile attitude and its relationship to aggressive behavior," *Journal of Personality and Social Psychology*, 5, 1967

Lorsch, J.W. - See Hower, R.M.

_____, - See Lawrence, P.R. (1967)

————, - See Morse, J.J.

Lowenstein, L., *What's Wrong with Wall Street* (Reading Mass.: Addison- Wesley, 1988)

Luft, J., "The Johari Window," *Human Relations Training News*, Vol. 5, 1961

Lusk, E.J., & Oliver, B.L., "American Managers' Personal Value Systems Revisited," *Academy of Management Journal*, September 1974

Machiavelli, N., *The Prince* and *The Discourses* (New York: Modern Library, 1950)

MacLaine, S., *You Can Get There From Here* (New York: W.W. Norton, 1973)

Mali, P., *MBO Updated: A Handbook of Practices and Techniques for Managing by Objectives* (New York: John Wiley, 1986)

Mann, F.C. & Dent, J., *Appraisal of supervisors and attitudes of their employees in an electric power company* (Ann Arbor, Mich.: Institute of Social Research, 1954)

March, J.G. - See Cyert, R.M.

Margulies, N. & Wallace, J., *Organizational Change* (Glenview, Ill.: Scott Foresman, 1973)

Markley, O.W., *Alternative Futures: Contexts in Which Social Indicators Must Work* (Stanford, Cal.:Stanford Research Institute, 1971) a research study for the U.S. Office of Education, HEW

Marrow, A.J., Bowers, D.G. & Seashore, S.E., *Management by Participation* (New York: Harper & Row, 1967)

Martin, A. - See Johansen, R.

Martin, W.F., & Lodge, G.C., "Our society in 1985 - business may not like it," *Harvard Business Review*, November-December 1975

Maslow, A.H., "A Theory of Human Motivation," *Psychological Review*, Vol. 50, 1943

————, *Motivation and Personality* (New York: Harper, 1954)

————, "Self-Actualization and Beyond," *Challenges of Humanistic Psychology*, (ed) Bugental, J.F.I. (New York: McGraw-Hill, 1967)

Mathys, N.J. - See Burack, E.H. (1977)

Mathys, N.J. - See Burack, E.H. (1979)

Mathys, N.J. - See Burack, E.H. (1980)

Mausner, B. - See Herzberg, F. (1959)

May, M.A. - See Harshorne, H.

May, R., *Power and Innocence* (New York: W.W. Norton, 1972)

McCaskey, M.B., *The Executive Challenge: Managing Change and Ambiguity* (Boston: Pittman, 1982)

McClelland, D.C., *The Achieving Society* (Princeton: D. Van Nostrand, 1961)

———, "Business drive and national achievement," *Harvard Business Review*, July-August 1962

———, & Burnham, D.H., "Power is the great motivator," *Harvard Business Review*, March-April 1976

McCoy, B.H., "The parable of the sadhu," *Harvard Business Review*, Sept.- Oct. 1983

McGregor, D., *The Human Side of Enterprise* (New York: McGraw-Hill, 1961)

———, *The Professional Manager* (New York: McGraw-Hill, 1967)

———, " An Uneasy Look at Performance Appraisal," *Harvard Business Review*, May-June 1957

McKenney, J.L., & Keen, P.C.W., "How managers' minds work," *Harvard Business Review*, May-June, 1974

Mechanic, D., "Sources of Power of Lower Participants in Complex Organizations," *Administrative Science Quarterly*, December 1962, Vol. 7, No. 2

Melden, A.I., (ed) *Ethical Theories* (New York: Prentice-Hall, 1967)

Meloy, C. - See Dale, E.

Mertes, J.E., "Case-Study - TRW, Inc., A Social Policy Statement," *Business and Society* (Cinn., OH: South-Western Pub. Co., 1976)

Meyers, M.S., "Conditions for Manager Motivation," *Harvard Business Review*, Jan.-Feb. 1966

Milgram, S., "Some conditions of obedience and disobedience to authority," *Human Relations*, February 1965, 57

Miller, E.C., *Marketing Planning* (New York: Amer. Mgt. Assn., 1967)

Miller, N.E. - See Dollard, J. et al (1929)

Mills, D.Q., "Planning with People in Mind," *Harvard Business Review*, 1985

Milo, R.D., *Immorality* (Princeton University Press, 1984)

Milton, C.R., *Ethics and Expedience in Personnel Management* (Columbia, S.C.: University of South Carolina Press, 1970)

Mintzberg, H., *The Structuring of Organizations* (Englewood Cliffs, N.J.: Prentice-Hall, 1979)

———, *The Nature of Managerial Work* (Englewood Cliffs, N.J.: Prentice- Hall, 1980)

Mischel, W., "Preference for delayed reinforcement and social responsibility," *Journal of Abnormal and Social Psychology*, 62, 1961

Mitroff, I.I. - See Emshoff

Mittman, R. - See Johansen, R.

Molander, E.A. - See Brenner, S.N.

Mooney, J.D. & Reiley, A.C., *Onward Industry* (New York: Harper & Bros., 1931)

Moore, J.F., "Predator and Prey: A New Ecology of Competition," *Harvard Business Review*, May-June 193

Moran, L. - See Osborn, D.

Morrisey, G.L., *Management by Objectives and Results* (Reading, Mass.: Addison-Wesley, 1970)

Morse, J.J. & Lorsch, J.W., "Beyond Theory Y," *Harvard Business Review*, May-June 1970

Mouton, J.S. - See Blake, R.R. (1969, 1978)

Mowrer, O. - See Dollard, J.

Moyer, K.E., "The Physiology of Aggression and the Implication for Aggression Control," *The Control of Aggression and Violence* (ed) Singer, N.E. (New York: Academic Press, 1971)

Musselwhite, E. - See Osborn, D.

Myers, M.S. "Conditions for manager motivation," *Harvard Business Review* January-February 1966

Nadler, D.A., & D. Ancona, "Teamwork at the Top: Creating Executive Teams that Work," *Organizational Architecture* (San Francisco: Jossey-Bass, 1992)

Nadler, D.A. & T.M. Limpert, "Managing the Dynamics of Acquisition," *Organizational Architecture* (San Francisco: Jossey-Bass, 1992)

Nadler, D.A. - See Heilpern, J.D.

Newell, A. & Simon, H.A., *Human Problem Solving* (Englewood Cliffs: Prentice-Hall, 1972)

Newman, W.H., Summer, C.E. & Warren, E.K., *The Process of Management* (Englewood Cliffs, N.J.: Prentice-Hall, 1972)

Nietzsche, F., *Thus Spoke Zarathustra* in *The Complete Works of Nietzsche* (New York: Macmillan, 1924)

Norman, R. & R. Ramirez, "From Value Chain to Value Constellation: Designing Interactive Strategy," *Harvard Business Review*, July-August 1993

O'Connor, R., *The Corporate Planning Department* (New York: The Conference Board, 1981)

Oliver, B.L. - See Luck, E.J.

Ornstein, R.E., *The Psychology of Consciousness* (San Francisco: W.H. Freeman, 1972)

Osborn, J.D., L. Moran, E. Musselwhite, J.H. Zinger & C. Perrin, *Self-Directed Work Teams: The New American Challenge* (Homewood, Ill.: Business One Erwin, 1990)

Paine, L.S., "Managing for Organizational Integrity," *Harvard Business Review*, March-April 1994

Parasuraman, A. et al, "Service Quality," *Journal of Marketing* 1988, p. 48

Parkington, J.J. - See Schneider, B.

Parsons, T., *Essays in Sociological Theory* (Glencoe: Free Press, 1954)

Pastin, M., *The Hard Problems of Management* (San Francisco: Jossey-Bass, Inc., 1986)

Patton, A., "Does Performance Appraisal Work?" *Business Horizons*, February 1973

Patz, A.L., "Performance appraisal: useful but still resisted," *Harvard Business Review*, May-June 1975

Paul, W.J., Robertson, K.B. & Herzberg, F., "Job enrichment pays off," *Harvard Business Review*, March-April 1969

Pavlov, L.P., *Conditioned Reflexes*, trans. by Anrep, G.P., 1927, first pub. in Russia 1897

Peabody, R.L., "Perceptions of Organizational Authority: A Comparative Analysis," *Administrative Science Quarterly*, Vol. 6, No. 4, 1962

Perrin, C. - See Osborn, J.D.

Peters, T.J., & Waterman, R.H., Jr., *In Search of Excellence* (N.Y.: Random House, 1982)

Peters, T.J. & Austin, N.K., *A Passion for Excellence* (Random House, 1985)

Pfaffenberger, B., *Que's Computer User's Dictionary* (Carmel, Ind.: Que Corporation, 1992)

Pheysey, D. - See Hickson, D.S.

Piaget, J., "The General Problems of the Psychological Development of the Child," *Discussions on Child Development* (New York: International Universities Press, Inc., 1960) (eds) Tanner, J.M. & Inhelder, B.

Plato, *The Republic* (Oxford University Press, 1945)

Pondy, L.R., "Organizational Conflict: Concepts and Models," *Administrative Science Quarterly*, September 1967

Porter, L.C., "Group Norms: Some Things Can't Be Legislated," *Laboratories in Human Relations Training* (Arlington, Va.: NTL Institute, 1972)

Porter, L.W., *Organizational Patterns of Managerial Job Attitudes* (New York: American Foundation for Mgmt. Research, 1964)

————, - See Lawler, E.E. III (1966)

————, & Lawler, E.E., III *Managerial Attitudes and Performance* (Homewood, Ill., L. Irwin-Dorsey, 1968A)

————, & Lawler, E.E., III "What job attitudes tell about motivation," *Harvard Business Review*, January-February 1968B

————, Lawler, E.E., III & Hackman, J.R., *Behavior in Organizations* (New York: McGraw-Hill, 1975)

Porter, M.E., "From Competitive Advantage to Corporate Strategy," *Harvard Business Review* May-June 1987

Posner, B.Z., J.M. Kouzes & W.H. Schmidt, "Shared Values Make a Difference," *Human Resources Management*, 1985, 24

Posner, B.Z. - See Kouzas, J.M.

Powers, C.W. & Vogel, D., *Ethics in the Education of Business Managers* (Hastings-on-the-Hudson, N.Y.: Hastings Center, 1980)

Pralahad, C.K. & G. Hamel, "The Core Competence of the Corporation," *Harvard Business Review*, May-June 1992

Presthus, R., "Toward a Theory of Organizational Behavior," *Administrative Science Quarterly*, Vol. 3, No. 1, June 1958

————, *The Organizational Society* (New York: Random House, 1962)

Pugh, D.S. - See Hickson, D.J.

Ramirez, R. - See Norman, R.

Rappaport, A., "The Staying Power of the Public Corporation," *Harvard Business Review*, January-February, 1990

Rathbone, A., *Windows for Dummies* (San Mateo, CA: IDG Books, 1992)

Reddin, W.J., "Management Effectiveness in the 1980's," *Business Horizons*, August 1974

Reif, W.E., et al, "Job Enrichment: Who Uses It and Why?" *Business Horizons*, February 1974

Reiley, A.C. - See Mooney, J.D.

Reisberg, D.J. - See Kirschner, W.K.

Reisman, D., *The Lonely Crowd: A Study of the Changing American Character* (New Haven: Yale University Press, 1950)

Remmers, H.L. - See Brooke, M.Z.

Rensberger, B., "What Made Humans Human?" *The New York Times Magazine*, April 8, 1984

Rescher, N., "What is Value Change? A Framework for Research," *Values and the Future*, (eds) Baier, K. & Rescher, N. (New York: Macmillan, 1969)

Rest, J.R., "Recent Research on an Objective test of Moral Judgment," *Moral Development*, (eds) DePalma, D.J. & Foley, J.M. (Hillsdale, N.J.: Lawrence Erlbaum Associates, 1974)

Robertson, K.B. - See Paul, W.J.

Rogers, C.R., *Client-Centered Therapy: Its Current Practice, Implications and Theory* (Boston: Houghton, 1951)

_____, "Toward a Modern Approach to Values: The Valuing Process in the Mature Person," *Journal of Abnormal and Social Psychology*, 1954

Rogers, F., "A Team Approach to Promotion at Rohr, Inc.," *Personnel Journal*, April 1992

Rokeach, M., *The Nature of Human Values* (New York: The Free Press, 1973)

Rotter, J.B., *Social Learning and Clinical Psychology* (New York: Prentice- Hall, 1954)

Roundstone, W., *Prisoner's Dilemma* (New York: Doubleday, 1992)

Ruh, R.A. - See Beer, M.

Saffo, P. - See Johansen, R.

Salmon, W.J., "Crisis Prevention: How to Gear Up Your Board," *Harvard Business Review* January-February 1993

Sayles, L.R., *Leadership* (New York: McGraw-Hill, 1979)

Schacter, S. et al, "An Experimental Study of Cohesiveness and Productivity," *Human Relations*, Vol. 4, No. 3, 1951

_____, *The Psychology of Affiliation* (Stanford: Stanford University Press, 1959)

Schein, E.H., "Management and Development as a Process of Influence," *Industrial Management Review*, May 1961

_____, *Organization Culture and Leadership* (San Francisco: Jossey-Bass, 1985)

_____, "The Individual, the organization and the career: a conceptual scheme," *Journal of Applied Behavioral Science*, 1971, 7

_____, "How Can Organizations Learn Faster?" *Sloan Management Review*, Winter 1993

Schmidt, W.H. - See Posner, B.Z.

Schmidt, W.H. - See Tannenbaum, W.

Schneider, B., J.J. Parkington & V.M. Buxton, "Employee and customer perceptions of service in banks," *Administrative Science Quarterly*, 1980

Schneider, B., (ed) *Organizational Climate and Culture* (San Francisco: Jossey-Bass 1990)

Schneier, C.E., R.W. beatty & L.S. Baird, *The Performance Management Sourcebook* (Amherst, MA: Human Resources Development Press, 1987)

Schon, D.A. - See Argyris, C.

Schull, F.A., Jr., & Cummings, L.L., "Enforcing the Rules: how do managers differ," *Personnel*, Vol. 43, No. 2, 1966

Scott, J.G., - See Kraut, A.I.

Sears, R. - See Dollard, J.

Seashore, S.E. - See Marrow, A.J.

Sekerak, F.J. - See Cottrell, N.B.

Serok, S., "Therapeutic Implications of Games with Juvenile Delinquents," *Game Play* (eds) C.E. Schaefer & S.E. Reid (N.Y.: Wiley, 1986). pp. 311-328

Shames, L., *The Big Time* (N.Y.: Harper & Row, 1986)

Sheldon, W.H., *The Varieties of Temperament: A Psychology of Constitutional Differences* (New York: harper, 1942)

Shepard, H.A. - See Bennis, W.G. (1965)

Sherwin, D.S., "Management of objectives," *Harvard Business Review*, May- June 1976

––––––––, "The ethical roots of the business system," *Harvard Business Review*, November-December 1983

Shorris, E., *The Oppressed Middle* (New York: Anchor Press/Doubleday, 1981)

Sibbet, J. - See Johansen, R.

Simon, H.A., *Administrative Behavior* (New York: Macmillan, 1958)

––––––––, - See Newell, A.

Singer, J.L., "The Influence of Violence Portrayed in Television or Motion Pictures Upon Overt Aggression," *The Control of Aggression and Violence*, (ed) Singer, J.L. (New York: Academic Press, 1971)

Sizer, N.F. & Sizer, T.R., "Introduction," *Moral Education, Five Lectures* (Cambridge: Harvard University Press, 1970)

Skinner, B.F., *Science and Human Behavior* (New York: Macmillan, 1953)

––––––––, *Beyond Freedom and Dignity* (New York: Knopf, 1971)

Skinner, W., "Manufacturing - missing link in corporate strategy," *Harvard Business Review*, May-June 1969

Smith, C. - See Stein, S.

Smith, A., *Wealth of Nations* (1776)

Smith, D.K. - See Katzenback, J.R.

Snyderman, B.B. - See Herzberg, F.

Sofer, C., *Men in mid-career: a study of British managers and technical specialists* (London: Cambridge University Press, 1970)

Solomon, R.C. & Hanson, K., *It's Good Business* (N.Y.: Atheneum, 1985)

Sommer, R., "Small Group Ecology," *Psychological Bulletin*, Vol. 67, No. 2, 1967

Spranger, E., *Lebensforman*, (Halle: Niemeyer, 1923)

Srivasta & Assoc., *Executive Integrity* (San Francisco: Jossey-Bass, 1988)

Stalker, G.M. - See Burns, T.

Stanton, E.S., *Reality-Centered People Management* (New York: Amacom, 1982)

Staub, E., "The Learning and Unlearning of Aggression," *The Control of Aggression and Violence*, (ed) Singler, J.L. (New York: Academic Press, 1971)

Stein, S. & Smith, C., "Return to Mom," *Saturday Review of Education*, April 1973

Steiner, G.A., *Business and Society* (New York: Random House, 1971)

Steward, R.B., "Behavioral modification techniques for the education technologist," *The School in the Community*, (ed) Sarri, R.C. and Maple, F.F. (New York: National Association of Social Workers, 1972)

Stone, C.D., *Where the Law Ends* (New York: Harper & Row, 1975)

Storey, W., *Career Dimensions* (IBM in-house publication)

Straus, D. - See Doyle, M.

Stringer, R.A., Jr. - See Litwin, G.H.

Summer, C.E. - See Newman, W.H.

Sussman, L. and Herden, R., "Dialectical Problem Solving," *Business Horizons* January-February 1982

Taguiri, R. - See Guth, W.D.

Tannenbaum, A.S., *Control in Organizations* (New York: McGraw-Hill, 1968)

Tannenbaum, R. & Schmidt, W.H., "How to choose a leadership pattern" *Harvard Business Review*, March-April 1958

_____, & Davis, S.A., "Values, Man and Organization," *Industrial Management Review*, Winter 1969

Tarnowiaski, D., *The Changing Success Ethic*, (New York: Amacom, 1973)

Tatge, W.A. - See Wilson, J.E.

Thomas, E.J., & Fink, C.F., "Effects of Group Size," *Psychological Bulletin*, Vol. 60, No. 4, 1963

Thompson, V.A., *Modern Organization* (New York: Knopf, 1961)

Thorndike, E.L., *Animal Intelligence*, (New York: Macmillan, 1911)

Thurow, L., "Let's Learn from the Japanese," *Fortune*, November 18, 1991

Toffler, B.L., *Tough Choices: Manager Talk Ethics* (New York: Wiley, 1986)

Tosi, H. & Carroll, S.J., Jr., "Improving Management by Objectives: A Diagnostic Change program," *California Management Review*, Fall 1973

Toulmin, S.E., *An Examination of the Place of Reason in Ethics* (Cambridge: Cambridge University Press, 1950)

Toynbee, A., "Will business be civil servants?" *Harvard Business Review*, September-October 1958

Trist, E.L. & Bamforth, K.W., "Some Social and Psychological Consequences of the Long-Wall Method of Coal Getting" *Human Relations*, February 1951

Urwick, L.F., *Scientific Principles of Organization* (New York: American Management Assn., 1938)

————, - See Dale, E. (1960)

————, - See Gulick, L.

Vance, G.G. - See Bonjean, C.M.

Vancil, R.F. & Green, C.H., "How CEOs use top management committees" *Harvard Business Review*, January-February 1984

Vernon, P.E. - See Allport, G.W.

Venkatesan, R., "Strategy Sourcing: To Make or Not to Make," *Harvard Business Review*, November-December 1992

Vickers, G., *Human Systems are Different* (New York: Harper & Row, 1984)

Vlastos, G., "Justice and Equality," *Social Justice*, (ed) R.B. Brandt (Englewood Cliffs: Prentice-Hall, 1962)

Vogel, D. - See Powers, C.W.

Vroom, V.H., *Work and Motivation* (New York: John Wiley, 1964)

Wack, D.L. - See Cottrell, N.B.

Walker, J.W., "Human Resources Planning: Management Concerns and Practices," *Business Horizons*, June 1976

Wallace, J. - See Margulies, N.

Walleck, A.S. - See Gluck, F.W.

Ward, L.B., "Do You Want a Weak Subordinate?" *Harvard Business Review*, September-October 1961

Ward, L.D., "Four Types of Learning," *Training*, November 1983

Warren, E.K. - See Newman, W.E.

Waterman, J.A. - See Waterman, R.H., Jr.

Waterman, R.H., Jr., *The Renewal Factor* (New York: Bantam Books, 1987)

————, - See Peters, T.J.

Waterman, R.H., Jr., J.A. Waterman & B.A. Collard, "Toward a Career-Resilient Workforce," *Harvard Business Review* July-August, 1994

Weber, M., *Max Weber: Essays in Sociology* (New York: Oxford University Press, 1946)

Weber, W.L., "Manpower Planning in Hierarchical Organizations: A Computer Simulation Approach," *Management Science*, November 1971

Weick, K.E. - See Campbell et al

Weil, R. - See Fordyce, J.K.

Weinreich-Haste, H., "Social and Moral Cognition," *Morality in the Making*, (eds) H. Weinreich-Haste and D. Locke (Chichester, England: John Wiley & Sons Ltd., 1983)

White, R.W., "Motivation Reconsidered: The Concept of Competence," *Psychological Review*, Vol. 66, No. 5, 1969

Whyte, W.F., "An Interaction approach to the Theory of Organization," *Modern Organization Theory* (ed) Haire, M. (New York: John Wiley, 1949)

Wikstrom, W.S., *Managing by - And With - Objectives* (national Industrial Conference Board, 1958)

Wilson, J.E., & Tatge, W.A., "Assessment Centers - Further Assessment Needed?" *Personnel Journal*, March 1973

Wolfe, D. - See Zaner, A.

Wolman, B.B., *Dictionary of Behavioral Sciences* (New York: Van Nostrand Reinhold Co., 1975)

Woodward, J., *Management and Technology* (London: Her Majesty's Printing Office, 1958)

Wylie, P. - See Grothe, M.

Yankelovich, D., *The New Morality* (New York: McGraw-Hill, 1974)

Yates, D., Jr., *The Politics of Management* (San Francisco: Jossey-Bass, 1985)

Yukl, G.A., *Leadership in Organizations* (Prentice-Hall, 1981)

Zaleznick, A., "Managerial Behavior and Interpersonal Competence," *Behavioral Science*, April 1964

Zand, D., "Trust and Managerial Problem Solving," *Administrative Science Quarterly*, June 1972

Zander, A. & Wolfe, D., "Administrative Rewards Among Committee Members," *Administrative Science Quarterly*, June 1964

Zemke, R., "Testing: Return of the Prodigal Process," *Training*, May 1983

Zenger, J.H. - See Osborn, J.D.

Zigarmi, D. - See Blanchard, K.H. (1985)

Zigarmi, P. - See Blanchard, K.H. (1985)

Ziller, R.C., "Individuation and socialization: a theory of assimilation in large organizations," *Human Relations*, 1964, 17, 341

Zysman, J. - See Cohen, S.R.

Name Index

Abernathy, J., 697
Achoff, R.L., 622-3, 710
Adams, W., 845
Adler. A., 49, 50, 53, 74, 242-4,
    248, 249, 260, 271
Adler, M., 185, 187-8
Adorno, I.W., 259
Alfred, T.M., 941
Allport, G.W., 38, 49, 53, 54, 73,
    74, 142, 154, 187-8, 223,
    243,385, 434, 559-560, 620,
    1049
Ancona, D., 614-15
Andrews, K.R., 1199, 1216
Ansbacher, H.L., 262
Ansoff, H.L., 515
Argyris, C., 14-15, 22, 88, 95, 98,
    114, 154, 189, 196-7, 222, 224,
    225, 256, 257, 260, 276, more
Aristotle, 149, 159, 165, 171, 185,
    187-8, 247, 260
Arnstein, W.E., 764
Atkinson, J.W., 230
Augustus, C., 448
Austin, N.K., 260, 341, 410, 418,
    495, 496
Axelrod, R., 225
Azrin, N.H. , 114

Babbage, C., 152, 439
Baird, L.S., 387
Bamforth, R., 438, 529, 559, 776

Barksdale, H.M., 437, 438, 454,
    715
Barnard, C.I., 438, 443, 473, 496,
    515, 954, 1064
Barry, V., 182
Bartunek, J.M., 188
Bass, B.M., 386, 1131
Baumhart, R., 182, 186
Beatty, K.W., 387
Beckett, S., 153
Beckhard, R., 443, 1005, 1007,
    1009, 1016, 1034, 1043, 1112
Beer, M. , 941
Bell, C.H., Jr., 1043
Benne, K., 973
Bennis, W.G., 450, 455, 468, 514,
    530, 540, 559, 965-9, 971, 974,
    1024-5, 1043, 1053, 1064,
    1129
Benson, S., 711
Bentham, J.S., 147, 149, 171, 1191
Bergson, H., 149
Berry, L.L., 341
Bertalanffy, L. Von, 226, 710
Bettelheim, B., 115
Blades, L.E., 1173
Blake, R.R., 614, 1012, 1043
Blake, W., 1218
Blanchard, K.H., 75, 1128-9
Bolt, J.E., 923, 931, 1043, 1089,
    1130
Bonjean, C.M., 259

Subject Index